# THE ZODIAC FAMILY

by
Julia Parker

THE AQUARIAN PRESS

First published 1988

© Julia Parker 1988

British Library Cataloguing in Publication Data

Parker, Julia, *1932-*
The zodiac family.
1. Parenthood. Astrological aspects
I. Title
133.5'8306874

ISBN 0-85030-723-6

*The Aquarian Press is part of the
Thorsons Publishing Group,
Wellingborough, Northamptonshire, NN8 2RQ, England*

Printed in Great Britain by
Mackays of Chatham, Kent

1  3  5  7  9  10  8  6  4  2

For Douglas and Helen,
Gemma and Adam,
and A.N. Other,
with love

I am grateful to the parents who have given permission for me to reproduce paragraphs from the astrological reports I have written about, and sometimes for, their children — especially the Bridgwater family.

In three cases I have unfortunately been unable to trace the families for whom the reports were originally written.

I would also like to acknowledge the constructive assistance of my husband, Derek, whose witty and incisive critical comments have contributed much to the production of this book.

# CONTENTS

# INTRODUCTION

Perhaps you have just become proud parents for the first time. Perhaps you have a growing family. In either case you will, I hope, find many of the statements in this book interesting and helpful.

If you have a tiny baby you will very soon see characteristics of his or her Sun-sign emerge, and as the weeks and months pass, these characteristics will become stronger, and more will develop. Recognition of them will help you to make use of your ever-growing experience of the complicated role of parenthood. Astrology is a discipline which even at this, its most popular level, can broaden our understanding of people, and can show us how to help children, in particular, to develop areas of potential which might not otherwise readily surface. It also helps us to acquire that sympathy, empathy and all-round understanding of our fellow human beings which makes us good partners, good neighbours and friends. Or — and this is the point of this book — good parents. And in what other relationship can understanding and sympathy be more valuable than in the enormously complex one between parents and their offspring?

This book will help you to keep at least a step or two ahead of your children — help you to make an informed guess at what they are thinking, how their minds are working and their emotions developing, how to appeal to the best side of their nature, and, most importantly, how to guide them so that they will be prepared to lead fulfilled and happy lives.

This is not a book from which you will learn how to bully and bluster: rather, it will suggest how you may drop the tiniest hint here and there which will germinate like a well-fertilized seed and have a good chance of growing into a lifetime interest or talent, or, rather differently, into some form of understanding — all of which will make your children better human beings.

In a lighter vein, you will have fun watching young Sagittarius's or young Capricorn's sense of humour emerge — Ms Leo's or Ms Libra's fashion sense — Master Gemini's constant chatter and enquiring mind turn into media skills . . . It is all there, all marvellous potential waiting to be tapped, and that tap can be turned in the right direction as early as you like!

So *The Zodiac Family* is a practical guide — a book to be used. I suggest that you place it alongside your favourite child care volume, and hope it will get as dog-eared — but its useful life will be much longer than the average guide to bringing up baby.

The old adage 'like father, like son' is only partially true, for even at a popular level astrology can underline the differences between parents and their children. You can compare yourself and your child by reading the section relating the signs to parenthood, which will show just how your children see you as a parent!

Natal astrology (in which the individual's birth-date, -time and -place is recorded and a precise map of the sky at that time and place is calculated and studied before statements are made) is extremely specific; obviously a Sun-sign guide to the family must be less particular; but nevertheless in-depth statistical research into the nature of Sun-sign astrology has had rather spectacular results, and reveals an impressive accuracy when one looks at the general characteristics, psychological traits, physical features of an individual Arian, Taurean, or whatever. So the Sun-signs in fact are a very good and revealing starting point from which to discover just how helpful and revealing astrology can be about personal relationships and traits.

It may well be that this book will get you hooked on astrology, and you'll want to learn more about it. If so, consult the bibliography on page 256. For the moment here are one or two very simple hints that could further whet your appetite.

Sometimes people (child or adult) are very typical of their Sun-sign — i.e., they seem to have a great many of the characteristics usually attributed to the sign — a number above average. This may be for one of several reasons, which will take a little time to explain. The most important is connected with the Ascendant — the first thing an astrologer calculates when working on the full birth-chart of an individual. As the earth turns on its axis, the Sun appears to trace a path around it every day; and around this path cluster the constellations familiar to all of us — Aries, Taurus and the rest — the Sun-signs. These, like the Sun, appear to rise and set every twenty-four hours: imagine a twenty-four hour clock, with the hands standing at quarter to three, but the dial rather than the hands revolving. The twelve figures on the dial would pass the hands one by one. Replace the figures on the dial with the Sun-signs, and you have the idea.

Now imagine the gold disc of the Sun painted in, within one of the signs — say, Leo — and let the line made by the two hands represent the horizon. You can see that, differences of season and latitude apart, if someone is born within an hour or two of sunrise — represented by the Sun's disc passing the hour-hand — the Sun-sign and the all-important Ascendant or Rising-sign will be the same, and that person will have a 'double dose' of the characteristics of that sign. If you are born at such a moment, you will be known astrologically as a 'double Leo', a 'double Cancerian', and so on.

Incidentally, due to one of the earth's motions known as Precession of the Equinoxes, the constellations with whose names everyone is familiar are no longer in the position in the sky which they occupied when development of astrology first began; some scientists claim that this devalues astrology as a system — but of course astrologers are entirely aware of this non-alignment, and take it into consideration when calculating a birth chart. The fact is that the constellations simply *originally* marked the sectors of the sky through which the planets were passing at a particular time — much as, if you were pointing out to someone in the room the position of a butterfly flying through it, you may say: 'Look, it's between you and the bookcase.' Of course the bookcase would have nothing to do with the butterfly, but simply be used as a reference point to describe its position. That is how astrologers use the constellations.

The Ascendant is more often, naturally, different from the Sun-sign. Someone born a couple of hours after Sunrise with, say, a Virgo Sun-sign will have Libra as their Ascendant; someone with a Capricornian Sun-sign who is born around sunset will have Cancer rising.

Another reason for people showing particularly strong characteristics of a Sun-sign is that they were born at the time of the New Moon, when both Sun and Moon are in the same sign. In such a case the individual will not only *react* and *respond* to all situations in the manner of the Sun-sign, but their *emotional expression* will be similar — so they will be 'very typical' of their sign.

There are two other 'hidden' factors which tend to make us 'typical' of a sign. These relate to the positions of the planets Mercury and Venus, whose orbits are closer to the Sun than that of the Earth, so that they are always relatively near the Sun, both astrologically and astronomically, when seen from Earth. Often one or the other, or sometimes both, fall in the same sign as the Sun, in much the same way that the Moon does when it is new. When this happens the individual will also *think* in the manner of the Sun-sign — due to an influence from Mercury, or *love* in the manner of the Sun-sign — because Venus is in the same sign as the Sun.

In this book I do not set out the mass of tables which would enable you to find out in which sign your children's Mercury and Venus stood at the time of their birth. But I nevertheless take this into account, and here and there hint at it. For instance, in the section headed *General Characteristics*, you will see two sub-headings: *The Three ways of Thinking* and *The Five ways of Loving*. In these short sections I interpret the influences of Mercury and Venus on your children. (It is worth remembering, by the way, that Mercury can only fall in the same sign as the Sun, the preceding, or the following sign, while Venus can fall in the same sign or in one of the *two* preceding or following signs). It shouldn't be difficult for you to identify the Signs relevant to your children, and these will add another interesting dimension to their Sun-sign characteristics.

Very often one hears talk of someone being 'born on the cusp.' There is a common belief that those who are born within a few days of the Sun entering a Sign or near the time when it is about to leave a Sign have a combination of the characteristics of the two signs in question. I have done a very great deal of research into this, and I am firmly convinced it is nonsense. I've examined scores of pairs of people born on the same day on which the Sun moved from one sign to the next, and their Sun-sign characteristics are quite different. It is as if the Sun almost clicks into each new sign as it crosses the imaginary line which separates them. The characteristics in question do not, I think, stem from the influence of the Sun, but are far more likely to relate to the influences of Mercury and Venus. In such a case it may well be that either of these planets were in a preceding or following sign, so that — as explained above — the individual will think or love in the way of the preceding or following sign. When they read the characteristics of the 'other' sign, and feel they share them, they will in fact be reading of their Mercury — or Venus — sign characteristics. The 'born on the cusp' theory is a myth — forget it!

People are sometimes troubled by the fact that different books or magazines often give different dates on which the Sun moves from one sign to another: born near the end of a sign, in some books they will be given one Sun-sign, and in another, the next. The confusion arises because of the existence of leap year, and the consequence that the Sun does not always change signs on the same day in every year. In popular Sun-sign books and columns, astrologers have to take a mean average.

If you have this problem, the only way to remedy it is to buy an *ephemeris* for the year of your birth. This is an almanac which gives the precise positions of the Sun, Moon and planets for noon or midnight each day. You can then, without too much difficulty, work out precisely the position of the Sun at the moment when you were born — and you will definitely be one Sun-sign or the other! If you have difficulty in finding an *ephemeris* — though they can be bought at many large bookshops — you will often find them printed in the more advanced astrological textbooks such as *The Compleat Astrologer*. Of course, a professional astrologer, or even a beginner, will be able to work out the Sun's position for you quite quickly. If you have a computer, software is available which will calculate for you the position not only of the Sun but all the planets, and the Ascendant and Midheaven as well.

Just as specialists can trace a genetic 'family tree', so a similar astrological pattern can be traced through the generations — though of course the precise birth data of grandparents, parents, children must be known before this can be seen. At the simplest level, some families have a great many members with one Sun-sign (in which case there's an expensive time when their birthday comes round!); but when an astrologer studies the fully calculated charts of several generations of a family, a pattern of repeated signs and planetary positions occurs. This often explains why, for instance, there are very strong ties between one grandparent and grandchild, or why in some areas father can be a more positive influence on certain spheres of a child's life while mother can be more constructively helpful in others.

The effects of traditional groups of signs often also emerge in an interesting way at Sun-sign level. One of the most striking of these relates to the 'polar' or 'opposite' signs. Each sign has its 'partner' lying opposite to it across the Zodiac (to return to the clock simile, at three and nine o'clock, four and ten, five and eleven, and so on). The *polar* signs are:

> Aries — Libra.
> Taurus — Scorpio.
> Gemini — Sagittarius.
> Cancer — Capricorn.
> Leo — Aquarius.
> Virgo — Pisces.

If you think of them in terms of their characteristics, the word 'opposites' is misleading, for they are really in many ways partners. There will not always be agreement between members of these opposing Sun-signs, but there is nearly always a good *rapport* — a strong bond between them. We find opposite signs often occurring within families. Perhaps you and your partner each belong to one of these groups, or if that is not the case where your Sun-signs are concerned, you may find (if you have your full birth charts calculated) that some *polarity* — as it is known among astrologers — occurs in other areas of your respective charts. If so, this is a terrific cementing bond between you — and the same thing applies to you and your children.

Another traditional grouping is based on the *elements*. Here the signs are divided into four groups, each governed by one of the four elements:

> *Fire* — Aries, Leo, Sagittarius
> *Earth* — Taurus, Virgo, Capricorn
> *Air* — Gemini, Libra, Aquarius
> *Water* — Cancer, Scorpio, Pisces

This very well-known grouping has perhaps been overemphasized in many popular astrology books, and you really must beware of those who try to tell you that, for instance, fire signs are 'good for each other' or that 'air and water don't mix'. Such silly statements are futile and even dangerous when applied to two people who are about to develop an emotional relationship, to parents and their relationships with their children, or to brothers and sisters. Like the theory about being 'born on the cusp', it comes into the category of a little knowledge being a dangerous thing; it can and should be ignored — except maybe at one level: when we are considering friendship. Very broadly speaking we can say that two friends who have Sun-signs of the same *element* do often seem to hit it off. But when your children are growing up and perhaps coming into contact with astrology for the first time, they may well read an article in a teen-age magazine which will tell them that they must try to date a boy or girl of the same element — or that some signs do or don't go with each other. This is nonsense, and can mess up a promising friendship or relationship. I have faced many questions on this subject in radio or TV phone-ins, and have always emphasized that one must never decline to get to know someone on the basis that their Sun-sign is incompatible with one's own. That is the way to miss out on a lot of very rewarding experiences; remember that no reputable professional astrologer who has calculated the precise birth-charts of two people forming a relationship will ever say whether or not they should get together; one can only point out areas of compatability or difficulty.

These are important points to note if and when you apply astrology to the pleasures and pains you and your children experience as they grow up. I cannot stress too strongly that generalizations of this nature are rubbish, and dangerous rubbish at that!

A third astrological grouping links signs by their *qualities*. This is less important for the purposes of this book, but it is of interest, for sometimes the quality concerned may emerge to your child's disadvantage, and it may be necessary for you to go in for a certain amount of correction. The three qualities are:

> *Cardinal* — Aries, Cancer, Libra, Capricorn.
> *Fixed* — Taurus, Leo, Scorpio, Aquarius.
> *Mutable* — Gemini, Virgo, Sagittarius, Pisces.

Tradition dictates that *Cardinal* signs tend to be 'outgoing' by nature. *Fixed* signs tend to stubbornness and become 'fixed' in their opinions. *Mutable* signs are adaptable. There is a sub-division here which can also be revealing and interesting: there are three *dual* signs — Gemini, Sagittarius and Pisces — and those with an emphasis on these signs really do seem to have an element of duality in their personality. Think of the Geminian twins, the Sagittarian centaur with his arrow, and the pair of Piscean fish swimming in opposite directions! As a general rule, it's no use telling members of these signs to 'do one thing at a time' — it won't work, and it's not good for them!

We come now to the last astrological group, which in a broad sense can be the most important. This is the tradition that divides the Zodiac into *positive* and *negative*, or *masculine* and *feminine*, signs. Modern research has added *extrovert* (positive) and *introvert* (negative). On a Sun-sign level I am not wholly convinced of this theory, though it obviously has some elements of truth. The grouping is as follows:

*Positive, masculine, extrovert* — Aries, Gemini, Leo, Libra, Sagittarius, Aquarius.
*Negative, feminine, introvert* — Taurus, Cancer, Virgo, Scorpio, Capricorn, Pisces.

At the end of each section are examples from my case-book: extracts from reports prepared for parents, together with my comments. Also included are short lists for each Sun-sign of its Rulerships. Over four hundred years of tradition has built up, linking many things with the Sun-signs: places, flowers, herbs, trees, foods, and colours. It is often the case that people born when the Sun was in a particular sign feel a special affinity with the places and things 'ruled' by that sign. You may find it interesting — and sometimes helpful (when, for instance, choosing a holiday destination or a gift) — to check the following list (which is not, of course, comprehensive). Note that many items appear under two signs (because the signs are ruled by the same planet).

Finally, when writing a book of this kind it is all too easy to slip into the universal 'he', thus offending women. I have no wish to do this, so while I refer wherever possible to 'they', I'm also making a general rule to use 'she', where necessary, for the feminine signs and 'he' for the masculine ones. It is not, incidentally, the case that subjects of the feminine signs are essentially feminine in expression, nor are they by any means introverted; neither can the opposite rule be suggested. But there are inferences to be drawn, nevertheless, and you may find them interesting. Remember, though, that my comments refer to both sexes, unless I specifically state otherwise.

# ARIES

## (March 21 - April 20)

Note: Aries is a masculine sign, so for the most
part I refer throughout to 'he', but most of my
comments refer also to girls.

## General Characteristics

Arian children are on the whole pretty uncomplicated. Above all, they are motivated
by a need to win and to be 'first'. They should be encouraged to achieve their goals
and objectives — but it is very important that they are not allowed to become ruthless
in pursuit of them; the dominant Arian fault, selfishness, should be watched for
and nipped in the bud as soon as you see it emerging.

Young Arians can very easily become bored. It is surprising just how often they
will say they 'can't be bothered', and we find them slumped in front of a television
set watching anything that happens to be on the screen. This seems to be particularly
true of the boys, and it is important that if they seem to have no objective or burning
interest you try to encourage them to find one, for Arians have a very high energy
level and a basically strong will. It is terribly important, psychologically, that these
children move steadily forward; otherwise restlessness and dissatisfaction will dog
their footsteps. Once these qualities are properly channelled and your Arian child
is hooked on a specific interest there should be no holding him back.

Their physical energy level is extremely high, and while many will enjoy all kinds
of sport, if your individual Arian does not happen to like it, you should try to find
some other way in which he can burn up all of that splendid energy. Positive
enthusiasm is another delightful trait, which should always be nurtured. The great
thing is that this interesting, lively quality is kept on the boil, for sometimes we
find Arians are terribly enthusiastic about a new idea, but their enthusiasm tends
to wane as the idea is developed — partly because they simply become fed up with
it and partly because they often find another interest which they feel is more exciting,
and which takes precedence.

Arians are passionate and in argument will respond very quickly indeed to suggestions — sometimes to the point that their emotions boil over and a stormy tantrum occurs. But as with all sudden storms, these will be quickly over, and young Aries will be ready to turn his attention to other matters.

It is their uncomplicated outlook on life which is one of the most endearing virtues of an Arian. For instance, while you are telling him about some complicated problem or discussing a very involved situation, Aries will instantly see a way through it summing the whole thing up in a few sentences, and coming out with many practical, simple suggestions for a solution. So when young Arians reach the age of nine or ten, their advice will already usually be well worth considering. They will have a freshness of approach which is straight to the point, and which will remain one of their most valuable attributes no matter how complicated their lives may become in later years.

You must accept the fact that Arians are impatient. As well as wanting to win and to be first, they want everything *here and now*. For instance, it is a couple of days before their birthday: a friend brings a present. If they see it, they will have to open it immediately — it will be up to you to decide whether they should wait until the big day or satisfy their curiosity and impatience.

Most young children like bright colours, and Arians are no exception. Red, the colour of the sign, will no doubt be a popular favourite. Perhaps more than most signs, they need to feel free and independent, to be able to make off on exploring expeditions, alone or with friends, to climb trees, to take what you may think are fairly ambitious risks. They will need tough clothes and shoes to protect them against the sign's tendency to be accident prone!

Because they take people at their face value, and tend to be trusting, they need particularly careful warning about talking to strangers. It is essential not to destroy their self-confidence and their openness to others, but they must be warned against taking silly risks, not only in their tree-climbing and exploring but in their attitude to people.

There is a certain amount of aggressiveness in the Arian character, and if it shows signs of emerging in a negative fashion, you should try to find a way in which it can be expressed without it damaging the child or others. Aggressive sports (see p.23) can often provide an answer. The Arian fighting spirit can be a marvellously positive quality, and it's not for nothing that for centuries those of this sign have been called the pioneers of the Zodiac. We almost always find a pioneering element in life-style, self-expression or career. It is another trait which should be recognized and encouraged; it goes hand-in-hand with powers of leadership and often physical and moral bravery — two more fine qualities which deserve positive expression.

It is sometimes necessary to encourage the young Arian to slow down when facing the important issues of life and to consider them deeply. In their hurry to resolve one problem and get on with the next, they can be thoughtless, and the sadly typical selfish streak can emerge. Try encouraging a caring attitude to (for instance) elderly relatives or neighbours; this will sharpen awareness of other people's needs and limitations. It is particularly helpful for an Arian to 'adopt' a pensioner, making visits and going on errands, perhaps doing the occasional chore. In a different way, taking part in sponsored charity sporting activities is also excellent, helping Arians to burn up their abundance of physical energy and at the same time increase their awareness of less fortunate people, thereby countering selfishness.

Money always tends to burn a hole in an Arian pocket, and it may be necessary for you to distribute it daily rather than weekly! But the Arian business sense may well emerge early in the children's lives, and it should certainly not be difficult to encourage them to be enterprising with what money they have. Whatever the family circumstances, they should be encouraged to make money in order to buy the things they want — at first by helping about the house and, as they get older, by taking a weekend job (a paper round, perhaps). They should put the money in their own savings account, watching it grow until they can take it out to buy whatever they have their eyes on. The passing of an examination or the achievement of a high place in their class at school can be made an excuse for a financial reward: this is one of the signs that reacts immediately to the clinking of pound coins in the pocket.

## The Three Ways of Thinking

Due to the influence of Mercury (see p.13), the Arian mind characteristically works in one of three ways.

★ The first group of Arians is sensitive and caring, delightfully kind and thoughtful, and aware of the suffering of others. These boys and girls often find the arts enjoyable and rewarding, whether as performers or members of the audience. They will tend to be forgetful in small matters, because their minds are wandering.

★★ The second group will rush in where angels fear to tread. If they are not to cause disaster by quick and perhaps thoughtless action, they must be encouraged to consider every aspect of a situation before making their decisions. A tendency to speak before they think should also be controlled.

★★★ The third group may be rather slow to learn, making less speedy progress than you would like. Don't worry: they just need time to ponder and absorb. Remember, what they learn will remain with them for life. These are the most practical members of this Sun-sign.

## The Five Ways of Loving

Due to the influence of Venus (see p.13), Arians will tend to express their affection in one of five ways.

★ Because of their independent spirit, the members of the first group will make good leaders of a gang of friends, but may tend to be rather cool in responding to individuals. This can mean that they may be slow to form a permanent emotional relationship later in life.

★★ Don't be surprised if your Arian child tells you someone has accused him of being 'soppy': some Arians are loving and rather sentimental, warmly affectionate and caring, and quite able to control Arian selfishness. Make him understand it's fine for men to cry!

★★★ The third group will be sexually inquisitive at an early age. Answer questions frankly and without embarrassment, as soon as they are asked. Emotions will tend to be physically expressed — but there may be sudden emotional reverses ('No, he was my best friend *yesterday!*').

★★★★ Loving and affectionate, other Arians may tend to be over-possessive. Encourage them to share toys, sweets, affections — and friends. Watch out for jealousy within the family circle or among friends, for this group can want to hug things and people too closely.

★★★★★ Members of the fifth Arian group will be irresistably flirtatious from an early age, using sheer charm to get what they want. They will never stop talking about what their friends have done, and how fond they are of them — but will then go on to criticize and complain about them!

## Health and Diet

Aries traditionally rules the head, and we usually find that those with this sign emphasized in their birth-charts tend either to get an above-average number of headaches, or none at all. If young Aries persistantly complains of them, it will be as well to consider what may be causing them — get their eyes tested, for instance; or there may be a slight kidney imbalance. There is another possible contemporary cause of headaches: if you hear a Walkman squeaking away at the other end of the bus, it is likely to be clamped to the head of an Arian. Watch out for damaged ear-drums.

Because members of this sign seem always to be in a hurry, they are somewhat accident prone, tending to bump their heads and knock their noses — and sadly, many will lose milk-teeth at an early age, as the result perhaps of a fall. They will tend to cut or burn themselves when the opportunity arises, and knocks and bruises will be everyday matters. The only thing parents can do is recite the motto 'more haste, less speed', until it really sinks in! The Arian glands are the suprarenal glands, and when they become angry these pump adrenalin into the bloodstream, which can make them even more impetuous than they are already.

Generally speaking the sign is not prone to tension or worry, and relaxation is no more of a problem than sleeplessness. Usually young Arians will get plenty of exercise simply because they spend much of their life rushing from A to B, and then back to A. As they grow up, they will be keen to exercise, though because of their full and fast lives, they won't necessarily consciously need to set time aside for it. They usually have wiry, muscular bodies, and will probably be keen to avoid the puppy fat which can collect at adolescence. Exercise gear will be a welcome present. They should in theory be totally exhausted by bedtime, and simply crash out until morning, when it may be difficult to rouse them. A few Arians may be positively hyperactive, in which case it will be good for them to learn relaxation techniques. When they are a little older, this type can benefit from yoga. Earlier in their lives, however, they can be encouraged to listen to music and relax in that way.

All that Arian energy is splendid, and must not be fettered, but you should try to encourage them to use it in a controlled way, and if possible in a regular, steady way rather than in sudden gasps of over-exertion followed by inertia.

When Arians go down with the usual children's illnesses, you may find that their temperature can mount rather higher than that of other children; don't be too worried about this — just take the normal precautions. They are people who get overheated rather easily. Make sure that there is a good supply of fresh air in their bedroom — this is always important for children, but if Arians in particular don't get it, they will tend to suffer from catarrh or sinus problems.

Aries often enjoy very tasty, spicy food, but you should be a little careful, for it tends to overheat their blood. They certainly need plenty of protein. You may find that your Arian baby is off the bottle and into solid food rather earlier than you expect. If, later, they go through a period of rejecting food, it will probably be because they are just bored with the tedious occupation of getting the spoon up to the mouth, rather than with what you are offering them. Or they may have their minds firmly fixed on the toys on the floor below them, the football outside in the garden, or anything other than the business of eating.

Perhaps the most popular quick winter snack for an Arian will be a bowl of onion soup; tomatoes and leeks are also ruled by the sign. They will probably love the spicy, Indian snacks which can often be bought in health food shops. Rather than mass-produced sweets, try them with dried fruits — pineapple or apricots. In general, happily for the teeth, the Arian taste is for savoury rather than sweet foods; try to keep it that way.

With an Arian child in the house, keep a well-stock first aid kit always available: plenty of dressings, calomine lotion, and witch-hazel!

## The First Five Years

Arian children can make their presence felt more than usual while still in the womb, and they always seem in a hurry to get into the world. They will tend to be premature, to arrive almost without announcing themselves, and they grow up so fast that they seem to spend hardly any time as real babies. In fact they will seem positively grown-up as soon as they can walk, when they will immediately look good in clothes which might seem too grown-up for them — miniature track suits, for instance.

It is never too early to help an Arian baby to start developing. Always assume that he or she is older than they really are: help them to walk, think, and act before they appear to be ready for it. They will constantly surprise you.

The favourite earliest toys will be animal rather than human — a toy dog or bear rather than a doll. A large red ball will be appreciated — or a large red fire-engine! Picture-books should be full of action and adventure, and brightly coloured. They may tend to be bored by the process of learning to read, and you will perhaps have to work at getting them interested in books: by reading to them and by encouraging them to learn bits and pieces and recognize the words and sentences as you go along. They'll like joining in action and movement games on children's television, and their natural sense of adventure will encourage them to meet new friends — child and adult — at play group, to which you could take them at the earliest opportunity.

The Arian sense of adventure will soon show itself, and it is more than usually wise to keep an eye on them if you take them to the park or the beach; if you doze off for two minutes, they will very likely be in the next county, or striking out for the coast of France. Similarly, it is always a little dangerous to let an Arian child loose in an action playground on his own while he is very young; a child must take his own risks very early in life, but the Arian child will positively rush at a climbing-frame or a swing, and his ready enthusiasm may all too easily lead to a fall.

In the same playground, try to encourage the young Arian to become part of the team which he or she will inevitably want to lead. Being leader is fine, but he must learn that it is often necessary to follow. Naturally, it is a good thing to encourage sharing, sympathy and care for others at the earliest possible age.

Rather than obviously helping mummy in the home, it will be best to give the impression that they are doing something completely on their own, without too much supervision. So in the kitchen, if you can bear it, give them their own cooking ingredients and let them produce their own grey and malformed pie or cake rather than just handing you the salt or pepper; let them polish an accident resistant piece of furniture rather than help you with the table or chair.

Buy them a toy-box and encourage them to put their toys away when they've finished with them. They will hate this, and more often than not it won't be done; but it's a good move, and the seed might possibly take root!

## School Years

Nursery school may be hell for the teacher, but it will be heaven for the Arian child, who at last — with any luck — will have plenty of space to rush about in and plenty of other people to bounce his energy off. He will make the slushiest mud pies in the district, and along with Leo friends he will mix the brightest colours with which to paint the biggest, showiest pictures.

Encourage him to take some of his toys to school with him — once there he will be forced to share them with other children, and some of the natural Arian selfishness will be knocked out of him. If by chance there happens to be a particularly shy or nervous child in his group, try to encourage young Aries to befriend him or her, learning to be helpful and kind and damping down the slight tendency to aggression which can be part of the Arian nature. He will need to curb this — and need, too, to come to terms with the fact that he is not necessarily always to be the leader, or to come first, either in the classroom or the playground. Recognition of this fact can be a serious blow to his self-confidence if he learns the lesson the hard way — having been pack leader at nursery school, suddenly finding himself put in his place by stronger, more assertive children at primary school. It is advisable from the very beginning to make quite sure that he recognizes that he has to fit in with others rather than always having his own way.

When it comes to choosing a secondary school, remember that a young Arian will need discipline but not overwhelming or too restrictive discipline. Ideally, the school should have spacious, open buildings and be in open grounds; claustrophobia can be a problem. Good sports fields and gymnasia are very advisable, as are good workshops and craft rooms. Arians are self-contained enough to cope with the right sort of boarding-school with a modern outlook rather than too much emphasis on tradition. Coeducation suits both boys and girls: each sex can accept the other on equal terms — and see p.25.

Such a lively, strong-minded child will only accept discipline if he can be sure that it is soundly based and doesn't exist solely for the purpose of keeping him in his place. Routine will always bore him, but since school must have a routine, he must be persuaded that it is for a purpose — and in any event one advantage is that if he hates the maths period, he can be quite sure that games will follow shortly.

Arians will tend to be rather slapdash, rushing headlong at problems rather than following a logical course. This may make maths and science rather problematical subjects — though their love of experiment may attract them to the latter. They will be interested in the more dramatic incidents of history. They are not specially patient and need to see quick results; so in craftwork, for instance, they will like to work on a fairly large scale rather than fiddling with small, intricate problems. They will enjoy working with metals, so maintaining machinery often fascinates them.

A good sense of humour is essential when dealing with Arians; sarcasm (never a good move with children) will go down like a lead balloon — but the average Arian likes a good, perhaps obvious, joke; a rather bluff, good-humoured, straight-forward and above all enthusiastic teacher will be most effective and popular.

The impatient Arian will leave revision until the night before the examination. This in fact can work well for them, provided they don't actually leave it too late. In the examination room they should try to pace themselves rather than dashing so quickly at the papers that they finish thirty minutes too early, but later find that they have omitted important facts. They must be encouraged to read questions two or three times, if in their haste they are not to misunderstand or misinterpret them. Their biggest failing is probably carelessness.

Arians are natural sportspeople. They will enjoy games, though they are not always the easiest and most disciplined members of a team. Parents and teachers should encourage their spirit of adventure; many of them make wonderful adventure scouts and will love the carefully organized perils of adventure holidays. They should enjoy boxing, judo and the other martial arts, and often make excellent modern dancers and speed skaters.

Provided they can avoid the difficulties which will arise if their selfishness is not curbed, their straightforward enthusiasm and sheer love of life is infectious enough to make Arians popular. They will make friends quickly (though they can drop them quickly, too, especially if the friend is even slightly uncooperative!) the Arian needs a friend who is sufficiently assertive and strong-minded to be stimulating and not boring, without giving way so often that the Arian comes to feel he is always naturally top dog. Parents and teachers should always watch for any tendency to trample on other people to get to the top.

## Out of School Activities

The fuller an Arian child's life is the better, and it follows that out of school he or she must have plenty to do. They must certainly not be allowed to slump in front of a television screen in an apathetic stupor. However much they may seem to want to do this, it will breed boredom, and from boredom will spring dissatisfaction and discontent. Despite their energy and enthusiasm for life, Arians can be inclined to take the easy way out, and it is not always easy for a child to find things to do unless he or she is more than usually inventive. When a young Arian has a blow to his self-confidence he will sometimes sink into inertia rather than make the effort necessary to recover from a set-back. Parents must be aware of this problem and work out solutions which match their children's inclinations and which fit in with the family finances and environment.

You will probably find that your young Arian will be most attracted to out-of-school activities which are physically demanding, and you should look around for the best local sports facilities. If there is a large sports centre in your area, it will provide the ideal environment for Aries. Don't worry if he seems undecided on one particular sport or exercise activity; he will probably want to try everything before making up his mind what he wants to concentrate on. An adventure holiday combining several activities will be a splendid annual present; and as I have hinted, scouting and guiding are to be particularly encouraged — they will develop the Arian's enterprise and self-assurance, while encouraging the need for discipline and an awareness of the needs of others. Some Arians will specially enjoy first aid courses.

Bear in mind that outdoor sports are on the whole rather better for Arians than those which take place indoors. I have already mentioned the martial arts, which are particularly rewarding especially to the boys — though Arian girls will perhaps be among the most enthusiastic of their sex when it comes to learning practical methods of self-defence.

Both boys and girls will enjoy such mechanical tasks as repairing their bicycles or messing about with any kind of machine — which in itself can become an engrossing interest; there may be an early enthusiasm and flair for engineering, which could of course become a career.

As far as hobbies are concerned we must always remember that patience does not come naturally or easily to Arians; while they should be encouraged to try to develop it, don't be manic about this, for it is important that they aren't frustrated by their efforts to work slowly and carefully, and quick results are essential, whether the individual is learning a musical instrument, sewing, or model making. Something simple rather than complicated with go down best: the drum rather than the violin, making a big felt cushion rather than a small piece of lace.

Don't forget Arian impatience will prompt your child to leap onto new subjects with great enthusiasm — but tend to drop them equally quickly. Don't buy expensive equipment or lessons until you're sure it's not to serve a temporary craze.

## Preparing for Life

Arians are quick developers and will want to be part of the adult world before, perhaps, they are entirely ready, psychologically.

The Arian girl, for instance, may tend to assume that her first period makes her, automatically, 'a woman'. She will soon find that there is more to adulthood than its physical manifestations. It may be that Arian girls need special sympathy from parents; mother should take care that the difficult days are made as easy as possible and that her daughter is able to carry on with her sporting activities and her ordinary life as easily as possible. This may be easier than with some other girls, for Arians are not likely to be shy about their bodies, and there should not be any particular difficulty with inhibition.

   The boys will show early on something of the typical Arian attitude to sex, which can unfortunately consist of making as many conquests as possible in a short period of time! The best lesson they can learn, or be taught, in this area of life is that which applies to friendship and social behaviour in general: consideration for others. Like the girls, they will have few inhibitions about their bodies, and there is no need to be at all pussyfooted in explaining the facts of life.

   Both girls and boys, then, will be ready to experiment, sexually, at a fairly early age. The problems that arise will depend very much on circumstances. Coeducation, which I have recommended, may seem dangerous in some ways, but is actually extremely good for young Arians developing their relationships with the opposite sex: girls may tend to be tomboyish, and the daily presence of boys will remind them of their femininity, while the boys will hopefully learn consideration and respect for the girls' academic skills. Propinquity will make sexual experiment easier, but the problems will be no more and no less than in any other area.

   Arians are interested in and enthusiastic about sex, and if parents are either shy or too restrictive in their attitude, the reaction is likely to be a determination to kick over the traces. A completely open attitude is best, both in explaining sex and in discussing any difficulties. The young Arian will almost inevitably want to experiment in all sorts of ways. It is vital to be frank about the consequences, both in psychological and physical terms. If you find it difficult to discuss all this with your Arian child, *don't* just give them a book about sex and hope for the best; make absolutely sure they they receive proper sex education at school. When the time comes, they should be encouraged to carry and use condoms; Arians are creatures of the moment, and in sudden enthusiasm must, for the sake of their health, be prepared.

   When they begin to form real personal attachments, you will find their reactions will fall into one of the groups I describe on p.19-20. In general, Arians really need to share an emotional relationship and require a great deal of harmony in this sphere of their lives. Arguments and disagreements will occur — maybe triggered by Arian selfishness — but will blow over very quickly, for this type will have nothing to do with lingering, petty resentment. The Arian enthusiasm will mean that they want to share activities with the boy- or girl-friend.

   The best possible partner for an Arian is perhaps one who is a little bit cleverer than themselves, thus nudging them on to higher attainments. There will almost always be an element of competitiveness in an Arian relationship, and it is very good for them.

## Further Education

Further education is something which never comes amiss with an Arian, and if young Aries is not involved at university or on some advanced course, rather than spend any time unoccupied he or she should look at every conceivable Government or private scheme to help him occupy his time profitably: as I point out later, wasting time is the worst possible thing for the Arian character.

   Having said that, 'education' as such is perhaps not invariably at the front of the Arian mind. At university, look for the Arians on the football field, on the river, in the gym. Of course they can make fine students, but there is no question that they can also be seduced all too easily into a greater preoccupation with sport than is good for their academic career — especially if it so happens that they are among the best athletes of their year, when they will tend to concentrate on proving that they are *the* best. And they will be prepared to spend not only every moment of spare time on this, but time which should really be spent in study.

The extent to which they can be persuaded into the lecture room will depend entirely on the lecturers. At college, as everywhere else, an appeal to the Arian's enthusiasm will be answered immediately and in no uncertain way. Conversely, the slightest indication that a tutor is bored with his subject will have the opposite result. Arians are never backward in setting out their opinions and ideas, and this should endear them to intelligent teachers. It will also tend to involve them in political activity and in any debating body which exists.

It is not in the Arian character to start worrying now about an examination in nine months' time. But as the exam approaches, you can appeal to their love of proving their ability; they will want to make their mark, to get a good degree, and will settle down to serious study — if belatedly — for a poor result will damage their sense of pride.

An Arian studying perhaps at a polytechnic and living at home will darken the domestic doors less and less; they will get enthusiastically involved in school business, both formal and social. When they are at home, studying, it may not always sound like it; there will be plenty of noise — noise is in many ways an Arian's natural environment — and perhaps plenty of leaping about, as an Arian with a book in his hand needs to get rid of that abundant energy somehow. His desk will overflow with things and will be intolerably untidy — except that the Arian will know precisely where everything is. The work-bench will be covered with tools apparently scattered at random — except that in fact each will be just where the Arian hand can fall on it. Parents can only stand back helplessly — except that they should constantly warn their children to be careful with sharp tools; Arian hastiness has resulted in the loss of many a fingertip. Protective clothing should be worn in circumstances which demand it — goggles when using welding tools, for example; harness when working in dangerous places. In theory, Aries is all for self-preservation; in practise, forgetfulness and carelessness can be real problems.

Talking of carelessness, the Arian driver will be fast and skilful, but must learn to recognize the circumstances under which danger can occur — and know how to cope with it. There is perhaps no other sign which benefits more from advanced driving tuition; they will enjoy this and will enjoy the sense of security which stems from knowing just how to deal with emergencies when they occur. This in itself will make them safer and better drivers.

Arians are at their best when they have two sources of income — this seems to satisfy a need for additional security. So in the vacation, any holiday job which will give them experience in a previously unknown area will be not only interesting but rewarding, giving them perhaps an insight into a possible future spare time interest which could be developed into an additional source of income.

# Unemployment: Stresses and Strains

The superabundant Arian energy and enthusiasm really needs an outlet, and any Arian caught in the unemployment trap will feel the awful frustration of that situation perhaps more acutely than most; if some way is not found of easing the problem it will lead to anger, resentment and despair.

So it is absolutely necessary that the Arian should look for every way of occupying himself, rather than sitting about doing nothing. Follow every possible lead. Look at Government schemes, and accept what seems unsuitable temporary work (it may lead to something better); even unpaid work for charity is better than nothing, for the Arian. Far better for him to dig someone's garden or clear away rubbish for nothing or for an inadequate payment, than to spend the day waiting for the phone to ring. This seems unfair, and often *is* unfair, but better to keep in good psychological shape at the cost of working for next to nothing than to be inactive and allow all sorts of pressures to build up.

Parents too should do everything they can to prevent despondency setting in, encouraging their children to be patient and persistent in looking for work. One of the best things they can do is suggest that Aries adopt a systematic approach to the problem: taking the right sort of magazines, going daily to the job centre and looking at the advertisements, letting no day pass without writing a letter, adjusting the CV, doing *something* to promote himself and his prospects. In this way his will to win will be kept alive. He must at all costs preserve his self-respect and self-confidence. The motto really should be 'Never say die'.

There will of course be long stretches of time when even the most lively and involved Arian will flag. These gaps must be filled, and you could suggest, for instance, that he get together with people of his own age who are in the same situation and work out a community project for their district which will help others and occupy themselves. We should never forget the enormous amount of physical and emotional energy of the Sun-sign Arian; if it stagnates there will be trouble. There is unlikely to be premeditated violence, but impatience and frustration might boil over and lead to sudden outbursts of verbal or even physical action. On the other hand if it has positive expression, even when career prospects are at their dreariest, the Arian will at least find some kind of fulfilment, and be physically tired at the end of the day.

For the Arian, the solution to the problem of unemployment may very well lie in self-help, and this must be impressed on individuals. If he realizes that he's out on his own and that only he can climb out of the hole he finds himself in, his energy and ingeniousness will see him through. Encourage him to blow his own trumpet; no one will blow it better.

## Coping with Drugs

Arians are not specially vulnerable to negative escapism. They like to face up to reality rather than looking for an easy way out, so they are not likely to turn to drugs for relief from problems. If they succumb at all, it will be because, like the denizens of some other signs, they are always ready to try something new and different, to broaden their experience of life. And if they start early — smoking while they're at school, for instance — they may find it all too easy to look for a stronger kick and will then really have problems, because they are whole-hoggers and not given to stopping halfway. But they should have the willpower to kick the habit, and not the least thing to put the boys off hard drugs is the realization that their sexual prowess will be affected. Once more, their self-confidence will be shaken!

Because Arians are not on the whole very complicated people, who really do know right from wrong, they are likely to respond well to a really logical argument; they may feign excuses, but a few well-chosen words should get through to them and hit home. Don't forget, incidentally, that hard drugs are not the only problem; the pint of beer after the match could grow to two or three, and then to too many. Again, logic — the fact that too much alcohol will depress their performance — should do the trick.

## Interests and Spare Time Activities

Once your Arian has found a boy- or girl-friend, you're not likely to see them moping about the house. Yes, there will be the excitement of finding out about sex, but that won't be the be-all and end-all of the relationship, for they will want to share all the things they like doing best — and this will mean, in particular, outdoor activities and sports of all kinds. Arians are doers rather than thinkers, so pretty well all those joint activities will be extrovert; they will be off and about, rather than sitting listening to music or watching TV.

They (both boys and girls) usually share an enjoyment of physical tasks. They will be at their best when, for instance, they have something to repair — car servicing or the restoration of old automobiles or planes will keep them happily occupied. But here, as everywhere else, it is the expending of energy that is important — they are not at their best trying to mend a watch, for instance, nor at modelling a delicate flower in clay — they would rather be hacking away at a large piece of wood or stone. Parents need not tremble in fear and trepidation when young Aries suggests that he wants to redecorate his or her room — the choice of colours may not be exactly what mother will admire, and the standard of painting may leave something to be desired, but full marks will be given for the sheer enthusiasm and energy (those words again!) put into the job; they usually want to see the end result of such a job, so they're unlikely to give up halfway through, even if they are rather too happy to take short cuts. They won't be bothered with two coats of paint if one will do, but the overall effect when the task is finished will be interesting and good fun. It is no bad thing, by the way, for the boys to be encouraged to make new curtains and the girls to put up shelves.

Arians like to be fashionable — they are always consciously aware of the latest trends. This can prove expensive if they are continually trotting off to their favourite boutique. The girls should be encouraged to make their own experimental fashion creations. These will certainly have considerable impact, and while we won't look too closely at the stitching, provided it is strong enough to withstand an energetic evening or two at the disco, all will be well.

The Arian, with his spirit of adventure, will often be attracted to canoeing and the more daring water sports. Water-skiing, surfing, diving and deep sea exploration are all excellent ways in which they can enjoy themselves (remembering that these are not sports to be carelessly enjoyed; in an aqualung, you're only careless once!). Many enjoy sailing in small boats, and with a stiff breeze, a life-jacket, and a well-equipped hamper they will make the most of a day afloat with friends.

Those Arians attracted to creative cookery (take care in the kitchen with knives and hot dishes) will probably excel in quick dishes — wok cookery, omelettes, and convenience food artfully tarted up with herbs and spices.

Arians are not specially good committee members, and while they will initially be keen to involve themselves in societies and organizations which attract them, they should be conscious that their lack of patience could annoy less enterprising and quick witted colleagues. They will have to learn that for their club or society to make progress in the way they wish, and for their suggestions to be accepted, they should curiously put their case calmly and rationally, and sometimes give way to others. As chairpeople they must not allow their emotions or their tendency to speak before they think to get the better of them; that is just the way to antagonize the rest of the committee — more perhaps than they realize. With this in mind they will certainly contribute much and get a great deal of satisfaction from the time spent in helping the organization.

The ideal pet for a young Arian is probably an Arian dog — or at least a dog with as much enthusiasm and lust for life as he. Arians tend to be dog rather than cat people — mainly perhaps because a healthy dog can share their outdoor activities. It is good for them to have the discipline of caring for an animal, or taking a share in caring for one, from an early age. It helps to mitigate against forgetfulness and selfishness. Later in life owning a pet will be a great source of pleasure.

And to end where we began, there will certainly be a great deal of sexual shenanigans. Whatever your moral view, the line with Arians — if you can persuade yourself to take it — is not to forbid anything; that will have quite the opposite effect than you desire. These days more than perhaps in any other age, and specially with impatient Aries, it is most important to underline the old adage: if you can't be good, for goodness sake be careful.

## Ideal Careers

Working alone in a stuffy, ill lit office, doing repetitive dull work is absolutely wrong for lively, enthusiastic Arians, who need to be able to communicate with like-minded colleagues, to work in a well lit and aired conditions and an invigorating atmosphere — and above all to put all their energy, physical and intellectual, to continual and rewarding use. If they are restricted in this, they will become bored, and boredom is anathema to them all. Members of the sign cope extremely well with noisy, even dirty conditions, if called upon to do so, but it is as well for them to have a job which gives them the opportunity to express a certain amount of individuality and enterprise.

Arians are generally ambitious and will be eager to lead their particular team or colleagues, even to climb to the head of a department or firm. They must beware of an equally strong tendency to be ruthless (remember the old motto, 'Be careful who you tread on on the way up; you may meet them again on the way down').

Their ability to be frank should be softened consciously by their characteristically jovial sense of humour, which will stand them in good stead when they are forced to criticize or rebuke colleagues or subordinates.

They are not averse to a certain amount of tension, at least as it is expressed in a confrontation with risks or problems; faced by any difficult situation, they won't expect anyone else to cope with it on their behalf, but will jump into the roughest water and strike out for the other side, confident that others will follow their lead. This leadership shows itself in another way: it is essential that Arians are able to use their pioneering spirit — in science, perhaps by experiment and the opportunity to diversify, perhaps in a somewhat off-beat way which will turn out to be valuable both to them and their employers. Arians interested in medicine often tend towards psychiatry and an exploration of the workings of the human mind. And following up the traditional connection between Aries and the head, work on the ear, nose and throat can also attract those who enter medicine; so can dentistry.

Engineering can provide a satisfying career, so can the motor trade — and any work involving the use of metals. Many Arians are to be found working for the railway systems and fire brigades of their countries.

If your Arians are deeply attracted to any branch of sport, there is no reason not to encourage them to develop this interest; a well above average number of people with this Sun-sign have become extremely successful professional sportsmen and women. They will be partly inspired by the challenging need to widen the boundaries of human physical endurance, and their desire to win is coupled with that pioneering spirit — a good recipe for success.

Linked somewhat to this is the proposition that Arians always enjoy physical work. An out of work Arian will generally not be afraid to take a labouring job and may even find it fulfilling; any parent whose son or daughter shows any desire to become a farm worker, a miner or a builder, however disappointed they may be at what they perhaps see as lack of ambition, can at least be confident that the young man or woman will stand up well to the physical demands of the job, and indeed will relish them. They may in fact be satisfied in such a situation but will still be likely to find their way upwards to a position of leadership. Women can cope with tough physical work, too — and might be specially happy as bus- or taxi-drivers or chauffeurs.

Remember that Arians are not the most patient people in the world, and this can sometimes be a disadvantage, for not only will they be impatient for promotion, but they may become impatient with themselves and their lack of progress. Parents should try to cheer them up when this happens by underlining their successes and encouraging them to persist with careful hard work.

The motto 'a change is as good as a rest' makes a great deal of sense to an Arian; if trapped in work which is boring and repetitive, they must have plenty of hobbies and social life to make life endurable. Stagnation is the great poison; as long as the natural enthusiasm and vivacity can be fully expressed, there will be no problems at work — whatever the work is.

## Travel

Arians love to travel, and rather sooner than you may like your son or daughter may announce the fact that they are off alone to walk the great wall of China with a sleeping-bag and a small haversack. Once having set their sights on a particular trip, they won't in the least mind putting up with any amount of discomfort — though they may tend to take slight risks just because of their eagerness to get there as quickly as possible.

And there are, of course, risks — but not necessarily the obvious ones. You might for instance point out to them that rather than having their passport or money stolen, they may lose them just as the result of personal carelessness, for they can be forgetful, and having sat down for a brief rest halfway up the mountain pass, press on without checking that they still have everything they had when they stopped. They are certainly not the kind of people to enjoy having to hang about in police stations or frontier posts waiting for that missing passport or wallet to be found or replaced.

As I have said elsewhere, you must learn very early on to keep an eye on your Arian youngster. His or her first holiday will provide a marvellous excuse to wander off in the direction of everywhere. Foreign parts, in particular, will provide just that mixture of strangeness and excitement that Aries will burn to explore. They will very much want to find out how the other half lives, looks, talks, and tastes. Quite apart from keeping within sight of them, try to protect them from the heat of the sun, for they love sunshine but can easily suffer heat-stroke. Humidity is less worrying but will drain their energy (not, come to think of it, altogether a bad idea where you are concerned — but it may make the younger ones fractious and irritable).

Choosing the kind of holiday which a young Arian will enjoy, keep in mind the fact that they may very much want to continue their normal routine of interests; so if they are into, say, one particular sport, try to find a resort which offers facilities for it. One which has good sporting opportunities will probably be popular — Arians enjoy wind-surfing and para-gliding and such excitements and, incidentally, winter sports, with their combination of sun and excitement. Remember that Arians do tend to be accident-prone, and while this should never be used to stop them doing anything (no chance of that succeeding, anyway), the wise parent of Arian children will take a good first aid kit wherever they go.

Excitement, indeed, is an excellent ingredient of every Arian life, and this has its advantages: there shouldn't be any problem on the journey, young Aries will be so excited by the travelling itself that they won't have time or energy to be travel-sick! The hovercraft, plane, train, car — the excitement of heading towards new places, people and activities — should be quite enough to keep them occupied.

## Arians as Brothers and Sisters

The main problem for Aries as a brother or sister will occur when he or she is overshadowed by the presence of a sibling; the tendency will then be to shoulder forward, taking the first place to which Arians always aspire, regardless of the feelings of others. Parents may find, when a younger child is born, that Aries will make a great clatter when too much attention seems to be focused on baby, seeking by any means to regain the consideration — and as they see it, the affection — which is now focused on someone other than themselves.

However, parents should realize that there is a great advantage in having an Arian brother or sister, for they will be encouraging and helpful, and their help can be asked whenever required — at bathtime, for instance — and will happily be given, because it will underline the Arian's feeling of being important to the family in general. And remember that it is not natural for an Arian to be spiteful or vindictive, so there will not be that problem — though in a moment of anger and impatience there might be a sudden violent instinct, so watch out for tantrums which might lead to this. It will be perfectly easy to appeal to the Arian good nature and conscience. Problems should be diplomatically and logically discussed and resolved; in many respects, fair play is important to Arians, and it is not difficult to get them to see both sides of an argument.

As with most modern children, it will be a good thing to involve them in mother's pregnancy, but don't be surprised if, having explained 'where babies come from' to as great an extent you think wise, Aries asks whether the baby will appear tomorrow — as with everything else, immediate action will be demanded! When baby does arrive, the best thing to emphasize is the fact that Aries is the 'big brother or sister', because that will appeal to the Arian need to be out in front of the field.

If your eldest child is rather sensitive, a younger Arian brother or sister should be encouraged to understand that just because a person is older, it doesn't mean that they are necessarily going to be more energetic or braver; people are different, in other words, and Aries needs to learn this at an early age. Encourage Aries to stick up for the perhaps less positive older sibling; they will not be in the least reluctant to do so once they realize that it is a good thing.

It may be that some problem arises at school because of the extrovert Arian need to show off, to prove themselves better than anybody else in the vicinity — and that will certainly include a brother or sister, whether younger or older. They need not be encouraged to 'let' the other win; but must learn not to be distressed or jealous if they do! If there are signs that the non-Arian sibling is living in a shadow, overpowered by the Arian strength of character, it might be an excellent thing to talk things through with a sympathetic teacher. But the other child should be involved too, and told that just because young Aries always wants to be out in front jumping up and down and making a fuss, this doesn't necessarily mean that they are any better, or more likely to be successful, than a quieter achiever. If this situation arises, it would be a good thing to arrange that the children's interests at school are as disparate as possible; this will mean that the competitive element becomes less obvious and important.

At home, it is sometimes necessary that children have, at least early in their lives, to share rooms. Aries won't be at all keen on this, and it may be necessary actually to mark out their own territory into which brother or sister will step at their peril — to give them their own toy cupboards, different coloured bed-covers; and if they have bunk beds, Aries had better have the top one! Though you needn't tell them so, it is actually quite a good thing for them to share a room for a while — they will then not only learn that under some circumstances they have to share things but that it isn't always possible, let alone desirable, for them to have their own way about everything and to impose their will completely upon everybody!

Try as much as possible to underline what *fun* it is to have a brother or sister, encouraging the bouncy, extrovert side of Aries, which can be such a joy to everyone around them.

## Arians as Parents

Arians always being eager to rush at everything, there is a danger that they may rush into parenthood before they have really thought things through, and before they are necessarily ready for it. There is also the point that the male Arian will perhaps feel particularly under pressure to prove his virility (he would certainly be more susceptible than most to any raised eyebrows from potential grandparents about a decision not to have a child in the first year or two).

Ms Aries will be equally eager to have a child very early on, even if she is a committed career woman. This certainly won't mean that she will want to give up her career, and she will readily devise ways of coping with both situations — and will be more likely to have spare time and energy to cope with her children at the end of the working day. If this is the case, however successfully things seem to be working out, she should think carefully whether the children are really getting enough of her time and attention — but the frustration and boredom of coping with young and demanding children could have a very bad effect on her, and on balance it is probably better for the children to see rather less of a happy mother than more of a fractious and bored one.

The well-known phenomenon of father having his nose put out of joint by the arrival of baby will be more likely to show itself with an Arian than with a father of another sign, just because of the Arian personality. So mother must try more than usual to show that the baby isn't actually the whole of her life and that father is still 'pack leader'! Arian fathers are usually very popular with their children because they are eager for them to get as much out of life as themselves. The time they are able to spend with them will be packed with incident and will enrich their lives; there will be plenty of treats and outings to burn up that excess energy. But Arian parents of either sex should beware of imposing their own tastes on their children, carting them off to football when they would rather be at the ballet — this warning probably specially applies to Arian fathers who are into sport in a big way. They really must remember that not everybody is as involved in the physical life as much as they are. Of course it hurts no child to be brought up conscious of the importance of healthy and regular exercise; it's just that this should not take up a disproportionate part of their lives unless they are cast in the same mould.

As good achievers themselves, Arian parents should, if they have the time, involve themselves with their children's schools — with parent/teacher activities, for instance. They often have a natural instinct about how to encourage others.

Whatever their age, Arian parents should have no difficulty with a generation gap. They like to keep abreast of things and should not have to strive to discover just what their children's interests are; they will probably know as much about the subject, themselves. And if they do find, suddenly, that they are out of touch, the challenge of catching up will appeal. One of the most exciting things about Arian parenthood is the stimulation it offers — having to keep abreast of, and if possible ahead of, the children — from predicting the top of the charts next week or the next fashion change, to being on the winning side of the school vs fathers cricket match.

An Arian parent with one compulsive interest should be careful not to concentrate on it to the extent that their children are entirely excluded — not only from that activity but from father or mother's thoughts. The result can be a parent whose life is interesting and fulfilled but a child who spends too much time slumped in front of the TV screen.

There are some difficulties for children with an Arian parent, but if the parent gets things right, the relationship can be wonderfully rewarding — full of excitement and energy, enthusiasm and push. Yes, there will be occasional squalls, but they will be soon over. There will be no resentment or lingering anger — no punishment going on for weeks; a quick word or even a blow then all will be forgotten, and the excitement and joy of life will once again take over.

## Case Study

**Debbie** - Sun, Mercury, Venus in Aries; Mercury Group 2, Venus Group 3.

**From the Report**: 'I gather that Debbie may go into private education. If this is so, do try to find a school that is not too claustrophobic or restrictive. While in many ways she may need a little 'taming' at times, she will thrive on lively, positive encouragement, and will hate any over-strict teachers who tend to nag or carp. Some care is needed here. If you find that she has suddenly not done as well one term as in the previous one, it could well be due to her not getting enough encouragement or inspiration from a teacher, and nothing to do with the difficulty of the subject. When she is working with a teacher she likes, admires and respects, she will sit taking in every word that teacher says and go ahead in leaps and bounds; otherwise she may get easily bored, and you'll get used to seeing the phrase 'could do better if she tried' in her school reports.

'She may well have potential for some form of craftwork, and enjoy making and designing jewellery or working in some way with metals. She could well be musical, but — dare I write this? — don't be surprised if she wants to play the trumpet or percussion. Sorry about that!'

**Comment**: Debbie's analysis was written immediately after her birth in the late seventies. At the time her parents thought my comment about trumpet-playing extremely funny; however, a brass band was formed at her school, and she started to play the bugle, soon graduating to the trumpet, for which she not only has great enthusiasm but considerable talent.

## The Sun-sign and Its Rulerships

*Countries and areas*: Denmark, England, France, Germany, Japan, Poland, Syria.

*Cities*: Brunswick, Capua, Crakow, Florence, Marseilles, Naples, Padua, Utrecht, Verona.

*Trees*: holly, some types of fir; thorn-bearing trees or bushes.

*Flowers and herbs*: arnica, bayberry, bryony, broom, capers, cayenne pepper, furze, geranium, honeysuckle, hops, juniper, leeks, mustard, nettles, onions, peppermint, rhubarb, tobacco, witch-hazel.

*Food*: all fish; cereals, especially wheat; onions, tomatoes, and leeks; beer.

*Cell salts*: Kali Phos., Nat. Phos.

*Animals*: sheep and rams.

*Stone*: diamond.

*Metal*: iron.

*Colour*: red, scarlet.

# TAURUS

## (April 21 - May 21)

Note: Taurus is a feminine sign, so for the most
part I refer to 'she', but most of my comments
refer also to boys.

## General Characteristics

Faced with having to think of a single word which characterizes the Taurean, one would probably come up with 'solidity': the best sort of Taurean is a good, solid citizen — reliable in a crisis, with a sound personality and background. But in order to become so reliable and dependable, the Taurean needs, above all, security — both material and emotional — and if this is threatened she will become worried and upset; a Taurean child, for instance, faced with the breakup of her parents' marriage — or even something much simpler and less traumatic like moving house — is more likely than most to react by behaving uncharacteristically, becoming disruptive and ill-tempered. It is always advisable to keep them in the picture, and whenever a major change seems likely to warn them at the earliest possible moment. (Don't worry: if you tell a Taurean child something in confidence, they are not the sort to blurt it out embarrassingly to Grandma or anybody else.)

Young Taureans are among the most practical of children, and you can appeal to this quality in difficult situations — they will always see reason if things are properly explained to them, slowly and carefully. They are not usually terribly quick at grasping things, or indeed in reacting to them, so a leisurely approach is best. They tend to be more than a little stubborn — another good reason to be sure that logic is kept well to the fore. They are very good at cloaking stubbornness with charm and will use that charm — which is often considerable — to win parents round to their way of thinking. Taureans indeed have the reputation of being the most charming people in the Zodiac, so this really is a danger to watch out for! They are good-looking, too, and often have delightful, warm speaking voices. All these are great assets, of course, but it is a good idea to point out that it is better to use them honestly than as weapons!

Taureans should be encouraged to be flexible, to bow gracefully to others' opinions when necessary, and not to take a dogmatic view of life. Thus, stubbornness can be modified into determination, a slightly different but infinitely more preferable quality which will be a help rather than a hindrance to them.

Taureans rarely lack energy, but it is often slow to get going; they will hang around indefinitely at the breakfast table or after supper, rather than getting up and on with whatever needs to be done. They enjoy a lazy life. The way around this can be found in their love of a steady routine. Once this has been set and they have accepted it, they will hate, because of their need for security, to break it. Parents who set a home timetable just as rigid as the one at school will find that they will adhere to it. If they know for a fact that particular hours are set aside for homework, cleaning their room, or taking exercise, and that only a real emergency will alter the routine, they will happily stick to it and flourish — a predictable, set pattern to their lives is just what they need.

You can and should trust your Taurean child with regular tasks; again, the routine will attract them, and they are extremely reliable and responsible. If in a careless moment they forget what is expected of them, an appeal to conscience will have vivid results, and their future standards will be higher.

The basic Taurean fault is possessiveness, which extends to people as well as things: father will be 'my daddy' rather than mummy's husband; toys will be *mine* and not to be shared, and so on. Throughout their childhood, in as many ways as possible, parents must watch out for this unattractive trait, which in extremity can lead to jealousy and storms, which apart from making the child wildly unpopular with her peers, can lead to emotional problems later in life. It is not an easy trait to combat, but certainly Miss Taurus should be encouraged, however much she hates it, to give some of her old toys to charity — and even some of her pocket-money. She will hate this even more, but remember that she is loving and kind, and you can appeal to this side of her nature. Since Taureans can have a considerable preoccupation with money, any effort to loosen their grasp on their piggy banks early in life will make it far easier for them, when they are grown-up, to take a reasonable attitude to finance. It's not that they're mean; it's just that they enjoy saving and even investing. Their natural business sense, however, should not be stifled; encouraged at an early age to start saving, the earlier they have their own bank account and learn to administer it, the better. And as for charity, why not encourage them to use their natural business sense to help raise money? And they make excellent treasurers of charities or leisure organizations, for they are trustworthy as well as reliable — while it would be silly to suggest that no Taurean treasurer has ever absconded with the funds, this does not on the face of it seem very likely!

Taureans are on the whole very conventional, and this affects their attitude to people, to whom they may react in a somewhat old-fashioned way. These are not necessarily children who will enjoy calling their parents by their forenames, and while of course they should be warned about predators, their natural caution and good sense make them perhaps less susceptible to the stranger offering them a sweet than children of some other signs. Taureans are naturally cautious, in fact; they are not risk-takers. This can be excellent, but it can also hold them back, for a much-loved routine can easily become a rut out of which you may need to jolt them.

It is often necessary to point out that change is a good rather than a bad thing and that one should look forward optimistically rather than apprehensively.

Because they are rather conventional, Taurean children won't object to school uniform, and indeed if it is reasonably attractive it may be quite difficult to get them out of it. But they will also look good in leisure wear; the girls will enjoy choosing clothes, and both sexes will like wearing track suits in attractive shades of pale blue, pink or green — the Taurean colours.

The adult Taurean will look on home as the baseline, beyond which there is no retreat and from which the world can be faced and if necessary outfaced. The Taurean child needs to have the same confidence that home is a rock which cannot be shifted. If any problems do occur — emotional problems between parents, for instance — it is far better to bring these out into the open, explaining at the same time that home is still home and that the child's security is an absolute priority.

## The Three Ways of Thinking

Due to the influence of Mercury (see p.13), the Taurean mind characteristically works in one of three ways.

★ Some Taureans are decisive and have the ability to think very quickly. The combination of these qualities with their sound judgement will of course be extremely useful. Taurean bulls do sometimes rush their gates, but at least when they do so their energy will see them through until the stiffest obstacle is down.

★★ A second group will be much more deliberate in its approach to problems but once having made a decision, will be difficult to shift from it — stubbornness can even become bloody-mindedness and can certainly be a problem. These Taureans must be allowed all the time they need and not be rushed into decisions.

★★★ A third group has lively, quick minds but are surprisingly changeable. These children's powers of concentration are not terribly good, but they are less stubborn and more open-minded and reasonable than their Taurean brothers and sisters. Their lively minds add a lighter side to their personality.

## The Five Ways of Loving

Due to the influence of Venus (see p.13), Taureans will tend to express their affection in one of five ways; because Venus is the ruling planet of Taurus, its placing also has an important psychological influence.

★ One group of Taureans is tender, loving, romantic and somewhat sentimental. Their emotional level is high, and falling in love for the first time they will be particularly starry-eyed. They cannot be expected to take a practical view of the situation or of their lovers.

★★ The second group is passionate, highly sexed and highly emotional, with a tendency to fall in and out of love very quickly. They will get a lot of happiness and sheer fun in an affair, though there may be an element of selfishness to mar their relationships.

★★★ Some Taureans are very romantic, with the charm and good looks to win them almost anyone on whom they set their heart. But they must be careful that possessiveness or jealousy does not end the affair as soon as it begins. They must stifle these negative qualities if their positive side is to dominate.

★★★★ Others show a delightfully light-hearted, flirtatious streak which can be enchanting. There may be a tendency for them to involve themselves with more than one relationship at a time — but at least possessiveness will worry their lovers less than other Taureans. They enjoy friendship as part of a love affair.

★★★★★ The final group of Taureans has a strong caring quality which may make them over-protective and over-possessive. Their marvellously loving quality can be stifling. But they tend to judge every man or woman as potential father or mother of their children, which may not always go down well. They often tend to worry, too.

## Health and Diet

One of the strongest characteristics a Taurean child displays very early in her life is a voracious appetite and love of food. Generally speaking there should be few problems in this area, and you will find that your Taurean baby will happily devour whatever you set before her. The most important thing, and this cannot be too strongly stressed, is that you should very carefully watch your Taurean child's intake of sugar. They love very sweet food, and as we know this is not very good for them, so the more you can discourage it the better. Of all the twelve Zodiac signs, this is one whose members put on weight most easily, and it is only common sense to keep the intake of sweets, cake and chocolate to a minimum. Pocket-money will tend to be spent on sweet snacks — of course all children do this, but anything you can do to persuade Taureans to have, say, an apple or a banana rather than a bar of chocolate, will be worthwhile. If they must have sweet foods, honey is preferable to sugar. Certainly if you are packing lunch for them, this should be kept in mind.

Should your young Taurean seem inordinately plump or inactive, it might be worth having your doctor check up on his or her thyroid gland. This gland is associated with Taurus, and when it is faulty can slow the metabolism and cause inaction and hence a build up of weight.

The Taurean metabolism tends in any event to be somewhat slow, and they need to increase it; exercise will help. Just being out in the fresh air is good for them, but heavy sports are excellent, and they should enjoy them. If they do not, they could be encouraged to work in a garden, digging and growing plants (if this is possible); if they live in the country, farm work could help their physical well-being, build up muscles and help to prevent an accumulation of fat spoiling their good looks!

They will enjoy their sleep and shouldn't have any problems provided they are living balanced lives. Don't be surprised if you hear young Taurean snoring — the body area emphasized by this sign is the throat, and they may tend to lie on their backs with their heads thrown back on their pillows — an ideal attitude for the trumpet blast. Remember that their throats are vulnerable; colds will inevitably start there, and sore throats will be provoked by worry. This — whether actual or psychosomatic — will be the classic excuse for not wanting to go to school. Certainly it may be a genuine sign of tension or worry, so try to discover whether a problem may be provoking it.

A sick Taurean will be quite good at staying in bed, partly because she enjoys her creature comforts anyway and will appreciate the extra attention. All this may tend to encourage them to make a spectacularly slow recovery, just so that such a comfortable life can continue, but their powers of recovery are actually quite strong.

Fond of food, they won't be especially eager to experiment; you won't easily be able to persuade them to try a curry or a Chinese meal — their chief loves will be steak and kidney pie, traditional roasts, and so on. Trying to make a Taurean into a vegetarian might be considered a conscious act of cruelty! Fatty foods should be avoided if possible. High-fibre foods are a positive necessity; if they need an additive, brewer's yeast is an excellent idea (apart from anything else, it benefits the thyroid gland).

If you regularly drink wine, they won't at all mind trying this; why not take the French view, and give them wine-and-water early on? They will enjoy beer, too, eventually. But they will be discriminating; they are one of the signs which will drink for the pleasure of the taste rather than for the effect. They are not among the natural drunks of the Zodiac!

Although some Taureans are extremely wiry and active, if there is one area of health to stress, it is the tendency to put on weight, so diet and exercise are both something to watch. A subscription to a health club or membership of the local sports centre are among the best presents you could give young Taurus — they must be encouraged at the earliest possible age to watch their diet, watch their weight, and keep active.

## The First Five Years

The phrase 'a bouncing baby' was probably invented for a Taurean, for these babies may possibly arrive late but will certainly arrive large!

Taurean charm will begin to make itself felt in the pram; when you hear strangers cooing over your beautiful baby, rest assured that they will be telling the truth. That first smile — always a very special moment for parents — will be particularly delightful, and the contented expression after feeding-time and before she drifts off into her afternoon snooze will be seraphic.

Building bricks will be much enjoyed early presents. Picture-books of farm animals and flowers (remember Ferdinand the Bull and his predilection for flowers?) and plants will help interest them in reading.

One can't really see Taurean children making gleefully for the door when they first set off for play group. Best get them used to the company of other children at home by inviting them around to play or for parties, where communal nursery rhymes and singing games will be popular. The play group won't then come as too much of a shock. It is important to get Taureans involved with other people, and nursery school is an excellent idea — but there must be a tactful introduction to the idea, and the leaders of the group should try to get young Taurus to help, actively, by clearing things away or setting out materials for the next game or lesson.

Out in the playground, teachers should watch for the Taurean temper and any storms that may result, for (as with the adults) while these will not occur often they will be fairly impressive and can distress other less tough-minded children. If you see a young Taurean going red in the face, or indeed around the neck, prepare for trouble. Once again, they should be encouraged to share their toys, games, and books if their inherant possessiveness is not to make them unpopular.

Group leaders must expect them to be slow to react, but if they are given a task to be regularly performed this will help them to develop a sense of responsibility, which can be among their most solid virtues. They may be very determined on their own way, especially when it comes to getting at sweets or bars of chocolate, and it will be quite difficult for adults to resist their charm or to take a strong line when they need to be placated. When you know that a bar of chocolate can purchase five minutes' peace, it seems a small price to pay, especially since young Taurus is perfectly happy to promise anything in order to obtain it. But it really is best to resist, for Taureans are easily spoilt, and once the pattern is set they will all too readily seek the easy way out.

It is never too early to devise a physically demanding task in the home which can be assigned to Taurus on a regular basis. They like routine and accept sensible discipline, and you constantly need to find ways of using up their considerable physical energy in order to avoid laziness and combat time-wasting.

## School Years

Friendship is important to Taureans, and they may well make their first secure friends at nursery school — and keep them perhaps for the rest of their lives.

Because they are good company, it is not difficult for others to respond well to their advances, and once they are over the hurdle of learning to share toys and books they should find little difficulty in enjoying friendships, which will benefit the friends quite as much as themselves. You may find that Miss Taurus will not have a very wide circle of friends, but that is perfectly alright, for because of her need for emotional security she may feel that she wants a few good friends rather than a lot of less intimate ones. It will be important to her to know just how her friends will respond and what their attitude is likely to be in any particular situation.

It is sometimes the case that young Taureans accept discipline rather too readily. This is not to say that they are teacher's pets, but there can be an inherent fear of stepping out of line, of being really original and inventive, of doing anything to upset the status quo. It comes naturally to them to toe the line; they are not always so ready to show originality. The only exception will be if they are really upset, when the need to rebel can take over. Within a disciplined environment they know what to expect and what is expected of them, which is just the way they like it — and the way they need it to be if they are to make progress, both at school and at home.

Your Taurean will have a particular approach to learning (see *The Three Ways of Thinking*, p.39, for how this may work). Don't expect young Taurus to leap suddenly from the bottom of the form to the top. He or she is far more likely to make gradual progress from a low place to a slightly higher one, and so on. The sky may well be the limit, but it may take some time for them to get there — and on no account should you try to push them. Gentle, firm encouragement is the best thing, and do remember that once facts have been learned and absorbed they will be in the mind for good; so it is worth waiting while the process is properly completed. It is not a specially good idea to rely on the Taurean sense of competition, which is not strong. They should be encouraged to be proud of their own accomplishments, of the place they have made for themselves, rather than made to think that it is vitally important that they should overtake the person in front of them.

This Zodiac group is not on the whole terribly original in outlook; really brilliant new ideas or new approaches to school projects are more likely to come to other people — though occasionally there may be a flash of originality. Taureans will not respond well in class to teachers who resort to gimmicks or short cuts. The Taurean approach to learning is slow but steady, and you can rely on its thoroughness. When examination time comes, try to encourage them to start revising in good time; a last minute dash is not a good idea.

Taurus is a sign that produces people with a keen appreciation of beauty, which they like to express in some way. There is also often a love of singing (remember the Taurean body area is the throat), and they should be encouraged to join the school choir. Physical activities are tremendously important to them, too. Dancing (whether ballet, modern or simply pop) is excellent for them. Many Taureans make very good team members and could be involved in a team dancing effort — or team sports of almost any kind but particularly 'heavy' sports. It is important to them to keep moving and to increase their ability to move quickly and adeptly — so sports where dexterity of movement and strength are involved should be encouraged.

You will have gathered that since discipline is not too much of a problem for young Taureans, the chances are that they will make good progress at schools run along rather conventional lines. You may have wished that you had the chance to go to an unconventional school where the discipline was easier and there were not so many rules. Remember that the Taurean, at that sort of school, would tend to suffer — the lack of discipline would make her feel rather insecure, she would have nothing to 'push against', and her character would not be as securely developed as in a school where a fairly strict (but not restrictive) attitude was taken.

Taureans may not like the idea of leaving home for a boarding-school, but if they must be sent away, once they have made the break they should cope fairly well. It will simply be a matter of exchanging the safety of one environment for the safety of another and of getting them set within a new routine, looking on the journeys to and from home as part of a new but firmly planned pattern.

Choice of schools is restricted in all sorts of ways, but remember that a Taurean will probably intensely dislike surroundings which are not reasonably neat, clean and easy on the eye; they are not likely to be at home amid pieces of torn paper and other rubbish or within graffiti-covered walls.

## Out of School Activities

Taureans have enormous energy, both physical and emotional, and it is the greatest pity if this is not used. But they need to be guided and directed in its use, otherwise their tendency to laziness will get the better of them — and once that pattern is set, it is all too easy for it to last the rest of their lives. The best way to help them to dispel their energy is to devise a routine for out-of-school hours. In doing so, aim to build as much variety as possible to help develop versatility.

I have already said that Taureans may well be interested in music — especially singing — and if there is no school choir it will certainly be a good idea to find an outside one which they could join. If they show a special interest in one particular musical instrument, they should certainly be encouraged to take it up if finances allow. Alas, financial cuts have severely reduced the number of schools with their own orchestras, but some local authorities can still help in this respect. Many Taureans also have a talent for working with natural materials, so clay modelling and wood carving are excellent spare time occupations. They generally have plenty of patience, and are often very good at careful sewing, embroidery, weaving and model making.

Taurus is one of the 'earth' signs of the Zodiac, and for psychological as well as aesthetic reasons contact with the earth is extremely rewarding — so if you have a garden, do give your young Taurean a piece of it for her own as early in life as possible. If there do not seem to be sufficient sporting activities at school, consider getting Taurus involved in an outside club where for instance cross-country running and athletics are a specialization. In quieter moments some Taureans do well at chess and many enjoy Monopoly.

Thinking about their love of food, it might be quite a good idea to allow them to do a certain amount of entertaining at home; this will encourage them to increase their circle of friends as well as developing an interest in cooking — as useful for the boys as the girls.

Taureans react well in a crisis; they keep their cool and are capable of bravery. But in everyday life they may lack a spirit of adventure, and any effort you can make to develop this will not be wasted. As with the initial idea of going away to school, they may not automatically greet the idea of an adventure holiday with great enthusiasm, but if one can be found which fits in with their interests, it will probably do quite a lot of good, nurturing what individual qualities of enterprise, leadership and team spirit they have.

As with physical action, so with intellectual energy: it can tend to lie fallow unless encouraged, and your Taurean child may be more than a little conservative, just tending to repeat your views without bothering to think out their own. So it is an excellent idea to encourage them to join a school debating society or even a junior political party (which, after all, they can always leave later!) just to make sure that they get their minds working.

## Preparing for Life

A sound sex education is important for children of all signs; with young Taureans, it is particularly important to underline the relationship between sex and the emotions and to counter any suggestion that sex can or should be an end in itself, for Taureans are deeply emotional people, and first love may be a more traumatic experience for young Taurus than for many other signs. When they fall, they will fall deeply

— and the opportunity may not be long in coming, for not only do they have the reputation of being the best-looking sign in the Zodiac, but they will probably be quite conscious of it and will make the most of themselves. One of the results of this may be that other boys and girls will be deeply attracted to them and begin flirtations before young Taurus has actually begun to think about sex as other than a sudden inexplicable urge. There is the danger, then, that (for both sexes, but maybe especially with Taurean boys) the sexual itch may provoke them into early experiments. Underlining the fact that sex has its place as a necessary element of everyday family life will help to ensure that they don't plunge in above their heads. Because they tend to be rather conventional and devoted to routine, they should readily accept the proposition that in a sound relationship sex has its place and is not the only ingredient.

They are unlikely to be madly experimental, despite the fact that they are — like their Zodiac partners, the Scorpios — usually sensual and passionate. They are emotionally mature and should behave responsibly and well, however young they are. The boys will like to give the impression that they are more experienced than they are and will find that easy; they will probably be quite good at carrying off difficult situations with a remarkable display of self-confidence. Girls may tend to fly straight to the chocolate bar when disappointed in love.

The possessive trait — which is never far below the surface of most Taurean personalities — can lead to real danger in a relationship, for Miss Taurus can think of her boy-friend as her property, and if he so much as pauses to say hello to another girl she may be deeply — and really — upset. This will not be a pose, and she should learn as soon as possible that you cannot actually possess another person as you possess a thing.

It should not be necessary to nag a young Taurean about his or her personal appearance — for they will want to make the most of themselves. You can use this as a handy weapon against their love of sweet things, pointing out the connection between these and the discomforts of puppy fat or spots! They will probably have a natural sense of style — which could lead to rather expensive tastes in clothing. Their wardrobes will tend perhaps to be rather unadventurous and conventional — at least within their generation. Not being particularly original, they will tend to copy the style of people they admire (and indeed their behaviour). One can only hope that they admire the right people!

One can never chose anyone else's partner, but Taurus would certainly benefit from a slightly unconventional partner or friends, who would hopefully encourage them to extend their horizons, to break away from convention and see that it is not necessary always to think or behave as others think and behave. This includes you; it is an uncommon child that does not sometime rebel against her parents, but your Taurean child probably knows when he or she is well off, and though they may privately disagree with you, why should they rock the boat and find themselves having to do their own washing or pay their own rent? It will do no harm to encourage them to express their own opinions, quite as important as cleaning their own room, but young Taurus may not be specially keen on either task!

Anything you can do, in due course, to get young Taureans to leave home and start making a nest for themselves will be worthwhile. They sometimes tend to cling to their parents rather too much (and laziness certainly plays a part in this). If you can see your way clear to helping them, financially, to establish their first flat, make it a businesslike proposition, pointing out that apart from anything else, their own place will provide them with valuable security. Their conventional attitude to life should respond well to this.

## Further Education

As young Taurus has made slow, steady progress through school, you will have realized that she has the mind and the determination to cope with the demands of learning, so if she shows signs of wishing to go on to further education, you can be sure that any investment this means for you will be worthwhile, and that while final grades may not be spectacular they will stand her in good stead for the future. She will certainly have a conscientious approach to her work and even if this seems a little too laid back, you can be sure that she will in fact be fully conscious of what is demanded of her.

Taureans are unlikely to play hookey from lectures and often impress their tutors with their methodical approach and the neatness of their work. They can be less forthcoming in debate than some of their contemporaries, and their opinions may lack the spark and originality of more forward-looking students.

Much the same applies to their life in any education faculty, but if Taureans are living at home and at the same time involved in considerable study, you may find them neglecting their social life and tending to become reclusive. It may be necessary to encourage them to entertain their friends and get out into the fresh air from time to time.

Creatures of habit, Taureans tend to make friends for life, but when they go from school to further education, unless they are very lucky, they will find themselves separated from most of their contemporaries and have to start afresh. They could find this difficult. The answer is to get involved in social life as soon as possible — in sports or music clubs, of course, but any other organizations which offer. They usually enjoy a good social life at college and generally get involved in the various societies which are available to further their spare time interests, though a slight shyness may lead to procrastination, and they may need a little extra encouragement during the first weeks at university. If they can, they should try to bring with them some new ideas with which they can make their presence felt, for the average Taurean unless she makes an effort sometimes gives the impression of slight dullness. Because of their love of food, they will seek out the best coffee shops, and these are of course excellent places for good chocolate cake and getting to know people. Their good taste and love of quality could lead them to, say, a wine society, of which they could soon become a pillar (the experience may be an asset later in life!)

It is absolutely essential to Taureans that they should build up mutual respect and trust with tutors and lecturers. Some students need the sort of tutor with whom they can readily exchange ideas and argue and who don't mind when their opinions are treated with scepticism. This is not the case with Taureans, who need to be able to take their teachers' words as absolute truth, trusting them utterly. Taureans in further education will know from experience that the best way forward, for them, is to allow plenty of time for revision rather than using revision time to pack information into their brains which could have been assimilated months earlier. On the whole, Taureans are not great worriers and do not readily panic; provided they keep their cool, they can take examinations in their stride. As in all spheres of their lives, correct pacing is absolutely essential.

Towards the end of their school careers, childhood hobbies can be important and rewarding, for it is often the case that early interests lead on to a career. A young Taurean, for instance, who has achieved a number of grades in the playing of an instrument — and perhaps played in a youth orchestra — may decide to go on to music college, and someone who has enjoyed gardening and working out of doors may develop an interest in farming which can lead on to agricultural college. The Taurean child's dexterity in handling her pocket-money will probably have shown itself early in her life, and parents should encourage any child who shows special interest in this to concentrate on maths and perhaps take a course at business college.

## Unemployment: Stresses and Strains

The Taurean common-sense attitude, their practicality, will make them less susceptible to the damage which can be done by prolonged unemployment. But of course they will suffer under such circumstances, as everybody must.

However busily a young Taurean starts looking for work, parents should watch out for danger signals and do their best to stir up the natural Taurean determination and persistance, for though in general Taureans are eager to make money in order to maintain the comfortable life-style which they so much enjoy, when they are unemployed they can sometimes tend to sink into lethargy, for there is an element of laziness in their characters, and this together with apathy can make it all too easy for them simply to lie in bed until mid-morning and waste the rest of the day away. (Taureans find no difficulty in relaxing, even under the least relaxed circumstances!)

The other danger — ironically — is the Taurean natural talent for finance. Whatever their income they will manage it well, so they may suffer less than other Zodiac types from the problems of having to exist on unemployment benefit, especially if they can live at home with parents. This is fine — except that such circumstances will not persuade them that there is much urgency about finding work. It is 100 per cent essential for parents to remember this and to be cruel to be kind; if you haven't the heart to throw your Taurean onto her own resources, she must certainly be made to pay her way, whatever the family circumstances, by making her contribution to the family budget, paying for her own telephone calls, and postage. She will then realize just how little she has to live on; it may be enough to keep her in coffee and buy an occasional cinema ticket, but it certainly won't buy the new designer outfit she has her heart set on.

A Taurean searching for a job should work out a proper routine: regular visits to the job centre, regular times for writing letters, and so on. They will find it a little more difficult than some not to regard each failure as a personal rejection and must realize that it is not so. The prospect of leaving school without going into a job will be as grim for Taureans as for all teenagers, but it will be much more hurtful if they go into a job which then folds, for their sense of security (so important to them) will have been badly damaged. They will need all the support that can be offered. But remember that support should be businesslike — loans, rather than gifts — for Taurus can take things rather too much for granted.

Taureans usually have many interests, and these will expand to take up the time available, so there should be no difficulty in filling their lives. The girls will specially enjoy dressmaking, and both sexes will enjoy spending as much time as possible out of doors. Their practicality will make them extremely useful in community service; there will always be tasks for which they will be suited — in particular, heavy chores which old people are no longer able to cope with: help with the garden or with DIY schemes, carrying coals, heavy housework and so on. Taureans are not on the whole tremendously eager to work for nothing; it should be emphasized that their payment is in the self-satisfaction of helping others.

Taurean common sense should keep them free from the tyranny of drugs. Indeed, they are less likely than many to indulge in negative escapism of any kind, and the problem should not arise provided their lives are reasonably fulfilled and stable. They will of course be more under pressure if they are out of work or if an emotional relationship has ended unhappily, but at such times they will not necessarily fly to hard drugs. They will be more likely to drink rather too much or to go on eating binges. Over-eating, starting innocently with the occasional extra chocolate bar, could really become a problem for them. They are creatures of habit, and habit dies hard with them; so if they smoke too much, or start taking even more seriously damaging drugs, they will certainly not find it easy to stop. Under such circumstances routine and security and the knowledge that they are loved are probably the only things that can help them.

## Interests and Spare Time Activities

Taureans have a great deal of patience; they also love the outdoor life, and a combination of these qualities offers plenty of different ways in which they can occupy their spare time. Many are forced to work indoors, or spend their days in the financial areas of large cities, and find it necessary to escape when they can to the countryside — or at the very least try to acquire a garden in which they can spend their leisure hours cultivating flowers and vegetables for the table. If the space is available, fruit trees will be popular — being decorative as well as productive. Those Taurean children who have to grow up in flats or high-rise buildings should be encouraged to cultivate window-boxes or grow indoor plants; they usually have green fingers.

Those Taureans fortunate enough to be able to work in the open should perhaps try to spend their spare time in more thoughtful pursuits. Many make first-class bridge players and enjoy all kinds of card games — or indeed chess — and we find a lot of Taureans, when they have saved a little capital and can afford the element of gambling involved, make a real hobby of studying the financial pages of the press, and playing the stock exchange in a small but satisfactory way.

Both male and female Taureans are capable of producing beautiful craftwork and should be encouraged to work with clay, wood and the other natural products of the earth (to which the sign is so strongly connected); in doing so they will be expressing their natural affinity with the earth — as they do in cultivating their gardens, often specializing in one particular species of flower.

Young Taureans can be safely encouraged to entertain their friends at home, learning how to set a table and make it look attractive. This will not be difficult for them, for they have natural good taste. It will be valuable experience, for later on in life they will often feel the need to entertain people they want to impress. In the kitchen they will probably score their greatest successes with conventional dishes — particularly good, rich casseroles, possibly involving good wine; they will really come into their own with the desserts — confections of dark chocolate and cream, all kinds of *gateaux*. They are not the types to take short cuts with their cooking, and parents who hand over their kitchen to a Taurean boy or girl must be prepared to give it up for the day!

If you feel your Taurean is not mixing sufficiently with new people, encourage her to ask her friends' friends back; remember, she will always feel more secure meeting new people at home than anywhere else. Taureans will tend, as in everything else, to be rather conservative, clinging to friends of long standing. They are always dependable; and while this is an admirable virtue, it can become slightly boring. They should cultivate the unexpected. Watch the danger that they may bang on rather too long about any accomplishment they may have achieved. Friends of either sex who can spur them to be original will be excellent for them; this applies to intimate friends — they need partners who can inspire them (the Piscean type springs to mind, for the signs share a high emotional level, and Piscean sensitivity can lighten Taurean solidity, while Taurean practical common sense can keep Piscean feet on the ground. This does not of course mean that only a Piscean will make a satisfactory friend, but Taurus could certainly welcome one particularly enthusiastically!)

The term 'the salt of the earth' must have been invented specifically to describe a Taurean! It is particularly true when Taurus joins a club or society, for on the committee they will be enormously hardworking and a continual source of sound and practical suggestions. They must learn, however, to speak up and shut up, for their tendency to go on and on can nullify all their good intentions. They should make careful notes and make sure they say what they mean briefly and pointedly.

However aware a Taurean may be of current fashion, they won't specially want to involve themselves in it — they'll tend to play it safe, and considering the shape their careers are likely to take, this is probably no bad thing. There could be some conflict when their contemporaries latch on to a new trend and they themselves feel forced to try it (they love conforming) and find themselves with drawers full of clothes they don't actually like very much. Parents should point out that they should cultivate their own personal style rather than always imitating others. Taurus has good taste; others are simply being imitative.

Think of Taurus and you tend to see them followed by a slowly ambling bulldog, but it is much better for them to own a pet that is going to set a pace which will help them increase their naturally slow metabolism — a lively dog needing regular exercise, one perhaps that will happily accompany a daily jog. Relatively few people can afford to keep a horse these days, but if Taurus lives in the country she should certainly think of riding as a hobby, and if near a farm all farm animals will interest her.

## Ideal Careers

I have mentioned money often enough to suggest that any career involving finance should suit most Taureans. Because of their need for security, a regular pay cheque is important to everyone of this sign, and work which brings in irregular reward is not a specially good idea. They are at their best in a career in which, starting at the bottom, they can work their way slowly and surely up the ladder without the prospect of finding any uncertain stages or missing rungs. Banking, insurance, finance houses, the stock exchange — city work in general — will always attract. The communicative type of Taurean will welcome a job which will offer the chance of studying national and international markets. While they may be somewhat worried at the idea of challenge — because there is, after all, always the possibility of failure, which would disturb them in all sorts of ways — they will welcome it because its successful resolution will mean an increase in income!

The influence of the earth element will again make itself felt in the area of Taurean careers, for many make extremely successful architects, surveyors, estate managers and estate agents. If your Taurean has an artistic bent she may well become a sculptor, or perhaps find a niche as an art or crafts teacher (embroidery or pottery). The young Taurean attracted to fashion may become a successful dress designer (though not a specially avant-garde one); if there have been examination successes in biology or chemistry a career as a beautician or make-up artist will also be rewarding. Taureans are often good-looking and physically attractive, and while the modelling business is by no means easy to get into, the good Taurean model, male or female, will always be in demand — for apart from their looks, they also have infinite patience, and the hours spent hanging around the studio will not prove unduly trying.

The typical interest in food married to the Taurean business sense could be shown in the management of a restaurant (rather than involvement in the actual cooking). Taurus' interest in wines would come in useful here too, and work in the wine trade would also be admirable. The Taurean who wants to start a business of any kind, in fact, should be given support and encouragement; their shrewdness and enterprise will be such that the chance of failure will be below average.

Taureans often have excellent singing voices and pleasant and sometimes unusual speaking voices. They could easily become stage-struck, and might well make an impact in their amateur theatre company — and even in the professional theatre. Very often it is an unusual speaking voice that is at the back of a successful theatrical career. I have already mentioned singing, and a Taurean opera singer is by no means set for failure. Though of course I do not need to underline the uncertainty of this career, Taurean natural determination and persistance will stand them in good stead. They will need these, because it is not a profession in which a regular pay cheque is available, and that is a real disadvantage for those of this sign. They should really develop a second string to their bow, so that they can make a little money in lean times. Having said that, when they do get a particularly well-paid job, they will be unlikely to squander their money and will make sure they invest some of it against lean times.

Farming, in these days, is almost as uncertain a profession as the stage, but it is another one to which Taureans will be attracted. They will find it tremendously psychologically satisfying but must remember that with changing times and techniques it is no use whatsoever being too conservative and thinking that traditional farming methods offer a secure future. Happily, many of them will be attracted to organic farming, which is becoming more and more popular with the consumer.

In any career, the Taurean love of security can be a drawback, for they sometimes let good opportunities slip by just because they fear the outcome, not that they are naturally pessimistic, but they simply do not welcome change of any kind — even for the better! They should try not to cling too desperately to the desk they know, the job they could do in the dark with one hand tied behind their back. This is not to say they should take unnecessary risks just for the sake of it, but they should try to develop enough self-confidence to explore interesting possibilities.

# Travel

A decision to holiday in a different resort this year will result in a wail of horror from young Taurus: 'Why can't we go to X again?' she will cry. Habit dies hard, for Taurus, in every department of life. And they don't much like the actual process of travelling either — the holiday may be fine once they arrive, but the journey itself will be tolerated rather than enjoyed — especially if it is by air, for the Taurean bull likes to keep all four feet on the ground! When they have money of their own, look for them in the Club or first-class lounges, for they will want to make the journey as comfortable as possible — quite apart from having an eye to the better food and wines!

If young Taurus decides to take off on her own, parents should encourage careful planning — not only because of any inherent wisdom, but because Taurus will be a great deal happier knowing that there is going to be a seat on the plane or a place on the ferry and a room at the other end of the journey. They aren't on the whole the kind to take off for the Kalahari desert with knapsack on their back; they are fairly unadventurous and like their comfort too much for that. They will enjoy beautiful, strange scenery — but they will enjoy it more through the window of an air-conditioned bus than from the saddle of a bike! And the girls in particular, won't welcome the idea of living in one skirt or pair of jeans for a fortnight.

Though they're not specially likely to go in search of adventure, Taureans will want a change from their daily routine — and if this involves simply swopping it for another kind of routine, what of it? They should be allowed, after all, once in a while to be thoroughly lazy, and (if they can afford it) to laze in style. They won't mind spending money on this, but they will expect value for their cash, and woe betide the tour manager who does not fulfil his promises. A working holiday is not altogether a bad idea because the Taurean will be quite happy to think that as well as relaxing she is also making a little money — or at the very least making new contacts which could lead to that!

With a generally rather slow metabolism, they will find that a hot, humid climate tends to overheat them and make it even more difficult to get their energies going. A holiday on a river or canal, or sailing, should attract them, as should a slow, comfortable walking holiday in a fairly cool though not cold climate.

They will enjoy trying out local food — especially new flavours of ice-cream, new confectionary and cakes, and the hotel restaurant had better be a good one! With their love of trains in mind, a journey on the Orient Express would probably be the ultimate Taurean holiday. But even if they have a uniformed porter to help them, they should watch the amount of luggage they take; they love being surrounded by familiar possessions and tend to pack everything but the kitchen sink in rather too many suitcases.

## Taureans as Brothers and Sisters

It is not an easy matter to tell a young Taurean that very shortly he or she is going to cease being the sole central member of her generation. Unless she is well-prepared in advance, the birth of a brother or sister can be truly traumatic, and there can be tantrums and stubbornness during the new baby's first months, when Taurus finds she now has to share the affections of mummy and daddy. As a protest, she could resort to angry foot stamping and cries of 'Won't!' or 'Shan't!'. Underline the fact that the coming baby is going to be 'a brother or sister *for you*', and that young Taurus is going, *of course*, to help look after them. But remember that Taureans can be extremely artful and adept at getting their own way by turning on their considerable charm. Don't allow this to lead to bribery and corruption and the purchase of peace by a vastly increased intake of chocolates, sweets or toys. Encourage Taurean children to make things for their brothers or sisters; the greater the degree of sharing at an early age, the better. Sensible, practical Taurus can be trusted to baby-sit at a remarkably early age — and will welcome the trust, for they want to be 'grown-up' and seen as a useful integral part of the family. Tell a Taurean that a child is '*your*' brother or sister, and the Taurean possessive streak will ensure that she becomes an absolutely trustworthy guardian. If she takes a small brother or sister out, she will be unlikely to wander off about her own business and leave them by themselves.

It is an excellent idea to encourge Taurus to put aside a few pennies from regular pocket-money to buy birthday or Christmas presents for a young brother or sister. Because of their possessiveness, Taureans can find it difficult to share toys, or pass them on, and rather than risk emotional agony over this, an emphasis on their good money management is a solution.

A younger Taurean can be a tower of strength to older siblings. A five- or six-year-old can be almost a father figure to a flightly eight-year-old girl, coming out with delightfully quaint and practical suggestions which will have a great ring of truth and be likely to make a considerable impact, especially when the older child has perhaps behaved rather stupidly. Taureans who have to share a room for a while won't find the situation very easy; they will want to guard their territorial rights and have their own storage space. The other child might be invaluable, however, when it comes to getting young Taurus up and about in the morning, and sharing will help Taurus develop a sense of the necessity for compromising and considering other people's feelings.

Their need for security means that having a brother or sister at the same school will be a great comfort for a Taurean child — even if the sibling is younger, when they will be wonderfully protective and comforting. This will not necessarily extend to doing everything together, for Taurus will not be the type to work very hard at sharing interests which are not naturally attractive. If a common interest can be discovered and emphasized, it will be an excellent thing for family relationships — if perhaps the children could play instruments together or be partners at tennis. Otherwise there is a possibility that they will grow apart, and while this does not perhaps particularly matter, it can be rather sad in later years. It is not always a good idea for them to share holidays — indeed, this could be absolutely infuriating for brothers and sisters of other, perhaps livelier and more extrovert signs; sharing a business interest, on the other hand, should work extremely well, with Taurus providing the strong anchor and steady hand and the brother or sister the flair and excitement.

A brother or sister who lacks steadiness or is perhaps not very good at managing pocket-money, will soon learn that the Taurean is absolutely to be trusted in such matters, and they can seek her help and advice — and this can be extended into adult life; a Taurean is the right person to go to for advice when investing or planning to buy or rent a flat or a house.

## Taureans as Parents

The Taurean parent will above all be concerned to make a good life for her children and will be prepared to spend as much time and as much money as she can afford on their education and the development of their personalities and interests. The creation of a secure home background and comfortable living conditions will be a priority.

There can be a Taurean tendency to think of a child as a possession, and difficulties and discord may arise when that child starts expressing her own opinion or showing a tendency to do things her own way. A Taurean parent is sometimes a strong disciplinarian and may tend to be too strict with children when they begin to show their own characters and express their own opinions. Apart from which, the desire to spend money on them can take the place of real love and family togetherness — Taureans will be out making money so that the child will have a better life than they did. This is certainly less true of Taureans than of some Sun-sign types, but it is nevertheless a tendency to watch, especially when the children ask for some expensive present and Taurus remembers herself being deprived, when a child, of something she longed for. Taureans make kind and affectionate parents who sometimes over-indulge their children with expensive toys or gifts, and it may be to everyone's advantage to compromise and encourage the child to save up in order to contribute to the price of the bicycle or computer or whatever. Guard against indulging the children's appetites, too, by allowing them too many sweet things to eat. The fact that you enjoy them may persuade you that they're not as bad for children as the doctors suggest. But be warned: they are.

Where pocket money is concerned, the Taurean parents' common sense and financial shrewdness will protect them from being too generous; they will probably be able to strike a good balance between meanness and over-indulgence.

Taurean family planning will be as rational as the planning of home buying. Children will be logically spaced, and provided there are no complications will arrive punctually on time. Leaving things to chance is not what Taurus is about!

Because of their rather conventional, even unadventurous, character, it is very important that Taurus parents should try to keep abreast of contemporary thought and opinion as the children grow up. This may not be too easy for them; they may even find it boring. But if they are going to have a proper relationship with their children and really understand them, they should know what is going on in their lives and what the influences around them are. If Taurus tries to impose the behaviour patterns and opinions of their generation on their children, the generation gap could become a yawning one, very difficult to close. Involvement in the childrens' interests is obviously important, and it will be particularly good if the Taurean parent can play her part in parent/teacher associations. She will score highly when it comes to fund raising or running the cake stall at the annual fete, but she should listen carefully to what the teacher has to say about her children, since she may be so concerned with their personalities at home that she finds it difficult to see them as their teacher does; ill behaviour at home is not always mirrored at school, and vice versa. Taurean mothers should try not to be too irritated at the sudden demands made on them by schoolchildren: 'Where's my football shorts?', when they hadn't realized they'd be needed. Try not to let that kind of thing get under your skin.

Taurean parents will be at their best when taking their children to concerts of all kinds, on visits to stately homes, zoos or safari parks, and on nature rambles. Even a simple walk in the local park can be an interesting botany lesson for the children, for Taurean awareness of plants and birds will be a source of inspiration. The outing will probably be concluded with an ice-cream or a fruit drink.

Taurean mothers will always be concerned that their children are well-dressed and neat, and this can obviously be a source of difficulty with an unregenerately untidy and grubby child. Again, try to strike the right balance.

The chores of parenthood may weigh somewhat less heavily on Taureans than on some other parents; they are normally well-organized and rational, and the pleasure they find in the whole business of running a family will more than compensate them for the difficulties, worries and sheer hard work involved.

## Case Study

Barry - Sun and Venus in Taurus, Mercury in Aries; Mercury Group 1, Venus Group 3.

From the Report: 'You probably know that a tendency to possessiveness shows itself in most Taureans. To counter it, try to encourage Barry to share his toys and best-loved possessions with his friends. If you do not do so now, he may well tend when he is grown up to think that he owns people as well as things — and in particular, his partners. I do not know whether you plan to have more children; if possible, you should prepare Barry for the role of elder brother well in advance. Most parents do that automatically these days, but it will be essential in Barry's case, if the situation arises; give him as much information as he is ready to cope with about the growth of his baby brother or sister inside mummy, and from their first meeting encourage him to take an active role in helping you to look after the infant and bring it up.

I say this not only because of his possibly possessive instincts, but because in some ways he could react rather jealously when and if another child comes on the scene. You will understand that jealousy can also seriously mar an emotional relationship, so the sooner it is treated, the better.

'Barry needs a fair amount of discipline, but also needs to be given his head, and this will be enormously important to him during school years. You should never forget that he will be far more adventurous and rather less conventional than he may seem.

'I think you will find that he has a pretty quick-thinking mind (not always the case with Sun-sign Taureans). He will be firm and decisive, and from time to time his thought patterns could be impulsive and erratic. He will in no way lack imagination, and there will be many ways in which he will be able to use this to its best advantage, later on.

'One of his negative traits is stubbornness. He is likely to be very stubborn indeed at times. There are ways of overcoming this, and it is possible that with care you will be able to change it from sheer bloody-mindedness to strong determination and a positive expression of will-power. The trait will need careful correction on your part; fortunately, he will develop a good sense of logic, to which you will certainly be able to appeal. His powers of reasoning may get a little buried at times, but are nevertheless real.'

Comment: Barry's report was written just after he was born. Although at the time of writing he is still very young, many traits mentioned are emerging strongly. His Taurean charm (referred to elsewhere in the analysis) is striking, and possessiveness is showing in a tendency for him to cling to his mother. He is not always obedient, so stubbornness is present. A brother or sister is now on the way, and his parents have assured me that he is being kept fully informed and is taking a great interest in the process. I suggested in the report that, as is the case with many Taureans, he needs a firm discipline. His parents are well aware of this, and he is getting it. He is already, to quote his mother, 'a bit of a handful.'

## The Sun-sign and Its Rulerships

Countries and areas: Capri, Cyprus, the Greek archipelago, Iran, Ireland, Ischia, Parma, Poland, Switzerland, Tasmania.

Cities: Dublin, Eastbourne, Hastings, Leipzig, Lucerne, Mantua, Palerma, Parma, Rhodes, St Louis (U.S.A.).

Trees: almond, apple, ash, cyprus, fig, pear, vine.

Flowers and herbs: alder, artichoke, asparagus, beans, brambles, cloves, columbine, daisy, elder, foxglove, marshmallow, mint, poppy, primula, rose, sorrel, violet.

Food: apples; all cereals, especially wheat; all berries; grapes, pears; spices.

Cell salts: Nat. Sulph., Calc. Sulph.

*Animals*: cattle.

*Stone*: emerald, moss-agate.

*Metal*: copper.

*Colour*: pale blue, pink, and green.

# GEMINI

## (May 22 - June 21)

Note: Gemini is a masculine sign, so for the
most part I refer throughout to 'he', but most of
my comments refer also to girls.

## General Characteristics

At some time or another, you're almost bound to find yourself telling your Gemini child, 'One thing at a time!' If you can possibly catch yourself before the words fall from your lips, do — because that's absolutely *not* what to tell a Geminian! If someone calls him or her 'a little monkey', it'll probably be an apt description, for Geminians are here, there and everywhere, and 'monkey tricks' are pretty descriptive of what they get up to when, as very young children, they are finding their way about the world — and perhaps finding out, too, just how much you will put up with!

Gemini is the first of the three 'dual' signs of the Zodiac, and we certainly find a strong thread of duality in all those of this sign, which emerges at a very early age. So get used to the fact that your very young Geminian will have many tasks on hand at the same time. The great thing is not to encourage him to do one thing at a time but to make sure if you can that he completes everything he undertakes — the most serious Geminian fault is superficiality, and he may well tend eagerly to start a new enthusiasm which will die on him rather too early.

It is part of the Geminian nature to want to know a little about a great many things, but it is good for them from time to time to have to study one thing in depth, otherwise they find themselves splashing about on the surface and never plumbing the depths.

Of equal importance is the fact that Geminians have a low boredom threshold, and you will soon know when your child is bored or fed-up, because he will tend to become extremely restless. In order to help him to fully develop his excellent potential, you should allow him plenty of freedom of expression — indeed, you could positively encourage him to change from one occupation to another as and when he feels he needs to — all the time making quite sure that in due course he completes all his tasks and so reaps the benefit of personal achievement.

Geminians never stop asking questions and many even invite *you* to ask them, in order that they can show off their own knowledge! They will not be put off by glib answers — though they sometimes tend to make use of these, themselves, in order to cover a lack of real depth of knowledge. You could stimulate them by answering their questions with another, or by giving the sort of answer which will prompt them to think more deeply.

Remember that youngsters with this Sun-sign are in general very high-strung and tend to get the fidgets. Watch out for this; it is another sign that they are bored and that their psychological restlessness is getting the better of them. They have spare nervous energy to burn. In encouraging their various interests, try to make sure that they have plenty of intellectually demanding ones — but at the same time remember it is equally important for young Gemini to be able to go out and bat a ball about or run around the block, in order to exercise both mind *and* body.

It is very easy for Geminians to talk their way out of difficult situations, especially if they have done wrong — and they will sometimes use extraordinary imagination in doing so. Of course, they know perfectly well when they have offended — but perhaps more than any other Zodiac type they have a very highly developed knack of coming out with all kinds of brilliant excuses and justifications for their actions. It is up to you to be on the watch for this trait and to be very firm and very determined, remembering that the way to help develop the best qualities of this lively sign is to be extremely logical in your approach and never beat about the bush. Say what you mean, and stick to it!

It is sometimes the case that the Geminian physical energy level is not terribly high; it is often outstripped by a powerful nervous energy force, and as a result young Gemini can get more exhausted than either you or he realizes. At bedtime, for instance, you may begin to see the eyelids droop — but the flurry of questions and arguments about it not really being bedtime and about what he *must* do before he goes to bed and the number of books he must read (he'll be an inveterate reader-under-the-sheets anyway!) will be extremely persuasive.

The world was clearly made for Geminians — or that's how they think of things. They love excitement, change, surprises — they hate boring routine; each day must be as different as possible from the one before and the one after. Their lively, bright expression and continual talk mirrors their never-flagging interest in everything around them — and they have an ability to tell you all about it with the utmost vividness and persuasiveness. All this will surface very early in their lives and makes them a delight in childhood. They're also great at cheering up both their contemporaries and their elders!

There is a Geminian tendency to talk to anyone and everyone — it's part of the overall communicativeness of the sign. Obviously it can lead the children into danger, and you must underline the fact that not every stranger is trustworthy. Every parent of a Gemini child must work out his or her own way of dealing with this without stifling their delightfully open personalities. The best way of doing so is probably by appealing to their logic — a highly valuable Geminian characteristic.

The traditional colour for this sign is bright yellow, but if you ask young Gemini what his favourite colour is, he'll probably reply that he likes them all — and that will more than likely be true. Remember the need for variety and change (in any case Gemini won't let you forget that in a hurry), and when it comes to choosing out-of-school clothes I suggest you go for tee-shirts, shorts or skirts in a great variety of colours, so that Gemini can ring the changes as and when he or she pleases.

There is no doubt about it, pocket-money will slip through Geminian fingers with great speed and freedom — though on the other hand many of this sign have everything it takes to become good salesmen including a certain bright business ability. They invariably strike a good bargain and when shopping, for instance, will recognize one immediately as they see it. Nevertheless, encourage them to start a savings scheme for presents, holidays, and so on.

## The Three Ways of Thinking

Due to the influence of Mercury (see p.13) the Geminian mind characteristically works in one of three ways. But Mercury rules this sign, and influences the whole of the Geminian personality, as well as the thinking process.

★ One group of Geminians goes in for very practical thinking; their sense of logic is strengthened and adds stability to their personalities. Watch out for stubbornness, which can become surprisingly apparent and will be forcefully denied when you accuse them of it!

★★ Members of the second group have minds which work extremely quickly, so that they give the impression of being very intelligent — whether they are or not! They will get away with murder, but in particular superficiality and a lack of depth can cause problems, especially if concentration is poor. Their need to communicate is extremely high.

★★★ In the third group are Geminians whose imagination and sensitivity are enhanced. This is the most emotional type of Geminian. Their memories are very good, but they have a tendency to become somewhat snappy — especially in argument. This must be controlled, since harsh words may inadvertantly upset other people and even make enemies.

## The Five Ways of Loving

Due to the influence of Venus (see p.13) Geminians will tend to express their affection in one of five ways.

★ While all Geminians will fall in and out of love very quickly, the members of the first group are extremely passionate and ardent and will express their feelings in a most fiery and emotional way. A tendency to put the self first can spoil the fun, but the love and sex life will be thoroughly enjoyed, and the individual will certainly chalk up an above average number of experiences and relationships.

★★ Kind, warm and affectionate, members of the second group will be surprisingly possessive — both of their family and of their lovers. They will be generous and enjoy the good life, spending a lot of money on their partners. Both emotional and financial security are most important to them.

★★★ It's not for nothing that Geminians are called the flirts of the Zodiac, and group three comprises the liveliest and most flirtatious of them all. The Geminian tendency to enjoy more than one relationship at a time will probably find plenty of expression. Remind them that fun now can cause complications and hurt later.

★★★★ Many Geminians have a delightfully sensitive, somewhat sentimental and old-fashioned way of communicating their love. They don't find it difficult to express their feelings and will positively enjoy writing love-letters and sending small gifts. They also possess a splendid capacity for caring, which their partners will find particularly rewarding and endearing.

★★★★★ A tendency to show off in front of the loved one, and perhaps to spend too freely in order to impress, must be controlled. These Geminians will want to take the lead in the partnership and need to be convinced that equality of choice is a better idea. Their great sense of fun will help them bring out the best in their partners.

## Health and Diet

I have already mentioned the Geminian tendency to be restless, and it cannot be too strongly stressed that this can take a toll of the health. The nervous system is traditionally associated with the sign and is therefore somewhat vulnerable. Once a Geminian becomes restless, the whole physical wellbeing can be affected; he often succumbs to nervous fears and apprehensions. It is not that he is a tremendously worrying type, but tension and a lack of inner calm can cause serious problems. These in turn may lead to skin rashes or perhaps digestive upsets.

The arms, shoulders and hands are the traditional Geminian body areas, and we tend to find that when Gemini is involved in any kind of accident wrists can be broken, hands cut or scratched, or perhaps a collar-bone injured.

When your Gemini child goes down with any of the usual illnesses, it will be very difficult indeed to keep him in bed! If the doctor says this is essential, you will surely have to have a really good supply of puzzles, word-games and extra books on hand, otherwise you shouldn't be surprised if you find him leaping out of bed and into the garden to attend to his pet rabbit or take the dog for a walk.

While all human beings should work like well-made machines, it's particularly important to remember that the Geminian body and mind are one, and they interact to a greater degree than with members of any other sign. If the mind stagnates, the body will be sick; if the body is lazy and unexercised, the mind will feel stale. In a stressful period, make sure that the Geminian has plenty of exercise and fresh air. At times, a vicious circle may develop, with tension over-winding the body's spring and inactivity and lack of stimulation causing physical restlessness.

All kinds of exercise should be invoked to offset these possible negative tendencies. Heavy sports which make no intellectual demands are best avoided — they are really not very suitable. But wholly intellectual exercise isn't much help, either. The sort of activities that are best for Geminians need dexterity of movement married to quickness of mind; these will be rewarding. If your individual Geminian is so highly strung that he finds it very difficult to relax, it will be good for him (as with some other Zodiac groups) to get involved in relaxation techniques. It will not be easy for him just to sit and listen to music, however much he enjoys it, but you should try to encourage him to do this. If it does not work, what about his learning one of those controlled Chinese exercise techniques which will occupy his body and his mind? Later in life yoga could well be beneficial.

It may be that your Gemini child is somewhat 'picky' over his food. The reason could be that he is simply bored with the whole idea of eating, but it is more likely that he isn't getting enough variety of flavours. He needs light, nourishing foods, especially those that stimulate and nurture his nervous system; a diet of mixed vegetables — or vegetable soups in winter — and salads containing nuts and a variety of fruit and fresh vegetables would be ideal. Fish is also particularly beneficial. Like many young people, he may turn to vegetarianism; he should respond well to this provided the level of protein is well balanced.

Favourite snacks will certainly include peanuts and raisins and dried or crystallized fruits. Gemini has the reputation of being the most youthful of the twelve signs and because Geminis are usually extremely active and have a fast metabolism, they are less likely to put on weight than most of their Zodiac brothers. If your child is true to type, he can be allowed the occasional chocolate treat, or perhaps on a day out a delicious meringue or cream cake, without fear of his putting on weight. But this should be the exception rather than the rule, if only for the sake of his teeth.

Remember that the Gemini lungs are usually sensitive, and the slightest cold will tend to hang on as a nasty cough, even in summer. This should not be neglected, lest it grow into a weakness in later life. No household containing a single Geminian should allow a cigarette anywhere near him — and certainly you should try to make absolutely sure that he does not start smoking himself.

## The First Five Years

The chances are that your young Geminian will be able to carry on a logical conversation before he can walk. Don't be surprised if he explains to strangers, from his pram, that he can't walk yet!

The urge to communicate will make its presence felt very early indeed in his young life, and no sooner will he give you his first merry little smile than you will find his baby cooing turning into 'Mamma', 'Dada', or the name of the family pet! Never talk down to him; treat him as a small adult, carrying on logical conversations which will encourage him to extend his vocabulary and positively enjoy the sounds of words — and indeed of his own voice — though you might in later life consider this a mixed blessing!

The earlier you get him interested in books the better; I suggest you start out with rag books so that he can learn the very act of turning the pages without injuring them, and recognizing the look of the letters and illustrations. Nursery rhymes and singing games are a must, and if you agree with teaching your children to read before they go to school, you will find you have a lively student in your Gemini son or daughter.

There is a powerful need in youngsters of this group to be mobile. Whether they walk early in life or not depends of course on their physical development, but the need to move around is very strong. It is essential, then, when you think he is about to start crawling, to make absolutely sure that the necessary gate is in place at the bottom of the stairs or anywhere else where there might be danger. And if you leave him alone in his pram, he really will need a safety strap — comfortable but firmly buckled. Of course his natural tendency to mobility must be encouraged, but I strongly advise you to exercise strict (if not too obvious) supervision.

Here is another Zodiac type that should be allowed to go to play school as soon as he seems ready for it. You will find that his need to communicate will make him extremely friendly towards his contemporaries, and he won't hesitate to come forward when given the opportunity to play with a whole new range of toys and to make interesting discoveries for himself with such things as sand, water and paint. There is no doubt about it, he will be very keen to tell the group leaders about Mummy and Daddy, about his toys, his brothers and sisters if he has them . . . and his life in general. Similarly, when he comes home, encourage him to tell you what he's been doing; if he is reluctant to do so, then there is probably something wrong somewhere — perhaps he's been naughty and doesn't want to spill the beans.

He will make friends very easily and interestingly will bring the best out of shyer, less extrovert children. Soon you will have plenty of additional guests for nursery tea, and from then on shouldn't expect much more peace and quiet! As far as discipline is concerned, encourage him to be truthful and don't allow him to make up excuses for bad behaviour. He will enjoy helping in the home provided he doesn't find what he has to do too boring or repetitive. Give him plenty of variety!

## School Years

Pity the poor teacher who, if he or she is not at least as lively as the Geminian child, will be led a dance up-hill and down-dale.

It won't be difficult to work up a Geminian's enthusiasm for school, and when the big day comes he will probably be wildly excited. But should he say, as he goes to bed that night, 'I don't have to go again tomorrow, do I?', sadly the chances are that he's been bored. What can be done in such a situation? Well, the great thing is to look particularly carefully at what the school is achieving; is there evidence of interesting science lessons? a good school choir? Are the paintings on the school walls happy, positive ones? Most important, is there a good school library?

Then there are the teachers; obviously these will vary in age, but what do they look like? Do they smile easily? Do they wear reasonably lively, colourful clothes? You really need to ask as many questions as your Geminian child — for while every parent needs to be properly curious about school conditions, it is perhaps most important where a Geminian child is involved, for once that versatile young mind begins to get busy it really must be kept bobbing about on a sea of questions and stimulating answers. If it is not, it will sink, and the individual will become sadly dull and damp. Stimulation is really vitally important if Gemini is to make progress.

It is probably as well at this point to consider the whole Gemini outlook on life (but see, also, *General Characteristics*). This is very much up-to-date, and often ahead of the child's contemporaries; members of this sign do not respond well to anything remotely out of date or fusty, whether it is someone's opinion, the physical surroundings, or most importantly, the other people who contact him every day.

It is not always easy to discipline a Geminian child. He can be extremely crafty and difficult to keep quiet! He will probably learn the hard way that when teachers say 'Stop talking', he or she means just that! I don't think there is very much you can do about this, except to impress upon him the fact that it is inconsiderate and impolite to go on gossiping to friends when someone else is trying to communicate something important which deserves attention.

Parents should encourage their children to revise for examinations slowly, carefully and over a long period of time. But unless your Gemini child has a really good memory, that technique may not pay off particularly well. It could be, indeed, that he will do splendidly by cramming during long hours for a few days before the examination, since remembering facts (always rather boring things to Geminians!) for any longer time than a week or so doesn't come easily to people of this Sun-sign. The trouble with the latter approach is that an element of luck is needed — the examiners must decide to ask only the questions to which the Geminian knows the answers. And of course there is nothing to be done about that! Try to encourage Gemini to work out his own individual system of *aide-mémoire* — perhaps some form of pneumonic, rhyme, or word association will help him to keep the facts, formulas, and dates in mind.

Expect your Geminian to have a very wide circle of acquaintances. He will chose his close friends on the basis that each has something special to offer which makes him different from the others — thus ensuring the all-important variety. He will have his bookish friend, his adventurous, sporting friend, and a friend for no other reason than that he's a good listener. But from time to time the chances are that he'll get fed up, and tell you that 'old so-and-so is really very boring', so he's not going to go out with him any more.

If he suddenly starts suffering from schoolitis on Thursday evenings, the reason is probably that he has to cope with a particularly boring teacher on Friday! Of course he will have to put up with that state of affairs at least until the end of the school year, when perhaps he will move up a grade; in one way or another you must get him to realize that an awful lot of people in life are going to bore him and that this is perhaps as much his fault as their's! The truth is that young Gemini's enthusiasm for a subject will be closely geared to the amount of stimulation he receives from his individual teachers and that if his end-of-term placing in some subjects is lower than you may expect, it will all too surely be because he and the teacher of that subject simply don't strike sparks off each other — and when that happens Gemini simply won't be concentrating, in class, on the subject being taught. Try if you can to keep his interest by purchasing additional books, tapes or whatever, in order that he can get involved in the subject in his own time, under your personal guidance.

As ever, physical activities and sporting interests should be encouraged along with intellectual development.

## Out of School Activities

One of the keywords for Geminians is 'communication', and while each will have their own favourite hobbies and pastimes, it's a fair bet that one of them will have something to do with the communication of ideas — he may be a prominent member of a debating society, run the school newspaper, work — at a very early age — for a local hospital broadcasting station, maybe become a radio ham. And an above average number of Geminians will not only have English language and literature as their favourite subject at school but will bring the interest into their outside life, writing for their own pleasure. As we shall see, these interests can in time become careers.

Though often dextrous in movement, Geminians are perhaps not specially talented, in a practical sense, with their hands; they may set out for instance to make model aircraft, but a combination of haste and carelessness will ensure that while the model may look fine at first sight (they are wonderfully clever at first impressions!) when you pick it up, the wings will come off (and that, of course, will be *your* fault!) Similarly, if they turn to music they will often be able to improvise cleverly — but may well lack the staying-power to stick at the hours of practice which alone make a really first-rate performer. In general, they like quick results — so anything requiring long periods of study or work is not likely to appeal. It is particularly important that parents encourage their Gemini children to curb their superficiality; it will not be easy to keep a balance between inner fulfilment through the completion of plans and avoiding Geminian boredom, but it is essential — otherwise the house will be full of unfinished models, sports gear which has been used only about half-a-dozen times, and so on.

So best, perhaps, to stick to the pen — and you should certainly encourage your Geminian to involve himself with the local paper, perhaps at first collecting small items of news from your area, and later beginning to contribute articles. There is no need to invite you to encourage him to use the local library — the trouble will be getting him away from it.

Mercury, the planet which rules Gemini, was in mythology the messenger of the gods — and very good messengers Geminians make (though they may tend to embroider your original words, unless you actually write them down!). Similarly, in the open air, one thinks of them as athletes and gymnasts; they will enjoy tennis and squash — though they probably won't specially like team sports.

To keep Geminian enthusiasm on the boil, try to concentrate on hobbies which offer plenty of diversification — a broad area within which there are many small trails to be followed. If young Gemini is into scouting or guiding, the greatest satisfaction will be in collecting a large number of badges for a vast variety of achievements; this is ideal, since the objective will be to achieve a higher rank within the group by learning a little about a great number of subjects.

## Preparing for Life

Geminians are of all the signs perhaps most likely to benefit from coeducation; most of them will simply be unable to understand why they should be cut off from half of their fellow human beings — just as, later in life, they will be the least likely to succumb to any kind of snobbery, taking people absolutely at their face value.

We must remember that Geminians are the great flirts of the Zodiac and they are the most youthful-looking of all signs. When they are growing up, this can be a disadvantage, for looking younger than their contemporaries they may not find it easy to make the same progress as rivals when it comes to attracting the attention of the opposite sex. However, they have the personality to counter such set backs; they are good at communicating their feelings and should eventually be able to win the objects of their affections without too much trouble, though there is a possibility that words will be readier than action (there will be a lot of boasting, no doubt). Sexual experiment will take place, of course — perhaps with members of their own sex; but this is common with all children and is often simply a phase in normal development. Inquisitiveness is a strong trait with members of this sign: 'What's it *like*?' they will wonder and may well attempt to find out without giving too much thought to the consequences. This can of course be dangerous, and Geminians profit from early, frank and informed sex education.

When Geminians do capture a partner, they should remember to pay a little consideration to them; occasionally, for instance, it is quite a good idea to listen to what *they* say, do what *they* want to do, rather than take it for granted that all they want is to listen to that ever-flowing stream of entertaining Geminian talk or fall in with the plans Gemini made on the way over. If possible, the partners should be warned to take things easy, emotionally. Gemini may be devoted to one boy- or girl-friend one day, another the next — yet the first will still be well in focus! Parents might think of ways of dropping a gentle hint on the subject.

While one would never suggest that any one sign is more or less suited to another, the thought of two Geminians together is fairly boggling — certainly it might well be all talk and no action! But Geminians need a partner; someone to bounce ideas off, someone to react to them, encourage them, listen to them. They won't respond well to an over-romantic, possessive person; they need their freedom — and their partner will have to get used to the idea that their eye is probably never going to stop roving! Understanding parents should watch this trait, in fact, when Gemini starts dating; they may need to be shown that too much flirtation, while it may be fun for Gemini (who often doesn't take life over-seriously) can do hurtful damage to those who are more romantic. Point out that yesterday's girl-friend may be in the past for Gemini, but *she* may well think she's in the present — the same of course also applies to flighty Geminian girls!

Their partners should ideally be one step ahead, the Geminian racing to keep up — perhaps initially in class and later maybe in career. This will encourage them to study a little more assiduously, to set themselves a goal and keep their eye more steadily on it.

Don't be fooled by the fact that Gemini often seems to treat things casually; they will for instance on the whole be concerned to do 'the right thing' — to dress properly, for instance. They can be devastated if you don't notice how good they're looking — so have a few compliments on hand, even if they're occasionally somewhat insincere!

Although all youngsters spend hours talking to their friends on the telephone, the chances are that Gemini will be way out in front of the field; if you find him making long-distance calls to someone he's met on holiday, I can't urge you too strongly to take him to task and make him pay for them! Encourage him to write, instead — he should have a natural talent for this, and Geminian love-letters can turn up on the 25th wedding anniversary, still tied with the original blue ribbon!

## Further Education

When young Gemini leaves school and starts going to interviews for further education, it will be very necessary to impress on him the fact that he may well spoil his chances by being too talkative and appearing too clever by half. When he is nervous the flow of words will become a torrent — it's one of the ways he has of attempting to cover nervousness — so it is specially important that parents encourage him to try to build a little inner peace and calm. Far better aim for a few well-chosen sentences than too many slick opinions, probably ill-founded and flung hastily out at an interview board whose members will at once see through them.

There is no doubt about the fact that the young Geminian — maybe more than many Zodiac types — will benefit from further education, either at polytechnic or university level. But their desperate need for variety, to express their natural duality, will cause many of them to change course in mid-stream, and thereby prevent some of them from getting good grades or a good degree. Yet again, the way round this is to choose either one subject which is very broad-based or perhaps two subjects which are as different as possible from each other.

The Geminian's attitude to his or her subjects and tutors will be extremely sceptical; they will devour books and delight in finding passages which disagree with received opinion — writers who take different views to everyone else's (even their own) will be avidly consumed and quoted. In the lecture room they will raise all kinds of questions and opinions in order to provoke argument — and will of course pass them off as their own! Needless to say, the experienced tutor will have been through all this before at the hands, no doubt, of other Geminians — but to encourage them will provoke them in turn and hopefully get them involved in original research which will stand them in good stead later in life.

Unfortunately, while this Zodiac group are capable of excellent research, the task can bore them, and the tendency to take short cuts — something ever-present in the Geminian make-up — will from time to time spoil the end product. If Gemini is preparing to write a thesis, it will be as well for him to set aside far more time than he actually needs in order to decide on a subject which is as unlikely as possible to bore him!

It would be idle to pretend that Gemini's notorious lack of interest in facts will be any help when examination time comes. They will tend to answer questions by giving their opinions. Care is obviously needed; they can easily get carried away and fail to supply what is required — results will then be disappointing. They should really settle down to getting at least a selection of hard facts into their heads — and hope that the questions allow them to display the answers.

Geminians who are not going to university might like to consider training schemes which could lead to positions on sales teams; they are naturally good salesmen with the gift of the gab and often abundant charm. There are still some training schemes attached to newspapers, though the larger papers increasingly recruit from university. Publishing and the broadcasting media also offer careers often entered from university — this all underlines the fact that however tedious, in some ways, Geminians may find the routine, it is excellent for them. In politics, if that career attracts them, they can be successful, feeding their need to communicate and put their ideas over to other people, but they have an ability to see all sides of a question and indeed to rock the boat (partly out of sheer boredom with convention), which does not make them particularly obedient to party whips or supportive of the opinions of their fellows.

Geminians who think of art school should consider specializing in graphics and book design, backed up by their natural interest in the printed word. Fashion design can also attract them.

One final word on 'further education': though they are not natural risk takers, Geminian minds are often on something other than the matter in hand, and this can be dangerous when they are driving — at the very least, they may drive faster than they think they are doing (though they love speed and may be all too conscious of it!). An advanced driving course will be particularly valuable to them — and would make a first-rate present.

## Unemployment: Stresses and Strains

As has no doubt emerged, a major bane to Geminians is boredom — and if they find themselves with nothing to do, they are likely to go to pieces very quickly. They should take the view that doing *anything* is, for them, a great deal better than doing nothing; it is really more rewarding for them to work for nothing, or for very little, than to sit at home on national assistance going steadily mad with inaction.

Happily, they have skills which they can use to climb out of the situation; they will be attracted to the local library and will normally know how to use the reference books there to point to possible employment, and of course they will be adept at combing the situations vacant columns in the newspapers and applying for interviews. They are very good indeed at writing persuasive letters and should badger away at employers until the latter grant them an interview either just to stop the flow of letters or — far more probably — because they have been impressed by the Geminian's tenacity and, more than likely, originality, for they are very good at devising unusual ways of bringing themselves to other people's attention.

Parents who notice that the letter writing has begun to slow down should try to whip up more enthusiasm — and perhaps to encourage them to seek something new to occupy their minds; if they show the faintest interest in writing a book, for instance, or trying to write for radio or television, encourage it. If they are already spending a great deal of time indoors at the typewriter, encourage them to get out into the fresh air — they will enjoy bicycling, for instance. They are very volatile people, waking up one day full of enthusiasm, and the next, in the depths of despair — they find it difficult to believe that nobody wants to make use of all that enthusiasm and must be encouraged to believe that indeed this is not true — that someone out there wants them. Encourage them to fill the time in by doing some charity work — they are open people who enjoy helping those less fortunate than themselves, and in many ways this is a tonic to them.

If Gemini turns to drugs it will not be because he wishes to escape from reality, but because he is always eager for new experiences and ever-willing to experiment.

Once hooked, it will be quite difficult for him to kick the habit — he will find it difficult even to give up smoking or drinking. A gregarious character, he may sadly have taken up smoking rather early in life — either because everyone is doing it, or he wants to try something new, or even in order that he has something to do with his hands! At parties, too, he will drink because he has a sort of nervous compulsion to join in — and it is this aspect of his personality which makes it all too easy for him to accept drugs if they are on offer. One of the ways of helping him to give them up is to demonstrate just how much they are slowing him down, just how much of an obstacle they are to his communicating with other people. He could try to sublimate the problem by writing, in detail, about it.

## Interests and Spare Time Activities

It would be very difficult indeed — you might think — to find a shy and retiring Gemini; they always seem to be so lively and talkative and 'with it'. But beneath the facade they can actually be apprehensive and insecure, even melancholic. Sometimes we find that for part of the time they are confident and make good progress — but at others inhibition and lack of self-confidence will emerge. This will only be noticed, however, by those who are really close to them — or who can see through the bright, intelligent facade.

This element helps to make them particularly good at amateur dramatics or any hobby or spare time interest which allows them to present the extrovert part of their personality, which shows them off to their best advantage. The psychological need to communicate is a key factor, and kindred themes like joining a debating society or maybe becoming involved in local government will give them the chance to display and express their effervescent opinions.

Travelling about the local area to pursue sporting interests is a good thing in itself; communication is once again a theme and is being physically expressed. Good neighbourliness is something that should be encouraged and will probably be enjoyed; they will be lively and skilful, for instance, at setting up community schemes such as Neighbourhood Watch. Gemini will get great pleasure from writing to newspapers and speaking on local radio phone-ins about controversial issues which affect his area in particular. Anything that gets him out and about and 'on the scene' should be encouraged — and more often than not will benefit the community at large. Gemini will be the one to raise most money of all the sponsored walkers.

Geminians are not necessarily fascinated by heavy sports such as football; they enjoy cricket, baseball, basketball — the challenge of dexterity and quick movement is attractive, besides which, they are good at it. They should be encouraged to take up tennis, squash and badminton, and perhaps volleyball, and if they have already shown aptitude for these sports at school, they should certainly follow them up later in life. They are less likely to put on weight than some signs, but as they grow older it is good for them to continue exercising (or to start exercising, if they have not done so before), in order to maintain their youthful appearance. Membership of a gym or sports club might almost be said to be essential.

Home hobbies for Geminian girls may certainly include dressmaking, for they are very good at achieving the desired effect with a minimum of sometimes unconventional means. Like Arians, however, they are not patient, and should avoid finicky designer patterns. 'Make it today, wear it tonight' is their motto — and indeed is the right one for them! They can do much to keep their trendy fashion image up-to-date if they are interested in sewing. On the whole Geminians, both boys and girls, are very fashion conscious; they enjoy owning a lot of separates and will mix and match them as much as possible. They need a lot of help, however, since there is an overall tendency for their wardrobes to lack co-ordination; all too often they have wardrobes full of clothes — but no garment teams well with any other, and they are always bemoaning the fact that they 'haven't anything to wear'! It will be difficult for parents to guide them; mistakes will be made, and they'll learn the hard way. But once a Gemini settles down and decides on his or her image, a lively *chic* emerges, and they can look extremely smart and very fashionable.

'Friendship' should be the Gemini theme song in love, for it is vital that they and their partner should be friends as well as lovers — indeed, if they are not the former they will probably very swiftly cease to be the latter. This does not mean that there won't be a successful and enjoyable sex life — but it will tend to be light-hearted, and the talk may be quite as important to Gemini!

Parents will find that when Gemini find a boy- or girl-friend, you'll see very little of them; their new enthusiasm will be all too obvious, and they will want to be with the loved one every waking hour, whether that is practicable or not! There will also be plenty of phone calls, and he is quite likely to hitch a lift if the new lover lives some distance away (this is not, however, such a good idea — especially for girls). The partner should keep in mind that there is some basis for the story that Gemini is particularly inconstant; they do tend to change partners rather more than average until they actually find their soul mate — and even then it is absolutely no good for the soul mate to be the jealous type. If a Gemini does move on, it will probably be because the couple has not enough intellectual *rapport*, and the Gemini has become bored. It is worth remembering that Gemini is not necessarily more promiscuous than any other sign, but problems can sometimes occur because this Zodiac type tends not to trust their emotions and takes a rather sceptical view of love and romance.

## Ideal Careers

Geminians seem positively to need an atmosphere of bustle around them and are unlikely to be entirely happy working alone or within a routine which immobilizes them in some sort of strait-jacket. They need to be able to express their lively personality, continually adjusting to new circumstances, a telephone in one hand and a pencil in the other. The picture that comes to mind is perhaps that of a busy newspaper office — and indeed working in the media is excellent for them, for as the whole of this section shows, they really do need to be communicators, in one way or another.

Here is the ideal person to deal with the general public, thriving at reception desks, at a switchboard or in some other form of telecommunications. The atmosphere of a large, modern department store is perhaps also ideal; Gemini will enjoy getting to know his regular customers, informing them when that new outfit has arrived, and making newcomers to the department feel at ease. But Gemini, in this situation, must be given his head — his style must not be cramped by older, finnicky members of staff. He will take great pride in developing the department, and when in a position of superiority will be a reasonable boss, always open to discussion and unlikely to underestimate the abilities of the people working for him. It must have been a Geminian who was first to sell a refridgerator to an Eskimo — they really have the gift of the gab, so useful to the salesman — and indeed in business in general. Advertising is an excellent career for them — again combining the idea of communication with persuasiveness and a connection with the public. When it comes to setting up their own business it is usually as well for them to have a stable partner somewhere in the background to cope with accounts and record keeping (which will bore Gemini) and steady the Geminian enthusiasm and slight tendency to be fool hardy. And I cannot too strongly stress the fact that Geminis do not suffer fools gladly and on contact with them will display a cutting and sarcastic tongue which will certainly put them in their place.

Many Geminians are now making excellent progress in international banking and on the stock exchanges; they can cope with the tremendously fast pace of this work, which certainly burns up a lot of their nervous energy, but their partners must be on the look-out for tension, since in many cases the individual Geminian will not accept the fact that he *is* tense or worried about his work. If restlessness occurs, or he finds himself unable to sleep well, this may be a danger signal and health could suffer as a result.

As I have hinted, the Geminian is the quintessential media person; ask around any broadcasting studio and the chances are you will find several members of this Zodiac group and its sister sign, Virgo (also ruled by Mercury). Here we have the essential need to communicate married to the capacity to connect with the general public, and careers in the media can be ideal, especially if the individual can work on public affairs programmes or in some other way is in direct touch with the audience. Gemini will be at his best in this profession if he can use his talents to spread the news of, or communicate a joy in, his own favourite interest.

As with all air signs, there is a fair representation of this Zodiac sign in the field of aviation, where the need to communicate is expressed in a very different but equally apt way, for Gemini will enjoy the life-style of an airline pilot or steward, at least for a period of his life.

In many respects Geminians make good teachers, but they are best working with children of about the age of ten or eleven since they can find the limitations of teaching the very young rather boring; they are at an advantage with slightly older children, because they have the unique ability to keep well ahead of current trends and opinions.

Geminians with an artistic bent should be able to find a niche in graphic design — or in publicity or PR departments of all kinds (but perhaps especially in publishing, the theatre or the recording industry).

They should not despair if they find themselves in a career which, on the face of it, does not suit them; one would usually expect them to be bright and inventive enough to create interesting opportunities within the dullest routine (and they will enjoy the intrigue that this may require!). If they cannot do so, their spare time interests will be all the more fascinating and engrossing, taking the weight of a dull daily job off their minds.

## Travel

Any suggestion that travelling is more interesting than arriving will probably be wasted on your Geminian child, who will be all impatience to get there — wherever 'there' is. The actual process of getting there will usually be considered pretty boring, for they are not ones to be happy sitting in the car looking out of the window — however engrossing the scenery. Any parent of a Geminian child who does not provide him with something to do during the journey is asking for trouble. Think up plenty of word games to play; this is one situation when books probably aren't a good idea — they tend to encourage carsickness.

The moment they arrive they will want to be off and away exploring. The idea that it would be nice just to sit on the beach for a morning will go down like a lead balloon, and watching young Gemini like a hawk will be the only way of ensuring that he's still in sight when you want him.

While of course you will want to keep an eye on your youngster, do provide plenty of encouragement when he wants to find out just what it's like in this new environment; let him collect postcards, shells, wild flowers and, of course, friends — he will be jabbering away to anybody he can find who is interested to hear what it is like where *he* comes from!

You might not think it, but your Geminian child may get slightly worried while away on holiday — not about the experience itself but about how things are at home: about the pet you've had to leave behind, or maybe about the apartment you've rented or the hotel where you're staying. The nervous system can be upset by such niggling uncertainties; try to calm him, and watch his food because a minor tummy upset may arise as a result of the strain. Food may be a slight problem, in fact, not that Gemini won't be fascinated at the idea of trying new and unusual dishes, but his digestion isn't necessarily all that strong, and a sudden change of diet can upset him.

One excellent thing about taking Geminians abroad for the first time is that it may well encourage them to learn a foreign language; if they are learning French or German at school, it is a very good idea to try to holiday in the respective country. Actually hearing the language naturally spoken by other children will increase their interest a hundredfold, and if you can rub in the fact, before you go, that by learning some more words and phrases he will be more easily able to talk to the local children, you may be amazed at the results!

When the time comes to think of sending Gemini off on a holiday without you, you'll find the many 'theme holidays' now available for children to be an excellent idea; choose one that seems suitable and Gemini will welcome the suggestion, which will appeal to his lively, inquisitive nature and enable him to spend time — but not *too* long — involved in some new and unfamiliar experience.

## As Brothers and Sisters

When brother or sister arrives, at least it will mean that Gemini will have someone to talk to, and you may find him hanging over the cradle giving baby an endless lecture on life long before there is any likelihood of a response.

The younger brother or sister of a Gemini, then, will get plenty of help in learning to talk and will be encouraged to move about, too — they will probably walk a great deal earlier than if they didn't have this lively sibling tearing about the place and giving them an example! You may well have to keep your eyes open, however, for you may discover Gemini pushing the pram a great deal faster than is safe, or even trying to perch baby sister on a bicycle.

A Geminian with a brother or sister only a little younger than him will be encouraged to develop, because in many ways he will want to show the way — particularly, he will want to read stories to the younger ones, so their reading ability may well leap forward. Similarly, a younger brother and sister will be useful in showing Gemini that everyone is not as quick as he, and as long as his natural impatience can be curbed, there is a good chance that he will learn something about coping with that situation.

Once he knows you are pregnant, Gemini will (perhaps more than members of any other Zodiac sign) be full of pertinent questions which should be answered as frankly as possible. Get him to listen to his baby brother or sister's heart beating, for instance. There is not much point in stories about finding babies in gooseberry patches, because Gemini will be off to find one and search it diligently — or will be asking what happens next, since you haven't got one. This is a situation, incidentally, which will help develop patience, babies being notoriously slow in arriving!

Once the baby has come, and Gemini is no longer the centre of attention, he may tend to show his jealousy artfully; there may not be storms and tantrums, but the conversation will be carefully slanted in an attempt to make sure everyone knows what Gemini expects of the family and to attract attention to *him* rather than the little one.

As a younger child, Gemini will be quite a challenge to elder brothers and sisters and under pressure could become extremely argumentative — very irritating indeed if the older children are less ready with words. As ever, the great thing to impress upon Gemini is that people are individuals, and it is important to *listen* to their opinions and feelings as well as putting over your own. In this way Gemini will contribute much that is lively and happy to the family unit as a whole.

Pity the child who has to share a room with a Geminian, which is rather like sharing with a small typhoon. The placid young Taurean who wants a quiet hour of study will be infuriated. There will be no lack of stimulation, however, which might be a very good thing — though the other child may be kept awake by chatter, plans for the future, descriptions of the plot of the latest book Gemini's reading, or whatever. Every idea Gemini has is the best yet. You could encourage them to share hobbies and thus obtain a cross-fertilization of interests; hopefully it would also encourage Gemini to be consistent and stick at things — if he doesn't, it will spoil it for brother or sister.

At school, while he may not physically be very tough, all Gemini's quickness will be devoted to sticking up for brother or sister, whether they're younger or older. Watch out that Gemini's quickness and brightness (not always supported by real depth of knowledge) doesn't put a slower but perhaps basically cleverer brother or sister in the shade. You could well encourage brother or sister actually to test Gemini's real knowledge and shame him into more thoroughness.

If the children get into trouble, you would be right to suspect that Gemini may be the driving force — more than likely the naughtiness will have been his idea in the first place. Once having established this, you should really be rather strict but logically so; it is no use whatsoever punishing a Geminian without explaining precisely *why* they are being punished. You should also listen to their side of the story — which they will present with all the skill and persuasiveness of a High Court lawyer! The point is, however, that unless you can show them precisely why their action was silly/wicked/hurtful, they are more than likely to dismiss the punishment as unjust and go right ahead and plan some other outrage!

## Geminians as Parents

It is absolutely essential for the prospective Geminian parent to consider every aspect of their situation before positively deciding to start a family. He should look at his friends' families. Prospective Geminian mothers should baby-sit and prepare themselves as thoroughly as possible to know just what they are letting themselves in for; while the Geminian will consider the challenge of bringing up children exciting (especially when they think of helping to develop their young minds and supervising their education), they must recognize the fact that there will be times when they will be bored out of their mind — however lively the child is and despite their very real love for them.

This of course can particularly apply to the Geminian mother, who will presumably spend the most time with the children; so it is specially important that father shares the chores — and I strongly recommend that the would-be Gemini mother should, like some other Zodiac mums, make quite sure that the moment she is recovered from the birth she has at least a couple of hours a week in which to pursue her favourite interests — preferably out of the house and well away from baby. In this way she will remain a lively, intelligent, stimulating mother, far less likely to get bogged down by the predictable routine of looking after baby. If this proves difficult, she might like to consider starting a play group or perhaps a baby-sitting circle in her district, so that all young mothers may benefit from a little extra free time.

When the Gemini father comes home from work, he can and should exercise his skills by telling or reading bedtime stories; it is at such times that he will be at his best as a father and will himself get special pleasure from parenthood. Organizing hide-and-seek or treasure hunts will also be great fun both for him and the children.

On the negative side, however, remember that the Gemini type is extremely critical, and it is sadly all too often the case that their critical tones are heard whenever the child presents them with anything they've made or anything they've done, and this can be soul-destroying. In your keenness for your child's progress, do think two or three times when your little one presents you with a drawing he's particularly pleased with, and try not to be destructively critical — remember, your verdict will be very important indeed, and a young child is not always able to receive an antagonistic verdict with equanimity. Try always to allow your natural enthusiasm and sense of humour to dominate over your carping critical characteristics — over-rather than under-praise, and you'll win your children's hearts.

The Gemini parent makes a wonderful member of a school PTA. Involvement in this — and all school activities — is fully recommended, for originality of approach and bright ideas for fund raising activities will be most welcome, and Geminian enthusiasm will ensure that it all happens!

Of all Sun-sign types, Gemini is the least likely to experience generation gap problems; indeed, quite the reverse — very often it's the case that the children will have to work quite hard to keep up with their lively parent! But it must be remembered that while it is important for Geminians to be aware of their children's interests, they should try not to involve themselves to the extent of running everything; a balance should be maintained between genuine interest and their children's freedom to do their own thing. If this is not achieved, the children will look on them as irritating busybodies.

The Geminian may find it specially difficult to understand that his youngsters are not necessarily going to be like him; a Geminian whose children are simply not interested in reading finds it almost impossible to understand how such a thing could be, but in such a situation absolutely nothing will be achieved by forcing or trying to force books down their throats — though if your child is almost entirely physical and spends all his time on the football field, it is well worth getting hold of some books on the subject and leaving them lying around. It is really quite a problem for the articulate Geminian to understand that words are not the most important things in everyone's life; it's the old story — learn to think of your children as small adults who have a right to their own amusements and their own approach to life.

# Case Study

Katie - Sun and Venus in Gemini, Mercury in Cancer; Mercury Group 3, Venus Group 3.

From the Report: 'Because Katie was born just after sunrise (the Sun rises extremely early in late May) the Sun and rising sign in her chart are both Gemini, so I think you will find that she is extremely lively and will probably start talking very early — and indeed start reading at an early age, too. Once she does start talking she will probably never stop! She will always want to be on the move, and in some respects is not likely to be the most patient of people. She has plenty of charm, and while she may well make good use of this, it won't be at all forced — it will just bubble out of her, making her extremely appealing and attractive to others. I'm sure you can see this quality emerging already, and it is one that will not fade as she grows up, for it is very much part of her, and absolutely natural.

'I think you will find that she will be enormously enthusiastic about anything that fascinates her; she'll want to put ideas into operation as soon as she has them, and once she sets her mind on doing or wanting something, there will be no discouraging her. She'll simply have to try everything for herself, in her own individual way, and while she won't lack logic, I think you will find she will learn to talk you into seeing things her way — and be most convincing in her arguments!

'You will have to see that she is kept busy. Remember that as she grows up she will develop a powerful element of duality which on a day-to-day level will express itself in her not wanting to do one thing at a time. While it seems right to encourage children not to flit from one task to another, in her case you must expect her to, say, want to start writing a story one moment, then the next to turn to sewing, model-making, sticking stamps in an album. Expect her to change within a week from swearing that the thing she likes best is swimming to wanting to dance (just the thing for her). This sudden switching and changing will be natural to her, and should not be rebuked!'

Comment: Katie was born just after sun-rise, so her all-important rising sign is also Gemini. Her parents tell me that she is *very* true to type, and extremely versatile. Six years of age at the time of writing (the report was written just after she was born) she constantly switches from one occupation to something quite different but is very good at completing all her tasks in due course. Due to the placing of Mercury she has an excellent memory but is also extremely impatient.

## The Sun-sign and Its Rulerships

*Countries and areas*: Armenia, Belgium, Lower Egypt, Sardina, U.S.A., Wales.

*Cities*: Bruges, Cardiff, Cordoba, London, Melbourne, Nuremburg, New York, Plymouth, San Francisco, Versailles.

*Trees*: all nut-bearing trees.

*Flowers and herbs*: aniseed, azalia, balm, bitter-sweet, bryony, caraway, elf-wort, fern, hare's-foot, lavender, lily-of-the-valley, maidenhair, myrtle.

*Food*: nuts (especially hazel and walnut), most vegatables (except cabbage).

*Cell salts*: Kali. Mur., Silica.

*Animals*: small birds, parrots, butterflies, monkeys.

*Stone*: agate, sometimes emerald.

*Metal*: mercury (I suggest platinum for jewellery).

*Colour*: bright yellow; most colours.

# CANCER

## (June 22 - July 22)

Note: Cancer is a feminine sign, so for the most
part I refer throughout to 'she', but most of my
comments refer also to boys.

## General Characteristics

Any baby born while the Sun is travelling through Cancer will be kind, sensitive,
imaginative and loving, and you will soon see those characteristics developing, but
there will also be problems, for the child will be extremely susceptible to external
influences and may be more than a little moody.

Whether boys or girls, young Cancerians will develop an intense love of home
and family life and will defend both themselves and their loved ones with remarkable
tenacity and strength of will. There is in every member of this Zodiac group a unique
inner defense system which springs immediately into action when they are challenged.
You will see this quality emerge in a sudden change of expression; one moment
young Cancer will be happily smiling — the next she will have sensed some kind
of danger, signalled perhaps by someone's casual remark. The gentle smile will at
once become a deep frown which begins with the formation of a hard line between
the eyebrows, and this will be followed by a flurry of words which will undoubtedly
put the offending person immediately in their place!

At its best this is a terrific quality, but as she grows up, you may need to correct
the tendency since it is all too easy for the Cancerian type to develop a snappy
temper which can result in some very harsh comments which are far more hurtful
than Cancer realizes. Indeed, if she had said them to herself before speaking them,
her own delicate sensitivity would have come into play, and she would certainly
never have uttered them aloud, rather retreating into moody silence.

On the positive side we have a personality who is very tenacious and will work
hard and long to achieve objectives. The powers of intuition will be second to none,
and if, when she's very young, your Cancerian comes out with some extraordinary
statement that seems to bear no relation to anyone or anything, you will be wise

to consider it very carefully, since the chances are that there will be more than an element of truth in what the oracle pronounces!

While the physical energy level of Cancer is not the highest, there is enough emotional energy for more than one person so the two must be balanced; if you can encourage your young Cancerian to become involved in activities which make gradually increasing demands on her energy this will increase her strength and her resistance to the normal stress and strain of life. Determination will most certainly help in situations where physical strength is required.

The influence of the Moon — the ruling planet of this sign — is really quite strongly pronounced. Cancer will probably be at her most energetic when the Moon is new and most tense, fractious and moody when it is full. Changing moods are very much part and parcel of the Cancerian personality — so much so that the characteristic can veer towards unpredictability. Of course this is so to a certain extent with most babies and young children, but do be prepared for these vivid changes of emotional colour with your Cancerian. At their best, these children will make life extremely interesting for you — but sometimes their moods can result in a build-up of tension which must be countered if they are not to affect you as well as your child. As she grows up, the root cause of these changes of mood can sometimes be seen to be related to an over-active imagination — not to mention that powerful intuition. If you find this happening, it may be that neither intuition nor imagination are getting as much positive expression as they should; in that case I suggest that you aim to work out practical ways of expressing them more fulfillingly. As you will see later, this will probably be through creative, artistic work of some sort.

The strong protective instinct in Cancer is really quite remarkable. Very early in life you will find her cherishing and carefully looking after her toys — not to mention her brothers and sisters, if she has them. This is a marvellous quality, but it can sometimes be over-emphasized, taking the form of a tendency to cling to the known and loved. While this Zodiac type is in many ways very brave, we can find her hiding behind mother's skirts and becoming fearful and apprehensive.

Encourage young Cancer at all times to have a positive outlook on life; build self-confidence — which may not be particularly strong — and encourage her to express herself in a practical as well as an imaginative way.

Of all signs, Cancer is perhaps least likely to take strangers at face value; caution comes naturally to these children, and they will take seriously any warnings you have to give. Watch out, however, or the pendulum could swing in the other direction; a friendly remark or smile from a stranger could give your young Cancerian's imagination a fillip, especially if you have recently uttered a warning, and false accusations could be made. There is however a fantastic shrewdness in this type which usually enables them to see situations clearly; later in life they often make excellent business people. They will be careful with pocket-money, so much so that you may need to counter what appears like meanness. You can always appeal, however, to deep-rooted kindness and compassion, especially when you are making collections for a favourite charity. At such times you will find they will respond particularly well to charities which raise money for less fortunate children — suffering of that kind hits right at the very core of Cancerian susceptibility.

Your Cancerian will probably look particularly attractive in pale, pastel colours, and her out-of-school image should be carefully nurtured and developed, for later in life, while many of this sign become extremely *chic*, all too often slight carelessness and lack of attention to detail will mar the whole effect. So I suggest that whether your child is a boy or a girl you should train them from an early age to check their appearance: are both their socks pulled up neatly? is their shirt completely tucked in? This may sound trivial, but I assure you it is quite important!

However happy they are at school, however happy their holidays with friends, you will always have the pleasure of seeing a smiling face coming through the door afterwards — home means a lot to Cancerians, and they are always happy to be there.

## The Three Ways of Thinking

Due to the influence of Mercury (see p.13) the Cancerian mind characteristically works in one of three ways:

★ The first group comprises Cancerians who are very quick-witted and have a natural ability to express their intuition and imagination forcefully, dynamically and originally. These are the natural story-tellers of the Zodiac but should be encouraged to be truthful.

★★ Cancerians of the second group possess vivid, colourful imaginations and remarkable memories and will be strongly influenced by the events of their early years. Hypersensitivity can be a problem, increasing moodiness. Kind thoughtfulness abounds.

★★★ Members of the third group have a tendency to show off, to dramatize almost every situation; here are colourful characters who think in a positive and extrovert way — they are less likely to be moody, more readily able than other Cancerians to take life as it comes.

## The Five Ways of Loving

Due to the influence of Venus (see p.13) Cancerians will tend to express their affection in one of five ways:

★ Members of the first group have a particularly high need for emotional security; you may notice a tendency to possessiveness and jealousy emerging. The expression of love and affection will be especially charming, adding a delightful element to the personality.

★★ A light-hearted flirtatiousness characterizes the second group, but may inhibit an expression of real emotion. The charm of this attitude, with a delightfully cheerful friendliness, will be pleasing, but the Cancerian concerned may lose out because she has not learned fully to trust her emotions.

★★★ The third group of Cancerians contains some of the most romantic and sentimental people of the whole Zodiac. There will be a tendency, however, to live in the past. So encourage positive thinking and a forward-looking attitude to life, especially when it comes to the building of new relationships.

★★★★ Cancerian meanness will not be shown by members of this group, who will spend freely on their lovers and will be generous to their friends; the expression of love will be full and uninhibited. But watch out for bossiness and a tendency towards domination.

★★★★★ A certain shyness and a critical tendency could spoil the fun for the fifth group; encourage them to accept people for what they are, and point out that we are not all alike. There may be a somewhat clinical attitude towards the affections.

## Health and Diet

Cancerians have basically strong constitutions, but this is often something which they and their closest family and friends would deny, for they also have sensitive digestions which can be easily upset, and there is consequently sometimes a preoccupation with what they should or shouldn't eat — to the extent that this can become faddiness and fussiness. If we look at the reasons for it, we often find that the problem lies with some emotional difficulty; something has upset them, or they are worried about some problem. They can under such circumstances pick and choose in an irritating fashion or even go off their food altogether.

We must not forget that the glands attributed to this sign are the alimentary, which control the diet, so the necessity for a well-balanced diet is particularly strong, especially as it affects the Cancerian's moods as well as her physical well-being. The best sort of snacks for this sign are those with a yoghurt base, and carob makes a good alternative to chocolate.

Naturally, the more persuasive you can be when they are young in getting them to regard food as something unlikely to do them any harm, the better! And indeed for the most part this is true. Dairy products and food which is high in calcium are particularly good for them. If you can possibly avoid it, do not fall into the trap of giving way, when your Cancerian child is very young, to their fads and fancies just because it is easier to do so than to help them overcome their pickiness! Try to nip problems in the bud, for very often they can inhibit physical development — especially when they result in an unbalanced diet.

A steady, predictable routine, while it may seem somewhat boring, is as a matter of fact especially desirable for Cancerians, for it helps to alleviate tension and sudden changes of mood and will develop an even rhythm and pattern to their lives which will be calming and settling. This will not only give them confidence to relax into ordinary eating habits, but once the rhythm has been established you will find that they should begin to sleep well and deeply. So if you are having problems with young Cancer waking up in the middle of the night, fractious and in tears, the problem may well lie with over-excitement or tension. Incidentally, once they are sleeping well they will probably regale you with some marvellous dreams, and this should be encouraged.

I am afraid I have to agree that Cancer is at the top of the league when it comes to worry (though I must say that their sister sign, Virgo, runs them very close!) and when they are worried they may well shut up like a clam, definitely not wanting to tell you what is wrong. Do everything you possibly can to encourage them to open up; if they do not, their digestion will suffer, and you could even find that their behaviour patterns will change for the worse. If they say they're not in the mood for some interest or hobby that they usually find particularly rewarding, there is a distinct possibility that they are worried about something — or perhaps apprehensive about someone else's reaction to them and their abilities. Try to winkle the real problem out of them because it is only when it is openly admitted and expressed that things will once more fall into their natural daily rhythm.

Cancer should be quite a good patient when suffering from the usual run of childhood illnesses; she will feel protected and warm within the confines of her own room. Indeed it is at such times that her natural maternal instinct and caring, protective qualities may begin to emerge; she will inevitably pretend that her favourite toy is also ill and will imitate your behaviour to her in caring for it.

When it comes to exercise, all those activities accentuating steady rhythm and a repetitive pattern are particularly good for Cancerians. True to their element young Cancerians are usually water-babies; why not take them to mother-and-baby swimming sessions at the very earliest age? The earlier Cancerians learn to swim, the better. Not only is this good exercise, but it has an emotional significance for them.

*Please note*: there is no connection between Cancer the sign and the disease of that name. Those of this Zodiac group are no more and no less vulnerable to it than members of any other sign.

## The First Five Years

Of all the Zodiac types, the young Cancerian is one of the most interesting. For instance, you will find her imitating your every word and action far more precisely than other children, and you will see reflected in her everything that is good and not so good in your own behaviour and attitudes. As a result, in caring for a younger Cancerian you will find out a very great deal about yourself!

Praise young Cancer generously for her positive actions, and almost immediately you will hear her passing the approbation on to her favourite toys; scold her, and the dolls had better look out for squalls! But remember, you should consider more carefully than usual whether a short, sharp smack at moments of crisis is a good thing or not; if you decide it is, the chances are that should she become fractious — at, say the supermarket — you are going to have to cope with the embarrassing scene of a young child giving you a taste of your own medicine and letting fly at you in a sudden moment of temper.

Their wonderful imagination should be developed early in young Cancerians. It will be a great pleasure to see it blossom. From an early age they will respond very maturely to nursery rhymes and fairy stories; indeed, you may even hear your child making up her own — and if you do, you can be confident that you are stimulating her in the right way. I would suggest that, as early as you like, you buy her picture-books with well-drawn illustrations: 'The Flower Fairies' or 'Thomas, the Tank Engine', for instance. The artist should leave just enough unexpressed to inspire the Cancerian imagination.

Cancerian girls can all too easily become *over*-feminine — in part because of their naturally strong maternal instinct. These days it is good for them to have a number of toys which appeal to both sexes. Similarly the boys should be encouraged to realize that they are not as different as all that from their sisters; they too should be encouraged to play with every kind of toy, not just the 'boyish' ones.

Interestingly, while in diet there may be problems with likes and dislikes, you should look out for an early fascination with cooking — this can become very important later in life to either sex.

When it comes to play group or nursery school, shyness could swamp your young Cancerian; if possible, try first to cultivate a friendship with another child who already attends — this will cushion the shock and build her self-confidence.

When it comes to helping out at home, I suggest that you encourage your child to be tidy, for Cancerians are notoriously untidy. This is not because the idea of untidiness delights them, nor are they particularly careless, they are simply natural hoarders. You will have to do battle here; it will be very difficult to get Ms Cancer to throw anything away. So when her toy-box is full of all kinds of rubbish and she can't cram anything more into it, you must encourage her to sort it out and throw or give away the things she does not want — which will be difficult because she'll claim to want everything.

## School Years

Assuming that your young Cancerian has attended play group — which, incidentally, I strongly recommend — when it comes to starting nursery school she should be feeling more self-confident, and the braver side of her personality should surface. She should be able to stand up for herself when coping with other children, and some of her fine, caring, imaginative qualities will stand her in good stead in the rather more rough and tumble atmosphere.

She should be able to enjoy a steady routine and accept reasonable discipline; however, her intuition will spring into action in her relationship to other children and especially to her teachers. She will know far more about them than she can adequately put into words, and those natural responses will undoubtedly colour her whole attitude towards school life and will indeed have their effect upon her general progress. No matter how clever a teacher may be at hiding his or her real feelings, you can bet your life that the young Cancerian will instinctively know exactly how that teacher feels about her! And if she picks up negative vibes, all her Cancerian self-defensive system will spring into action and the *rapport* between pupil and teacher will either be non-existent or negative. She may tell you that she 'doesn't awfully like old so-and-so', and if you can encourage her to rationalize and discover just why, that will be very positive; but it will not be easy, for she will be working and expressing herself on a purely intuitive level. As a result, progress in the subjects taken by the unsympathetic teacher could be considerably less than in cases where there is a marvellously instinctive, sympathetic feeling between pupil and teacher. This may sound like a generalization, and indeed is true for a great number of pupils, but in the case of Cancer it is something of which all parents must be aware. The last thing that should happen to a young Cancerian is for her to be driven into her shell; if she does retire into it, a great deal of effort and persuasion is going to be needed to inveigle her out of it again.

The excellent memory of most Cancerians stands them in marvellous stead when they are coping with classwork and examinations. Whether Cancer is quick or slow to learn facts depends on the individual child, but the chances of a Cancerian having good retention are excellent, so when it comes to settling down to long courses of study she will be well able to take them in her stride.

As in everything, it is a sense of rhythm that is important if your young Cancerian is to maintain steady progress at school. There will be storms and changes of mood along the way, and no doubt you will find your own special way of calming them. Cancerians will benefit from a diversion, and this can take the form of a change of occupation; when they are worried, you might suggest a visit to the swimming-pool, or if there is an ongoing problem, a course of dance classes could act as an antidote. It is often the case that Cancerians do extremely well in heavy, tough sports; their ability to defend themselves emotionally can be expressed in a tough, physical way in team games, or perhaps they will develop skills at boxing or wrestling or in the martial arts. Judo is particularly recommended for the girls and is helpful as a form of self-defence.

There is a good chance that friendships formed during school years will last throughout life, for Cancerians are extremely good at keeping in contact even when miles separate them from old friends. They are the sort who never forget birthdays or Christmas, and such events are good excuses for letters, phone calls, and reminiscences about old times. Indeed, you may be amused to find your young Cancerian referring to 'the old days' when she is scarcely old enough to have any past at all!

For various reasons it is sometimes necessary for parents to send their children to boarding school, and while under some circumstances Cancerians will prove able to cope with life away from home, children of this sign will probably suffer most as a result of being torn away from the family. The Cancerian love of home and the family circle is so much part of their psychological nature that they are almost bound to be distraught at being separated from it, and the result may be to do them considerable damage. It is much better for both boys and girls to be able to return to the family at the end of the school day. If a boarding-school is decided upon, it would be helpful if a compromise could be reached and they could be weekly rather than termly boarders.

Although the Cancerian will get through a great deal at school, she may not be particularly amenable to discipline, partly because she can find it bewildering and confusing. This is something to watch for as in time she may waste a lot of energy running around in circles, whereas more careful planning could save a lot of effort and achieve a great deal.

## Out of School Activities

It will prove easy enough to get Cancer away from school; it may not be quite so easy, perhaps, to get her away from home. Both boys and girls have a tendency to be over-domesticated, and in the best of weather it may be difficult to prise them away from the home patch.

All kinds of sporting activities are to be encouraged with the emphasis on swimming. Those Cancerian children lucky enough to have parents who enjoy boating will be sure to follow in their footsteps and participate in water sports. Fishing can become a popular pastime, though this will perhaps give Cancer a little too much time to sit and brood inactively.

Whether they are at home or away, always aim to encourage them to do everything you can think of which will stimulate their imagination. They will love fairy stories and literature with a strong element of fantasy, and these can act as a starting-point from which they can create their own fantasy world. It will be as well to remember that this world should be shared with parents and other members of the family, otherwise there will be a tendency towards introspection. Cancerians should have easy access to writing paper, pens and pencils and all sorts of drawing materials, for these will encourage the imaginative force to externalize itself.

It is particularly good for Cancerians to have a pet to look after; this will help them express their caring, protective instincts, which are a very natural and beautiful aspect of their personality. Should they forget to feed their dog or take it for a walk, it will be very easy to appeal to their sensitive natures, getting them to imagine how the creature feels when neglected. They will be unlikely to repeat the offence.

Away from the family, Cancerians should be encouraged to get involved in first aid. Many will eventually go on to become doctors or nurses, and this early training could be a real source of inspiration. Working with animals is also good, as is any work or hobby which requires the individual to give help and show kindness and consideration.

The youngest Cancerian will very often befriend a much older person; if you have an elderly neighbour it might be a good thing to suggest to your young Cancerian that they might visit him or her and find out whether there are messages, errands or jobs they can do.

As there is a tendency towards shyness in most Cancerians, all activities encouraging personal development and increased self-confidence are excellent. There is a natural lyricism which can be expressed through dance and music, and if they learn to play a musical instrument or go to regular dance classes this will help them develop these happy qualities.

Cancerians can sometimes lack the spirit of adventure, so out-of-school activities to help them develop this are specially useful.

## Preparing for Life

Without a sensible sex education the young Cancerian's imagination will run riot, and all kinds of strange and fantastic ideas will take root which will probably be difficult to shake off. Remember, this sign is high on the list of the romantics of the Zodiac, so the teen-age romantic phase will probably hit them when they are rather younger than you expect and may stay with them for longer than is usual — if not for life! So encourage your growing Cancerian to be practical and realistic about their sexual development, to counter any over-romantic ideas.

Most young people are rather shy when on their first date, but Cancerians particularly need confidence in themselves if they are to blossom forth as the excellent and caring partners they can become. Help by encouraging them to look their best, to tidy up loose ends in their appearance, to approach the occasion as calmly as possible, and not to be suicidal if things do not go precisely as they envisaged. They should also be warned not to be inconsistent, not to blow hot and then cold — in fact to be considerate to their boy- or girl-friend. They should also be discouraged from harbouring grudges; they can tend to latch on to some often imagined slight and nurse it until it becomes a major problem in a relationship. Live and let live is not a bad motto to quote at them.

Cancerians who attend a coeducational school will cope with the problems of adolescence more easily than those who have been confined to a single-sex school, though there will be an above average tendency for the girls to bunch together with girls and the boys with the boys during the first few weeks. The more you or the teachers can do to encourage your Cancerian to mix with the opposite sex the better it will be for them, and the easier they will find it to form social and later emotional bonds.

Though few Cancerians will be happy with a partner who does not care for domestic life or does not want children, they should not look at every possible new friend as a potential father or mother of their family; this can be more than a little off-putting. Neither should they shy away from people not so exclusively interested in home and family as they — for they can benefit a great deal from being torn away from domesticity and thrust into the rough and tumble of the outside world. Friends of both sexes should indeed encourage Cancerians to be daring and occasionally step out of line; once the Cancerian is brave enought to do so she will develop the ability to take calculated risks and combine natural caution with bravery, so getting the best of both worlds. This can apply to the Cancerian sexual life, too; they are sometimes inclined to get into so strict a domestic, maternal or paternal routine that they lose sight of the fact that in this as in all areas of life there is everything to be said for *avoiding* an invariable routine, which can become boring not only for the partner but eventually for the Cancerian herself. This is an aspect of marriage which can be extremely damaging and in the end contributes to the destruction of the substantial home environment they most need and desire.

The Cancerian temperament may give a little trouble when they have actually decided to devote their lives to someone, for then will come the time when they have to tear themselves away from parents and the security of their first family in order to form a family unit of their own. This is not an easy situation for them; to make things easier, parents should try their best not to show the slightest tendency to cling to a Cancerian son or daughter, realizing that the very fact that they have decided to leave probably means that they are ready to do so.

If all this sounds a little discouraging, there is no need for undue pessimism, for nothing I have said must detract from the fact that once they have achieved balance Cancerians make marvellous partners — not only providing a stable home environment but being wonderfully understanding, caring and protective, using their intuition to provide just the home their partners need.

## Further Education

Once your young Cancerian has got used to the very different life style of university she will settle down and make good progress, but she must remember that she is likely to feel homesick longer than most people. She should be encouraged very early on to join societies and out of class activities; there is a tendency for her to hide her light under a bushel, and if she does this she will not enjoy the full advantage or excitement that a university education has to offer.

The girls of this sign will be particularly conscientious and will not shy away from lectures, taking full notes and going on to write interesting and intuitive essays. It will be best for both sexes to specialize in subjects which will allow their imagination full rein. Even if they are of a scientific bent they should have the opportunity to participate in research which demands an intuitive, imaginative approach. Nevertheless, those who opt for history or literature will probably do extremely well, since this is in many ways an ideal form of expression for the Cancerian personality. Although Cancerians can be chaotically untidy, because they have retentive minds they not only make good students but can do extremely well in examinations provided they do not allow apprehension, worry and tension to prevent them from being confident when faced with the papers. Neither must they allow concern for their love lives, or any external worry, to catch up with them since this kind of thing can distract them rather more than members of other Zodiac signs.

Cancerians need the kind of tutor who has a very incisive approach. The lecturer who asks searching questions and helps them express their real reasons for the opinions they hold will be the best possible person to bring them out. If challenged in this way they will enjoy getting down to basics, and their more intuitive talents will be nurtured.

If they do not wish to go on to university, the sort of training that a local polytechnic can offer will stand Cancerians in very good stead, especially if the individual concerned is somewhat introverted and rather reluctant to participate fully in a university's social life. Attending a local polytechnic will mean that leaving school won't necessarily mean leaving home, which is a good compromise, bridging the gap between domesticity and total independence.

On leaving school many young people take a year out for travel and self-discovery. This is a particularly good idea for young Cancer, and it will certainly be worth parents' while to suggest it, if practicable. Any Cancerian who jumps at the idea will be demonstrating that she has come to terms with her possible shyness and introversion and is ready to face the world. Hesitation probably indicates the opposite, so let the matter rest and don't force it — though as an alternative some kind of charity field work or community service might be an excellent idea.

I have already mentioned first aid, which might lead to the very Cancerian idea of a career in medicine, but anyone who has read a description of the characteristics of Cancer will remember that here are the natural cooks of the Zodiac, and no doubt by the time your young Cancerian has left school and is ready for further education she will already have experimented in the kitchen and may well have shown considerable flair. An ideal hobby which could lead to an extremely successful and lucrative career might be in the area of catering. Neither you nor she should ignore this — and here, as usual, I use 'she' very loosely indeed for this applies to young men as well as women; indeed, young male Cancerians often take the lead in the kitchen!

Many young Cancerians are particularly capable baby-sitters — here too is perhaps an indication of a possible career. From helping out in this way, they may well like to go on to become pediatricians or take up nursery school teaching or child nursing as an expression of this aspect of their caring instinct.

## Unemployment: Stresses and Strains

A Cancerian turned down by a number of prospective employers or just not finding a position for which to apply, will have her self-confidence undermined rather more than many other Zodiac types. As a result you may find that she will lose all assertiveness, tend to give up far too easily, and slip quite happily into a purely domestic routine.

But every Cancerian possesses powerful determination, if it can be ignited and kept alive. Should it tend to splutter and fade, you must try to find a way of blowing on the fuse! Encourage her to believe that perseverance will pay off in the end; once she gets the message she will think very differently about her situation and renew her efforts. The great thing is that she should believe in herself and her capabilities, and if she has worked hard at school and proved herself to be reliable, these fine qualities will stand her in good stead.

You can appeal to her shrewd business sense: encourage enterprise — perhaps she could start some small money raising scheme which at its most basic level will at least pay for phone calls, stationery and stamps while she applies for the jobs she has her eye on. Many Cancerians have an excellent ability to communicate their ideas; this is of course an enormous advantage if one is looking for work and is a trait you should always encourage. Meanwhile, your Cancerian must be helped to fill her day with activity. There are always charities, old people's organizations and children's play groups needing help — and such work gives most Cancerians a sense of inner satisfaction and a feeling that they are needed. So here are some worthwhile avenues to follow.

You may have to encourage your young Cancerian to continue to meet her friends, especially those who have been lucky enough to find work. She may feel that she is at a disadvantage, and her self-esteem will have been so wounded that she tends to keep away from them; but in fact they will be able to encourage her to keep looking and may even come up with some practical suggestions, or perhaps hear of a job that would be suitable. Remember that tenacity is a strong characteristic and should be a help in this particular situation.

One possible reason for a Cancerian to get hooked on drugs is that she wants to escape from reality into a more comfortable world. She will probably find that her imagination is stimulated so that she can enter an exciting fantasy life which will relieve the tedium of unemployment. Cancerian tenacity will help her kick the habit once she realizes where it is leading, and parents will then be able to help strengthen positive determination; but this could go both ways, for there can be a touch of pig-headedness and insistence on going her own way.

It is of course, as with all addicts, important to discover the real reason why Cancer has gone onto drugs in the first place. Rather than relating it to something as obvious as unemployment, it could be rooted in an emotional disturbance in her love life or some other area of her personality. We must never underestimate the very powerful emotional forces within the Cancerian personality; if these are not positively expressed or are misrouted, there can be serious problems. Sometimes outlet through creative work is of enormous benefit.

## Interests and Spare Time Activities

The strong protective instinct which is so much part of the Cancerian make-up will undoubtedly be expressed towards friends, and you can expect your teen-age Cancerian to be very keen to go off with them — perhaps renting a large apartment together, with Cancer going off to market to do the necessary shopping, and spending the rest of the day in the kitchen.

Activities making physical demands on Cancerians are extremely good for them; in a strange way they help them to develop determination and the stronger side of their personalities. An element of competitiveness is also useful in that respect. Water sports of all kinds may fill part of Cancer's leisure time, and if, as I suspect, she learned to swim when she was really tiny, you will find that she will naturally progress to diving, underwater swimming, surfing and wind surfing; all of these can be competitive.

To develop the quieter, more sensitive areas of the Cancerian personality (if indeed it needs development) some form of involvement in music might be encouraged. Many Cancerians get a great deal of pleasure from belonging to a choir or choral society, others enjoy country and folk music, and some make excellent string instrumentalists of one sort or another. It is in this kind of interest that their tenacity of purpose can be so rewarding, for many hours of practice are involved, and they often have the will-power to devote the necessary time to their hobby. Esoteric studies are also often rewarding.

Developing good taste is sometimes a difficulty. Many Cancerians tend to make glaring errors — often there can be a very sketchy colour sense, clutter, and untidiness. However, having realized that the problem exists, they should be encouraged to employ their keen powers of observation and acquire dexterity; in the end they will be able to achieve quite remarkable effects with great economy of means.

Fascinated by the past — sometimes tending to live in it — Cancerians love history at school and go on to read historical novels or social history and enjoy historical plays and films. Every Cancerian has a collection of something: the wealthy will go for antique silver, some for postage stamps, yet others for some unusual objects of very limited appeal. A craze in recent years which has especially appealed to the young Cancerian woman has been looking around street markets for antique clothes. This can be great fun, and Cancerians often have the ability to devise a unique and interesting (if sometimes somewhat ragged) image based on them. The talent for making good collections — of whatever sort — should not be underestimated, for it has been known to yield quite large sums of money when those are needed! What should be discouraged is the accumulation of unmanageable clutter — which often amounts to useless rubbish.

Cancerians profit particularly from keeping a pet of some kind. On the whole, they tend to be cat rather than dog people, but a dog with a nice, smooth, silky coat — a cocker spaniel, maybe — will appeal to most of them. Dogs will encourage exercise, of course, which is no bad thing; a cat will tend to play up to Cancerian preoccupation with home, which (while an excellent attribute) scarcely needs encouragement in members of this sign!

The Cancerian who becomes involved in a society or on a committee will be a great asset; here is someone who will work extremely hard. She is unlikely to have joined the committee if she did not believe in its work, and when elected (possibly with reluctance) she will get on quietly and efficiently with any tasks given her. There may be a tendency not to speak up, especially if things go wrong; she should be careful not to exascerbate the situation by grumbling on behind the scenes rather than bringing things out into the open. The chances are that she will shun the highest office.

It is sometimes a little difficult for Cancerians, male or female, to enjoy simple ties of friendship with members of the opposite sex. Their high emotional level tends to invest every friendship with an element of loving and caring. This of course is absolutely admirable, but even if they are 'just good friends' the Cancerian may nurse the suspicion, hope, or belief that there could be something more, and this can be upsetting or irritating to the other person concerned. It is this which makes it very difficult for a Cancerian to remain on good terms with a former lover; she will simply find it hard to accept the fact that the emotional element of the affair can really be over. It is probably far more likely with this Zodiac group than with any other that their real friendships will be with members of their own sex.

## Ideal Careers

It would be quite wrong to think that Cancer's ideal life is as housewife, keeping the beloved home clean and bright during the day and getting into the kitchen in good time to prepare the evening meal. The idea wouldn't entirely revolt many of them; but in fact they also have a particularly wide choice of apposite professional careers.

At the top of the list are the caring professions. Cancerians (of both sexes) make very fine nurses, many of whom specialize in caring for the elderly, the mentally retarded, or sick children; the most excellent pediatricians and gynaecologists are, unsurprisingly, often found to be Cancerians. The caring instinct can be equally well expressed within the social services.

Cancerians frequently make very good teachers, especially of the youngest children. Perhaps surprisingly — for they can be short-tempered — Cancerians in this profession often prove to be particularly patient and able to deal with the most fractious youngsters.

The travel, tourist and hotel industries also attract Cancerians, and (for obvious reasons) they make first-rate stewards and stewardesses on aircraft and cruise ships, and as couriers take great pleasure in looking after their flocks — expressing in all these jobs the characteristics which make them so devoted to their homes and families.

Cancerians are often attracted to a career in cookery — not only because they are usually excellent natural cooks but because they recognize that this can be one of the best-paid and most secure careers possible. Interestingly, the general idea of a chef is of a rather moody and temperamental individual — maybe because so many Cancerians are to be found in the kitchen! And to follow the food trail for a moment, those attracted to the outdoor life will find farming — particularly dairy farming — enjoyable.

I have already mentioned the Cancerian love of history and the past; the antique business can be very rewarding for them. Both the man who has the junk shop round the corner and he who is a knowledgable dealer in 18th century paintings are likely to be Cancerians; others will be working at restoring antiques.

One of the problems for a Cancerian is a particular sensitivity to atmosphere: they will instinctively know when colleagues are upset, and if forced to work in a large open office where there is a great deal of noise and bustle — to say nothing of noisy hotel foyers or the continual rush of a hospital — they will have to call on their defensive Cancerian shells to cushion themselves against the negative vibrations. The noise and bustle may not be too much of a problem, but in the long term there could be adverse psychological effects. Another problem rather more heightened for Cancerians than others is that of smoking; as non-smokers surrounded by smokers, physical effects on their health apart, they will find it particularly hard to put up with people poisoning themselves in that way — the simple stupidity of it will get to them, and while they may not speak out about it, their nerves will tend to be set on edge. Cancer will probably be at her best working in the peace and quiet of her own office, or at least in a little mini-environment of her own. She should be allowed to do things in her own way and will produce good results even if her own way may seem to others — especially superiors — to be pretty chaotic.

A creative Cancerian seeking the right form of expression — if it does not make itself obvious from the beginning — should think of their strong imagination and love of the past, together with intuitive qualities. Many are excellent visual artists and others are fine actresses and dancers, but perhaps the main emphasis is on writing — particularly writing romantic historical novels. Of course the chances of success are very small, but it can make an extremely entertaining hobby and in some cases has led on to glory. The long family saga will appeal enormously to a Cancerian. Other hobbies that could be turned to account would be working with silver or precious metals (silver is traditionally the metal associated with Cancer).

## Travel

The little pale face looking apprehensively out of the car window at the very beginning of the journey is more than likely to be that of a Cancerian — not that they dislike holidays, but they do tend to become very easily apprehensive about leaving home for the dreadful unfamiliarity of whatever lies ahead; and that is very conducive to travel-sickness. So make sure you have some travel pills from your doctor before you start. And be sure too to take with you some high-factor sun-screen, for the sensitive Cancerian skin is particularly likely to turn a nasty red and blister on the first day of the holiday if it is not protected.

Another casualty of Cancer's tendency to worry and to be unsettled can be their digestion; it is far better to allow them to starve themselves slightly than to force them to eat unfamiliar food which could upset them. Milk of magnesia or some other stomach-calming agent should form part of your holiday medical kit.

The Cancerian child will be happiest if the holiday accomodation is more like home than anything else; they will fit more readily into a self-service apartment than into a luxury hotel. Hard on mother, perhaps, but there you are. It would be nice if there were a swimming-pool somewhere nearby — if not the sea itself; they will specially enjoy swimming and snorkelling, and a seaside holiday will be preferable to an inland one — unless there is a large lake or river nearby! Cancer will enjoy both — and in fact will enjoy travelling on water whether in a rowing-boat, yacht, or cruise ship. If you are thinking of an adventure holiday which will take care of young Cancer while you go off on your own, one during which they could learn water sports, sailing or canoeing would be ideal.

Even the most conventional holiday can be turned into an opportunity to add to Cancer's collection — or series of collections. The boot of the car will be full of stones, shells and damp, smelly fragments of seaweed while many happy hours will later be spent sorting out bundles of postcards and photographs.

I have mentioned Cancer's love of history, and they will enjoy a holiday with some kind of theme, which could well be historical: a junior archaeology expedition exploring a particular site or historical event. They would also be very happy if they could follow a trail along which their ancestors had trod — a holiday in a town where their great-grandparents lived and worked might specially interest them, particularly if enough is known about them to enable young Cancer to relive their lives and experiences. They will always enjoy exploring ruins, old buildings, and old towns, or ancient Roman remains, even prehistoric caves. Encouraging this taste will stimulate their imaginations, apart from giving them a change of scene.

I have mentioned the dangers of sun-burn; otherwise, dry heat is well tolerated by Cancerians, but humidity is less good for them — and they will certainly need to take in plenty of liquid, and in really hot climates even salt tablets.

## Cancerians as Brothers and Sisters

If an elderly friend or relative exclaims 'She's the perfect little mother, isn't she!' when your Cancerian has been presented with a baby brother or sister, no doubt the remark will have more than a slight ring of truth. Young Cancerians — boys and girls — make perfectly splendid older brothers and sisters, and even from quite an early age can happily be trusted with many small tasks which will help their parents.

It will be most interesting for you to watch your Cancerian child's maternal instinct blossom endearingly — but when it does you should be a little careful that she does not begin to sacrifice her own interests, or become reluctant to mix with friends because of her love for her young brother or sister.

It is quite good for her to accept the responsibility of looking after baby from time to time; in doing so she will be expressing many important areas of her personality in a particularly delightful way, and if this fulfils and satisfies her maternal instinct she will come to terms with her adolescent personality more readily than in other cases — one must always feel that a Cancerian only child is at a slight disadvantage.

I have never yet come across real problems of jealousy with Cancerian children. Oh, yes, they will lose their tempers with their brothers and sisters from time to time, and there will be stormy weather — especially if the other child is an exuberant, extrovert type — an Arian or Sagittarian, maybe — but overall young Cancerians contribute much to the domestic side of running a family, and really will take a great interest in their brothers and sisters. This typical caring interest will indeed start very early on — it will make itself known as soon as they hear the news that a baby brother or sister is on the way; most parents now involve their children from early in the pregnancy, and you will find that from the very beginning young Cancer will be specially and intuitively sympathetic. But to return to the prospect of storms, there is a definite approach which will avoid tantrums: when they are angry they will no doubt come out with some pretty hurtful remarks — and you should show them that not only the brother or sister but you too are hurt (perhaps even over-emphasizing a little to make the point). Even their torrential emotion will not prevent their naturally sympathetic selves from appreciating the situation and seeing reason.

A Cancerian who is the youngest child in a family will tend to act as though she is the eldest — some Cancerians are rather bossy, in fact — especially to those they love! Do watch out for this negative trait, since in this particular type the bossiness can be expressed rather severely, and will not only hurt but may if it goes on inhibit the brother or sister, who in the end will deeply resent it.

The Cancerian child — and indeed her brothers and sisters — will benefit especially from attending the same school: here again, the protective side of Cancer will be at its most strong and endearing. If she hears of someone treating her brother or sister unjustly, she will at once spring to their defence. In such circumstances you will also find that her excellent memory will record details of the problem, and provided you make sure her vivid imagination is properly controlled you should be able to get a pretty clear picture of what actually happened.

When it comes to room sharing, the only real problem is the Cancerian hoarding instinct! This, as I have hinted, really is strong, and should not be underestimated — Cancer will need somewhere to store all her collections of bits and pieces, and will suffer if she does not have it, even if she seems to take up an entirely disproportionate amount of space with boxes of rubbish which really should be thrown out, but is, of course, absolutely essential to her! Even toys that she has outgrown and which are of no interest whatsoever to anyone else will be very difficult to banish! Appeal to the kindly, charitable side of her nature: get her to consider a visit to the Oxfam shop, pointing out how much pleasure she can give less fortunate children by donating her things. Once you have resolved the problem of clutter, there should be few difficulties — though no doubt you will hear your Cancerian child begging for just a little more space! She will read or create the most splendid bedtime stories for the brother or sister with whom she is sharing, and lights-out will not put a stop to them!

## Cancerians as Parents

It is obvious from what I have already said that Cancerians make first-rate parents. The only difficulty is likely to arise at times when they are too good — in the sense that their eagerness to build a family nest is equalled by their desire to keep it intact, so when the younger members of the family seek to express their independence, Cancerian parents can be seriously upset. Mothers in particular really must school themselves for this moment from the time the birth takes place, for the difficulties can scarcely be over-estimated, and are especially exacerbated if — as so often is the case — the problem arises just at the time when mother is experiencing menopause. They can then have the feeling that their life is over, that there is nothing left for them.

On the other hand because they are such good parents, providing a wonderfully comfortable home with good food and living conditions, and declining all too often to charge working children anything for it, a totally different problem can arise, with the children resolutely refusing to consider moving out! Cancer will enjoy this, up to a point; but when logic and common sense take over there will almost inevitably come a time when the Cancerian realizes she really is being put upon — and it may be too late to do much about it without creating a real row. This is a difficult problem to resolve, but obviously it must be resolved, and the very best thing that Cancer can do (especially mother) is make sure that during the children's last years at school she develops a really individual interest, or maintains an old one, so that life will not seem entirely empty when the children do decide to leave. If possible this should be an interest that takes her out of the home, in order that she can meet new people and get a whole new dimension into her social life — which she has probably neglected while looking after the young family. If she has had no job for years, she should consider getting back to her pre-marital profession, even if she does not need to do so, financially. She probably has a good mind, which should be used to the full. If this is not possible, I suggest she re-read some of the sections concerning careers and spare time activities, and apply them to herself. Could she start a small antique business, for instance, or study some aspect of history?

In most cases, of course, the Cancerian father will not have this problem. He will make an equally excellent parent, ever-ready to enjoy taking his children considerable distances to enable them to pursue their own compelling interests (he too, however, should be careful that they do not take advantage of his kindness). He may occasionally become rather short-tempered, especially at the end of a long and tiring day's work, and should try not to take this out on the children.

Because of the Cancerian tendency to look to the past, it must be remembered that the generation gap will almost inevitably become a problem. Try to be objective when it does, and consciously tell yourself that your opinions — even if they were considered rather advanced when you were young — cannot now be expected to coincide with those of your children. You tend to be nostalgic, and like things to be as they have always been (you are a natural conservative with a small c). Try not to react over-emotionally.

It may be the case that you will find you will most enjoy sharing with your children activities which centre on the home itself: fine, but should your children suggest that you go out more, together, do think about it. I think you would particularly enjoy picnics by river or sea, but also visits to stately homes, specialist museums, and safari parks. Trips on restored steam railways or steamboats would also appeal; so would an active interest in industrial archaeology — and the whole family could be involved.

Don't be apprehensive about involvement with your child's school's PTA. While you may not feel very inclined to take a very active part in it — or certainly to make a fool of yourself at fund-raising activities or bludgeon people into parting with their money — remember that you probably make far better cakes than any other member (though Taurean mums may give you a run for your money!) and your ability to organize the tea tent (to say nothing of the white elephant stall) will be second to none. (Think: is there anything in the attic you could be persuaded to part with, on such an occasion?)

## Case Study

**Katherine** - Sun in Cancer, Mercury in Leo, Venus in Gemini; Mercury, Group 3, Venus, Group 2.

**From the Report**: 'Obviously as Katherine grows up it is going to be important that her emotions are not stifled or hidden deeply within her. If possible, a positive outlet must be encouraged for her feelings. This can be done in different ways: she has for instance a very pleasant and natural desire to "take care of" and to "protect" others, and this is always a safe wicket for you to bat on. If she can be allowed, when she is a little older, an animal or perhaps a tank of fish to look after, this will be marvellous for her. Another way in which she can express her emotions is by channeling them along with her very lively imagination. Encourage her to let them run wild by writing fairy stories, painting fantastic pictures, and so on. You will find that she by no means lacks originality and inventiveness, and probably the best way for these qualities to be brought out is through the arts.

'I think that life will become very amusing and lively when Katherine grows up and starts going out with boys. She will have a very light-hearted attitude to them, and it is quite likely that while she will enjoy their company a very great deal, she will for a while prefer friendship to more emotional ties. However, once she has found the right person, that will very definitely be it! — the more sensitive, endearing and protective of her qualities will really come into their own, and she will give her more romantic side full rein.'

**Comment**: Katherine's analysis was written for her parents in 1968, when she was almost two years old. At the time of writing she is just embarking on her last year at University, reading modern languages. She is a very tender and caring person with a lively imagination which her parents think could eventually be expressed through literature. She enjoyed writing when she was very young.

Cancerian worry — always a problem for this Zodiac group — rears its head for Katherine at examination time, and although she has done well and her prospects for a good degree are excellent, this does not mitigate her concern. She has a very steady boy-friend to whom she is deeply attached. Her chart as a whole shows many contrasting features which run contrary to her Cancerian traits: she was for instance always a very open child. I warned the parents that she could tend to bottle up her problems; having borne this is mind, they have helped her to counter the tendency.

## The Sun-sign and Its Rulerships

*Countries and areas*: North and West Africa, Algeria, Holland, New Zealand, Paraguay, Scotland.

*Cities*: Algiers, Amsterdam, Berne, Cadiz, Genoa, Istanbul, Manchester, Magdeburg, Milan, Stockholm, Tunis, Venice, York.

*Trees*: all trees, particularly sap-rich.

*Flowers and herbs*: acanthus, colvolvulus, honeysuckle, lilies, saxifrage, water-lily, white rose, white poppy.

*Food*: fruits and vegetables with high water content: cucumber, melon, pumpkin; mushroom, cabbage, turnip, lettuce.

*Cell salts*: Calc. Fluor., Calc. Phos.

*Animals*: creatures with a shell covering.

*Stone*: pearl.

*Metal*: silver.

*Colour*: smoky grey, pale blue, silver.

# LEO

## (July 23 - August 23)

Note: Leo is a masculine sign, so for the most
part I refer throughout to 'he', but most of my
comments refer also to girls.

## General Characteristics

If the lion is the King of the Jungle, the boy or girl born with the Sun in Leo will
certainly think themselves the king or queen of the nursery, and of course the problem
is one of keeping them reasonably under control without damaging their pride and
self-confidence.

One of their finest qualities is their natural enthusiasm and zest for life. The Sun
is the ruling 'planet' of Leo, and at best the Leo child has a sunny disposition —
we at once know that something is wrong if a cloud crosses their face; their inner
psychological sun will be obscured and their behaviour will become darkly sullen.
But because the Leo type is positive in outlook, the cloud should soon pass, and
natural exuberance will reassert itself in a keenness to become involved once more
in his usual run of favourite interests.

The Leo organizational ability is famous: but parents of children of this Sun-sign
must be prepared to control it if they do not want Leo to become extremely bossy.
There is after all a difference between encouraging your friends to share your own
enthusiasm for living and ruling the roost in such a way that nobody else gets a
look in.

Leos have an abundance of physical and emotional energy — indeed sometimes,
because they hate to waste a moment of their lives, they can tend to exhaust
themselves. However, it is important to keep them extremely busy at all times: apart
from anything else, they are among the most creative Zodiac people, and it is vital
to them, psychologically, that they have some form of creative outlet in order that
they may express their potential: if they do not, they become restless and all too
obviously unfulfilled. This is part of their general outlook on life: they can see nothing
going on without feeling that it could be improved were they to have a hand in

it — and the infuriating thing, for the rest of us, is that that is probably indeed the case!

These qualities will emerge very early indeed in a Leo life: the children, as I have said, do of course need to be controlled and directed — but above all you should avoid carping criticism or nagging, which by deflating them and undermining their self-confidence can actually cause serious damage. Remember that when you criticize your young Leo, you should do it in good heart, showing a sense of humour. Then he will actually be helped to improve his efforts rather than be discouraged from pushing himself. Interestingly, much as he likes to be boss — King of the Castle — he can be a remarkably willing slave to anyone he really respects and admires. But true admiration and love must be won.

Another quality to emerge quite early in life will be the leonine organizational ability: again, he must be given his head — you will soon realize that he will readily accept responsibility and carry out instructions to the letter. If he happens to make a silly mistake, his own conscience and fury at his own stupidity will be punishment enough: shame, especially over his mistakes, really hits at the core of the Leo personality, and the error will not be made again.

Along with Sagittarius, Leo is perhaps the most optimistic of Zodiac creatures, and will be very bored indeed with people who constantly grumble and can find no joy, beauty, or hope in the world and its people. Finding himself in the company of people who simply decline to be enthusiastic, he will move on to others to whom he can communicate his own vivacity and *joie de vivre*, for only with them will he feel really at home.

Leos have expensive and very luxurious tastes. They don't waste money on kitch, but they love quality. The young Leo girl with a collection of junk jewellery will convert it to the real stuff as soon as she can possibly afford it! Generally speaking, even very young Leos are quite good at making the most of their pocket-money. They will set their sights on the most expensive articles, for nothing but the best will be really desirable; but they are sensible, and if necessary they will save for a long time rather than plunging into debt. They are extremely generous, and parents may need to offer guidance, especially when young Leo wants to buy a gift for a friend: they really do get pleasure from spending money on other people, and there are of course occasions when this can be misguided — those on the receiving end may think that it's just another example of the undoubted Leo tendency to show off. When it comes to giving to charity, Leo would on the whole much prefer to create something and give it for sale or auction rather than simply handing over cash: he then feels he has given more than mere money. This is something that should be encouraged.

I have mentioned the leonine tendency to show off: indeed, here is Mr Show Business himself, who will take centre stage at the faintest provocation — and if we think of this in relation to the kind of clothes he wishes to wear outside school, we will find that they will be chosen to attract admiring attention. Nothing specially wrong with that — but remember that while Leos have marvellously good natural taste, this needs a certain amount of control when they are very young because of the tendency to go over the top, with perhaps too much glitter and stardust! Leos look best in the colours of the Sun, from the palest pink of sunrise to the brightest orange of sunset.

Because Leo is himself open and frank and takes people at their face value, there is a tendency for him to be over-trusting; so this is yet another sign which you should be careful to guide about relationships with strangers, especially when they are out by themselves. It is quite difficult to inhibit a Leo, but there is an obvious necessity in this case. However, if you frighten a Leo you can call up a certain retiring quality which may indicate that he is losing self-confidence — leonine self-confidence is in fact less strong than many people realize.

One of the finest Leo qualities is the desire to make other people happy and to share with them enjoyment of life — to impress on them the fact that every minute of every day is a gift to be enjoyed. But we must also remember that Leos at their worst can be stubborn, dogmatic, and very autocratic! This is usually a cover up for lack of self-confidence — and that usually stems from mismanagement by parents (probably involving forcibly putting Leo down) so it is obvious that early training and reassurance is very important indeed.

## The Three Ways of Thinking

Due to the influence of Mercury (see p.13) the Leo mind characteristically works in one of three ways.

★ Many Leos have considerable imagination and think intuitively; watch out for these qualities, which can considerably enhance leonine creativity and self-expression. There is sometimes a tendency to be resentful and to live in the past.

★★ The second group thinks very positively, but will sometimes become blindly optimistic, dogmatic, and stubborn. But the mind will be capable of extremely creative thought, and its expression will be vivid. The organizational abilities of these Leos are generally second to none.

★★★ The Leos of the third group have a powerfully critical, analytical streak, and are capable of dealing with the details of problems and projects — something other Leos find boring. Their mind is incisive and intellectually inclined; there may be a tendency to worry.

## The Five Ways of Loving

Due to the influence of Venus (see p.13) Leos will tend to express their affection in one of five ways.

★ Leos of the first group have a delightfully light-hearted, flirtatious approach to love, and as well as needing to express their fiery, passionate emotion require a high level of companionship and intellectual rapport with their partners.

★★ In a second group are those with a marvellously caring, warm and tender attitude to love; but here is also a tendency to be too nostalgic and sentimental — and perhaps difficulty in accepting the fact that a relationship has ended.

★★★ Here are people who can enjoy great passion and exuberance in a rewarding relationship — but the tendency to dominate can cause problems. From an early age these Leos should be warned against their negative traits when they show up in the context of childhood friendship.

★★★★ The fourth group includes those who have a tendency to be critical and even clinical in the attitude to lovers. Sometimes reluctant to display emotion, this group needs a high level of intellectual rapport — a lover who continually challenges Leo is a good thing. Occasional coldness and sarcasm are unlovely traits which might appear.

★★★★★ Leos of the final group may tend to rush prematurely into a permanent relationship, for there is a strong psychological need for partnership. It is the most generous group, both in the giving of love and in material things. There is a tendency to idealize the partner.

## Health and Diet

Writing about leonine health and diet presents the problem that on the whole members of this sign are a healthy lot who enjoy their food! Apart from the medical problems which might arise with anyone, the thing to realize is that with Leo there is almost always (and more than usual) a connection between physical illness and psychological disturbance. This can show itself very early on. It is necessary, for instance, for Leo to have regular, sound sleep, for in one way or another he will burn up a great deal of energy. Apart from a small group of Leos (see the preceding section) this is not a Zodiac sign which encourages its inhabitants to worry, and it is fair to say that tension should not be a serious problem, either. But do keep a careful eye on your Leo child, for if he does become tense or worried, something will be pretty seriously wrong — he will either be being nagged at school, or brutally teased — something will have made his normally high spirits sink, and the situation must be remedied as soon as possible, for Leos are far more sensitive than others imagine, and when they are hurt, like the lion of their sign, their reaction is to retire to their lair to lick their wounds in solitude.

The body organ traditionally associated with Leo is the heart, so obviously it is important to take regular exercise in order to keep it healthy. It should not be difficult to keep your young Leo active: he will probably enjoy many forms of sport, and more creative active interests such as dance.

It is important to watch out that in his continual activity — and he will be a very active child indeed — your Leo does not outrun his strength; when this happens, all sorts of aches and pains may develop, especially perhaps in the back (the Leo body area). Any exercises which strengthen the spine will be helpful, and good posture is also a necessity (it should, with Leos, come naturally).

When it comes to childish illnesses, young Leo will certainly enjoy being the centre of attention — that's almost necessary to him. If you can provide him with some drawing materials or an interesting game he has not played before, he will be reasonably patient when bedridden. Once you find him out of bed and running round the room, you can be confident that he's well on the way to recovery, and that his energy level is restored.

Leo children will usually enjoy themselves at the table, and tend to like rather rich food. If they can be encouraged to eat plenty of well (not over) cooked vegetables and light salads this will help to maintain a balanced diet. For the between-meals snack young Leo should enjoy as much citrus fruit as possible — oranges are, by the way, ruled by this sign!

It is absolutely essential that young Leo's circulation is in good order: poor circulation can lead to rheumatism, even in the very young, and perhaps later in life arthritis might develop. People with this Sun-sign have serious problems when they feel cold — they will feel positively ill, and their psychological outlook will become negative. They thrive in hot, sunny weather; you can see their faces light up as the sun comes out — so in winter they really need warm rooms. They hate wearing heavy clothes, and should be encouraged to wear several layers of light clothing rather than solid, massive coats or sweaters.

Remembering that the Leo polar or opposite sign across the Zodiac is Aquarius (see p.14), we must not forget the fact that as Aquarius rules the ankle, so the Leo ankles are somewhat vulnerable. If your young Leo girl makes good progress at her ballet lessons and is told she is ready to go *en pointe*, do watch her very carefully when she is practising at home: the chances are that she will try something far too ambitious after her first lesson and possibly injure her ankle.

Most Leos have a wonderful mane of fine hair — the Princess Royal is a fine example. Encouraging them to take good care of it is especially worthwhile, since more than with any other Zodiac group it will be their crowning glory.

## The First Five Years

The admiration of mother's friends will be meat and drink to a Leo child, who will soak up all he can get. If most small children show off from time to time, Leo will seem to do it most of the time — you may find him grasping any article of clothing that comes to hand, for instance, putting it on and dancing about to attract attention. Dressing up will indeed be an enjoyable pastime for all Leos — perhaps all their lives!

But we must not forget that the tendency to show off is not always as endearing to the audience as to the performer, and parents must make quite sure that young Leo allows his friends to play their part in the games rather than hogging all the limelight all the time! The best way to instil in Leo a sense of discipline will be to allot him some specific task which allows him to express his excellent organizing ability — perhaps making him responsible for keeping one particular part of the house specially tidy, or setting him to do a specific task at the same time every day.

You will find the smallest Leo child pretty reliable; but he will probably claim to be able to do things which are still rather beyond him (or any child of his years); while not squashing his self-esteem, it will be as well to try not to over-burden him.

Leo should adapt very well to play group, and will delight in getting busy with paint and paper, creating lively pictures which will certainly include the sun (in a prominent position!) and flowers. If he produces a picture with the sun only partially showing behind a cloud, this could be a clear indication that all is not well, and there may turn out to be an underlying problem which needs sorting out.

Leo will be just the one to get games organized — in activities calling for a leader, or for someone actually to start the ball rolling, there he'll be (no doubt arguing with a young Arian as to who is to have first go).

Leos are not on the whole unruly, but like all children need discipline from time to time, and the more constructive your approach can be to this aspect of his training, the better. Aim to allot him tasks that will sharpen his consideration for other people, and encourage him to understand that he is very definitely not the only pebble on the beach.

He will particularly enjoy looking at picture books — even after he can read quite well — and his lively imagination will be sparked off by fairy stories of noble princes and their brave deeds on behalf of beautiful maidens. Leo is not basically aggressive, but should he find himself embroiled in a fight his fiery temperament will take over and he will express his anger without reserve. If and when this happens, remember that Leo has the reputation of being a particularly magnanimous sign: all should be forgotten very quickly, and no grudges held — the chances are that the rivals will become good friends. Outgoing and sociable, he should be encouraged as much as possible — and from the earliest age — to help other people in whatever way is most apt.

## School Years

Just as young Leo should adapt reasonably easily and readily to play group, so when the time comes parents should not have too many problems when he makes the transition to ordinary day school. We must not forget his tendency to show off, and if by chance he has a teacher who is somewhat uptight and critical of this aspect of his personality it could tend to suffer. On the other hand, he will flourish and make marvellous progress with teachers whose enthusiasm and enjoyment of their subjects is infectious, and who are happy in the company of children.

It is during early school days that Leo's organizing ability and powers of leadership will begin to emerge — and of course as they are fine, strong, positive qualities they should be encouraged. The only way to impress upon him the fact that he should not become a big-head is to make quite sure that he realizes that many other people — even of his age — are probably cleverer than he is, and that he should learn to listen to their ideas and consider their opinions. If he consistently comes top of the form, the problem of course is a slightly more difficult one; but again, emphasis on consideration for others is an excellent thing.

The leonine creative potential is generally considerable, but it is not always easy to find just where this lies — creativity can take so many forms! If he is fascinated by taking a toy car to pieces and putting it together again, that is one signal — his creativity may well lie in a mechanical direction. Readers will gather that it is not necessary for the creative Leo to be a painter or a writer or an actor; creativity does not only exist in the area of the fine arts.

Leo will be a particularly friendly child, and next only to giving love and affection to other children, will need to receive it. He will also want to make sure that his friends are happily enjoying life — he will be the one, for instance, to organize a summer picnic, or camping in a tent on the front lawn; making other people happy is something that is always important to Leos, to the end of their lives.

The Leo child likes to know where he stands when it comes to discipline: he will soon become positively furious if he thinks rules are stupid or made only to signify who is in charge! An element of stubbornness can show up even when he realizes that rules have been made for the best of reasons. He is not necessarily rebellious — he just feels that the rules would make a lot more sense if he had made them. And he may be right.

Self-expression is arguably the main requisite if a Leo child is really to thrive at school: fascinated by a subject and respecting the teacher, there will be no holding him — he will make almost incredible progress. Uninterested and bored and not trusting his teacher, he will lose self-confidence and his position in class will plummet. Even if he decides to take a scientific course or specializes in maths he should always have some kind of creative interest as well — if necessary out of the classroom (the dramatic society, for instance); this will balance the more intensive side of his studies. Needless to say, if he wants to specialize in art, whether it be painting, music or whatever, he should be encouraged as much as possible. If you discover that your Leo child has well above-average creative potential, then it will be as well for you to enter him for scholarships which could lead to free or assisted places in a specialist school. The young musician or actor would flourish at the Yehudi Menuhin school or at the Arts Educational schools.

Though over-confidence may be a problem, there should be little difficulty in encouraging young Leo to spend extra time studying before an examination — always provided he is interested in the subject. Help him to work out a steady schedule for revision, starting well in advance, so that he is not rushed and won't have to sacrifice his many leisure interests to make extra time for study as the examination draws near. Don't allow him to think that he is too clever by half: big-headedness (not necessarily a stranger to him) might have a disastrous effect when conveyed in an examination paper!

On the whole, Leo is fairly team-spirited and will certainly do well as a team leader, chivvying his team to success; team games will be enjoyed, though rough and tumble doesn't specially attract them — nor are they particularly happy to get really dirty! Pleasure will come from physical activity itself, and of course from the prestige of winning — something else that is quite important to them. They can, alas, be rather bad losers, and will in later life consciously avoid competitiveness rather than lose face; it will always, however, be far beneath them to even think of cheating.

As I have said, Leos make good friends, and like their Zodiac cousins the Cancerians, will continue childhood friendships throughout their lives.

## Out of School Activities

The Leo child's ideal weekly routine would consist of getting out and about — preferably in the sunshine — on one day, painting on another, rushing off to the ballet class on a third, maybe ice skating, and in between, visiting the most expensive department store in town to spend his pocket-money. In other words they enjoy a full life — and the more exciting it is, the better! Indeed even if their activities are to all intents and purposes rather dull, they will see to it — partly by using their imagination — that life is exciting and fun!

Even if money is scarce I suggest that you make a very special effort to encourage your Leo child to fill his spare time with activity, rather than lying around daydreaming or watching TV. Leos respond very well to scouting and guiding, and make excellent patrol leaders when the time comes: any occupation that touches on their sensitivities and helps them develop kind, humanitarian qualities is also particularly desirable.

We must not forget that here are the great performers of the Zodiac, and the chances are that your Leo child will definitely be in his element when he comes and tells you he is going to be in the school play.

It is difficult to recommend a sport, for Leos on the whole tend to regard competitive sport as slightly boring; in need of exercise, they should be encouraged to dance — whether they prefer ballet, break-dancing, or whatever. Not only do they always seem to enjoy this, but they are usually naturally good at it, and of course it does involve a certain aesthetic sense which will make it attractive to them. Any activity which engages the leonine dramatic flair will attract them as a pastime.

They are not very keen on detail, but they are always eager to reach a very high standard, in whatever field. They may attempt short cuts from time to time, but soon learn that this is no way for them to prosper. An element of self-satisfaction may catch up with them; when this happens, if it becomes obnoxious, simply point out their limitations and encourage them to progress. They don't lack determination or ambition, and indeed Browning's suggestion that one's reach should always exceed one's grasp was made for a Leo: 'If at first you don't succeed, try and try again' is certainly one of their mottos; except that they would not emphasize the word 'try', because they believe too surely in success for the idea of failure ever seriously to present itself.

Leo girls soon become fashion-conscious, and will want to spend a lot of money on clothes. It is good to encourage them, as early as possible, to sew: they will be very much inspired by working with beautiful materials, perhaps making a party dress or a fancy dress for a special occasion. They will be particularly in their element if they are elected Carnival Queen — or if some older relative asks them to be chief bridesmaid.

# Preparing for Life

As young Leos grow up their enthusiasm for life will be coupled with an enthusiasm for experimenting in relationships with members of the opposite sex.

It's likely that most Leos will retain a child-like quality, but at the same time be capable of giving their partners a great deal of surprisingly mature love and affection. These are members of one of the more romantically inclined Zodiac groups, and if their attraction to a partner is reciprocated, a tendency to idealize them will most certainly make its presence felt — and the inner Leo sun will shine very brightly indeed on their boy or girl-friend.

There is also a tendency for those of this sign, especially when they are young and relatively inexperienced, to put the object of their affections on a pedestal — the loved one is brilliant, can do no wrong, and so makes young Leo's life complete. Until, that is, he is rejected or — because he has expected too much — disappointed; the partner, failing to come up to expectations, will be thought to have let him down, and Leo's life will crumble about his feet; because of the high level of sensitivity I have mentioned he will be extremely hurt. The great expectations Leos have of their partners, and the high respect they bestow on them usually cause problems — not only when they are very young, but when they are older. If your Leo child becomes moody and gloomy, the chances are that the loved one has let him down or deserted him.

Looking at it from the loved one's point of view, it may be that Leo has simply been working too hard to 'improve' her, or has behaved bossily, and made her recoil. You can point this out to him, or at least ask him to question himself about it.

Leos are passionate by nature, and their sexual experiments are likely to start early. But they love comfort, too, and won't want to conduct their affairs in the back seat of the car! — it's simply not their idea of the right setting for romance, and they'll want much more pleasant surroundings than that. Another potential problem they'll have to resolve.

Leo will be marvellous at encouraging his partners in their own fields of interest or study, and injecting them with his own wonderful enthusiasm and zest for life.

Although both sexes will enjoy a great many relationships, and it is good that they should, there is a strong element of faithfulness in this sign, and while a relationship lasts the Leo will be totally involved, and life will be very much geared towards the partner. Even the most flirtatious Leo will have the element of fidelity as a backbone — though his reactions will also be those of his Venus group (see p.99-100). Of all signs Leos actually rather enjoy the excitement of the periods of change when one relationship ends and the next is just beginning. A Leo girl makes a very strong partner, but should be careful that the accent is on 'partnership', for there is a tendency for her to wear the pants. She can, and should, always bring out the best in her partners, and it is for parents strongly to impress upon her that it is very important indeed to keep a balance between encouragement and domination.

Young Leos will have their idols, and will want their partners to reflect some of the qualities they admire in their favourite pop star, or whomever. Leos will tend to see these qualities even in partners who conspicuously lack them — and this may not be a terribly good thing, tending to pander to the Leo sense of hero-worship and edge them out of reality and into fantasy. We must never forget just how easily hurt Leo is — and this is one of the ways in which they can hurt themselves. Do not be deceived by the brave face they wear in public, making themselves 'have fun' to the point of being the life and soul of the party — then, when the party's over, going home to cry themselves to sleep. The cover up can be successful, though; at least it ensures that Leo is out and about, meeting new people, rather than hiding in their lair.

## Further Education

Young Leo will be in a high state of excitement on leaving school: full of optimism and enthusiasm and very ready for the next phase of his life. He will feel that at long last there is an end to his being bossed around by teachers, and always told what to do, and that he can now begin to express his own personality in his own way.

He should have a wonderful time at university, where all his organizational skill and powers of leadership will come into their own — unless he is a very uncharacteristic Leo indeed! On the whole, he is an extrovert type and will already have found that classmates have pushed him forward when for instance there has been something difficult to explain to a teacher, or if someone has had to take the lead in almost any enterprise.

At the very latest it will be at university that he will realize that he is a natural leader; when he joins the college drama group, the union, or whatever, he will soon express the ambition to be a member of the committee, and eventually chairman or president. Other people tend readily to recognize his powers of leadership, and his own exuberant enthusiasm will put him in the spotlight; other less assertive types will eagerly take up his suggestions and be led by him.

It is important that he study a subject or subjects that mean a lot to him; it is difficult for a Leo to fake enthusiasm. If pushed, they can find something interesting in any project and make much out of little, but if their hearts and souls are not engaged in what they are doing they will fail to make the kind of progress they should; if they can put themselves completely behind a course, then they will leap forward.

They should be encouraged to develop their natural sense of pride; this will strengthen their conscientiousness, especially in study — loss of pride (through failure in examinations, for instance) is terrible to them, and difficult to bear; one failure will be enough to keep them on course for the rest of their time — they will be systematic, and will enter the examination room with a clear conscience and do well.

Leos need teachers, tutors, lecturers they can admire and look up to; this is more important to them than to any other Zodiac type — they really will progress spectacularly under the right instruction. Without respect, there will be boredom, and the student will not realize his full potential. He will not be particularly argumentative in discussion, and his mind will be selective about what it chooses to retain; but what is retained will be important, and will be with him for the rest of his life.

The Leo going to art or drama school will be even more enthusiastic about further education than the university student: he will really feel he has been 'chosen', and will know exactly where he's going — at the same time being sufficiently versatile to spread his net as wide as he can, absorbing as wide a knowledge as possible of the history and development of his subject. His is not a narrow mind, but one eager to grasp every facet of anything he studies.

There is really no such thing as a Leo hobby. One tends to think of the word as describing something pursued just for relaxation, whereas Leo's view is that if a thing is worth doing, it's worth doing as well as it can possibly be done — so he will work just as hard at his hobby as at his career! One of the advantages of this attitude is that at any time a hobby can be turned into a career, should the need or opportunity arise.

I have already mentioned the strong vein of creativity in the Leo character; it really does offer a key to the personality, and at the risk of repetition I must again stress that every Leo somewhere in his or her life express an element of creativity; it doesn't matter what form it takes, but it should be there. Remember that we can have creative cake-makers, creative clock-menders, creative accountants! The Leo will have a creative talent of some kind lurking somewhere within him, and must be encouraged to discover and nurture it — particularly if parents realize that it is lacking in his life.

Involvement in further education will inevitably increase Leo's strongly independent streak. This is a good thing, but can sometimes encourage a little too much early surface self-confidence; it is necessary perhaps to point out that he is not yet ready to rule the world — but to do so tactfully, and without crushing his spirit. Young Leos' stubbornness, married to a tendency to be fixed in their opinions, can also be problems; rather surprisingly, however, flexibility should develop with age and experience.

## Unemployment: Stresses and Strains

If young Leo is finding it difficult to get a job, you should be able to impress upon him the fact that there is no need for a Leo ever to be unemployed — he should have some compelling interest which will fill his time and though it may not bring in any money, it should help to keep him occupied and fulfilled.

Leo's natural optimism has good staying-power, and even if he has been out of work for some time should not — at least at first — be bored by the writing of letters or scouring the advertisements in the newspapers. Of course if the situation goes on and on the time may come when he gives up, and if that does happen he will be very depressed indeed. Watch out for danger signals such as his not wanting to get up in the morning and not wanting to take part in a favourite sport. Once the rot sets in and he becomes reclusive, once his self-confidence is drained, he could easily slip into negative escapism which might take the form of drink or drugs. He is among the achievers of the Zodiac, and when he realizes that he is being offered no opportunity to achieve he can all too easily crumble.

Leonine organizational ability should be brought into play in the search for work, which should be planned like a campaign. You can encourage this in all sorts of ways — one of the best is to help him present himself properly, by preparing an impeccable c.v., well-printed on first-rate stationary (if you want to give a little financial help, there is no better way). Appearance is also important to him, so when he goes off to an interview you can be confident that whatever his image he will be presenting himself to the best advantage.

Leos thrive on praise and need it as a tonic to bolster their natural enthusiasm and optimism; try to find something to praise rather than carping and criticizing — which will drive him into some form of destructive isolation.

Involvement in community service is good, especially if he can be given his head; organizing entertainments or events for elderly people, for instance, will come naturally to him, and their gratitude will increase his self-confidence and self-respect, for it is particularly good for Leos to watch others enjoying themselves as a result of what the Leos have done.

Any Leo tempted to experiment with drugs should look very carefully at those who are hooked on them. One glimpse of the tragic physical and mental degradation brought about by dependence on drugs should put him off for life — for he has far too much self-respect to want to end up like that. And sadly, even the lightest experiment may end up that way for a Leo, because they do tend to start out on a course and pursue it to the bitter end. Once hooked, the stubborn element of their personality adds to the difficulty of treatment. The way through to them will be to show them, in their sober moments, just how degrading the habit is and rely on their self-respect to help them to start withdrawing. They may benefit more than some other types from creative therapy, for again they will want to be totally in control of their faculties — to be in control of themselves in every way not just physical but emotional, and being under the domination of a drug will be just as insupportable for them as being dominated by another human being.

It is possibly true that Leos are less likely — for all these reasons — to get the drug habit, but they should always remember that if they do succumb, it will be equally more difficult for them to climb out of the pit.

## Interests and Spare Time Activities

There is no doubt about it, young Leo will definitely become a pack-leader in whatever circles he moves, but he will also enjoy the company of his friends and they will enjoy being with him.

Although he is romantic, it is quite possible for him to have girl-friends who remain only friends, so the 'pack' will include both sexes. It will probably fall to Leo to organize outings to concerts, cinemas, sporting fixtures, and probably also group holidays — preferably in the sun.

Because his hobbies are so much a part of his life, he will specially enjoy friendships with those who share his interests. He will spark off their enthusiasm — though he may not be quite so keen on listening to, let alone acting on, their ideas! Basically, the interests he is most likely to enjoy will be those which enable him to show off himself or his talents. Here we have the natural amateur actor, painter, musician or sportsman. Whatever Leo does he will want to do well; if he can work towards some objective with a team, that will be specially rewarding, since not only he but his friends will reap the benefit.

His taste in clothes is extremely good. Just how 'fashionable' he is depends very much on his individual tastes; sometimes Leos are not so much concerned with the latest thing as with graduating from cheap, down-market copies to the designer label. This bolsters their self-respect and acts as a continual reminder that they are making worldly progress. It is equally true for both sexes, and the women will justify spending a lot of money on an outfit by saying that it's a good investment!

One of the reasons for existence, for a Leo, is cheering other people up and doing their utmost to make life easier, more pleasant and simply more fun for those who are perhaps less positive in outlook than themselves. The song 'Spread a little happiness' springs to mind! They can be awfully good at this and make a point of giving sad-looking people a nice, bright smile. On the most important level, they should be encouraged to remember that their positive, lively qualities are infectious and should be used to this end. If they can find a little time to devote to some kind of community project, people in their area will be all the better as a result of their efforts.

Leos are lavish cooks: double cream and brandy with everything! They may feel that it is not a good thing to spend a lot of time producing a dish, but the pleasure it gives their friends is an inspiration to further efforts and gives them a great deal of satisfaction. They are past masters at taking expensive and daring short cuts when preparing a meal, and the end product is often extremely impressive. Incidentally, most Leos positively hate housework but will throw themselves into it very energetically, partly because they take a pride in their homes and like to see them looking splendid and partly because they find housework an outlet for aggression.

Leos adore most animals; because of their liking for quality they will probably chose some high breed of dog or cat. But they should remember that they need to have fun with their pets and should perhaps be a little chary of choosing an animal that is more decorative than energetic!

In the section on further education, I mentioned that the natural place for a Leo elected to some committee is at the top of the table or in the president's chair. While they like to be in a position of responsibility, many are keener to get on with the job than to spend hours debating, thrashing out details and coping with long-winded boring committee members. In other words, administration will tend to clash with creativity and self-expression; they must remember this when agreeing to become an officer in any organization. Though they will enjoy the prestige such a position gives them, the time this will take up can cut into the more enjoyable time they can spend actually *doing* something.

Whatever spare time activity Leo embraces, the chances are that any love affair they have with an occupation will be a very long one indeed. This is worth remembering; you might quite inadvertantly spark off an interest when your Leo is very young — the chances are that it will be with him until his dying day. Leo will carefully give himself time to prove an interest before totally committing himself but once committed will be willing to spend a great deal of time and energy — and indeed cash — in developing it to the fullest degree.

It is important that Leos can swing between occupations which are entirely cerebral and those which involve some kind of physical activity; they should be encouraged to bring, if possible, a certain amount of natural physical grace to the type of exercise they choose. All forms of dance, as I have said, attract them and are ideal. Skating could well be popular, and athletics may appeal, together with anything that expresses their natural sense of drama.

## Careers

You will have gathered that Leos are the quintessential showmen of the Zodiac. Whatever their chosen career, they will bring to it flair and showmanship, and however menial the task they have to perform, they will make the most of it. The young teen-ager starting work as a junior in a large department store will see to it that his counter is beautifully presented and immaculately polished and will take a great pride in what he sells, be it diamonds or junk jewellery. Similarly the elderly leonine commissionaire standing outside the luxury hotel will be in his element ordering limousines for the wealthy, and of course collecting huge tips to contribute to the establishment of a proper Leo life style for himself!

Any Leo running his own business will know exactly what he wants and how he is going to get it. He will be a demanding if very fair employer. He will certainly order people about, but he will also be extremely generous, especially when it comes to rewarding good service. Loyal himself, he will expect loyalty from employees. Superficiality is something he does not find easy to cope with in business (or anywhere else). He always says what he means and is reliable, and he expects everyone else to be the same; he is frequently disappointed.

The leonine working environment must be warm and comfortable, clean and colourful. The chances are that your young Leo's spirits will flag if he finds he has to work in a dowdy, dirty or dark environment. If it is also cold, he simply won't survive!

Leos — like all Zodiac types — are found in all walks of life; in particular they are good organizers and leaders, coping very well with other people. They make splendidly enthusiastic teachers (especially of the arts), though their own creativity can get the better of them so that they feel they must move away from teaching and work entirely for their own satisfaction. It is obviously not a good thing to over-encourage anyone to go into the theatre, the profession is such a difficult one, but many Leos seem to be born stage-struck, and if your young Leo is inclined that way, the best thing you can do is give him the most practical training you can afford and ensure that he has a skill through which he can earn money when acting jobs are thin on the ground.

We sometimes get the impression that because Leo likes to be boss, to express his qualities of leadership, he is power mad. This is by no means necessarily the case — indeed many Leos are extremely uncompetitive but are (through no real fault of their own) thrust into positions of power. If this occurs they should make the best of leaders, but if by some chance the power does go to their heads, they will need firm handling.

Leonine creativity is often expressed with great panache and flair, and we find many people with this Sun-sign making the grade as fashion designers, jewellers and illustrators. A high standard of craftsmanship will always emerge when Leos are involved in either the fine arts or craft work in general. They are not usually particularly innovative or glaringly original, but the quality of their work and their great eye for beauty outweighs this slight disability. Many Leos achieve high rank in the armed services or become professional sportsmen, and if they are inclined to science they should aim to become involved — rather like their Cancerian neighbours — in a branch of it which allows them to express their imagination and creativity. Laborious analytical research could be much less attractive.

Because they are very keen to help improve the lives of others, many Leos do extremely well as counsellors, and if your Leo finds it quite difficult to put down this book you may well have an embryo astrologer on your hands; the sign does tend to contain a good many professional astrologers.

In general, Leos are ambitious and will certainly aim to get to the top. Ruthlessness is not usually part of their character, but they do need a job in which they can be seen to shine (in the law they will be the showy barrister rather than the industrious clerk) and which gives them the opportunity to inject others with their own brand of enthusiasm. Working quietly behind the scenes is not for them.

# Travel

Wake up from a doze in your deck-chair to see that all the children in sight have been dragooned into forming teams for some beach game, and you can be confident that it will be your Leo child who has organized the whole thing!

You can make good use of your Leo son and daughter when you are planning your holiday; try to involve them in all the arrangements. You'll find them amazingly helpful in making sure everything is packed economically and sensibly; they'll remember important items you may have forgotten, and you'll probably find yourself sitting down with two hours to spare before you leave, everything absolutely ready! They'll not only enjoy giving you a hand, but it will sharpen their already first-rate organizational abilities.

Leo children usually enjoy their holidays — if with certain reservations. They will certainly expect to be at least as comfortable while away from home as they are in their usual environment; if they end up with a lumpy bed, a small claustrophic room with indifferent food, look out for squalls. And while *you* may enjoy camping out in a tent on the side of some drizzly Welsh mountain, your Leo child will certainly not! Neither will he enjoy being crammed into the back of a small car with four baskets of picnic food, the dog, and the snorkelling gear. The front seat, at the very least, is what he'll want; if he ends up in a seat on a first-class French *rapide*, with wonderful scenery gliding effortlessly past the train window, and the promise of good food coming shortly, so much the better!

Leo will on the whole want to be confident that there is a real reason for holidaying in a particular place and that there is something to enjoy while he is there; castles and beautiful cities will certainly attract him, and he should be encouraged to take sketch-book and pencils with him, because the chances are he will want to make his own record of the landscape. He may well want to look at the local museum and art gallery; Leo is usually in some way interested in culture — maybe not conventional culture, of course.

Though Leos aren't always mad about sport, if they find themselves in a resort where there is nothing much else to do (a ski centre, perhaps) they won't at all mind experimenting — but they do hate making fools of themselves, so be prepared to pay for them to have good lessons if they're to enjoy themselves. Though they really dislike the cold (and indeed it's not good for them) they will bear it provided the sun is brightly shining onto the snow, but they will really prefer a day on the beach to a day on the ski-slopes. In both cases watch them when they first arrive, for in their love of the outdoors and particularly the sun, they may overdo things and end up with a nasty case of sunburn. This will be because of simple leonine enthusiasm rather than rashness — they are usually quite good at looking after themselves, and are not innately foolish.

They'll enjoy looking for really good (not necessarily expensive) souvenirs, too.

## Leos as Brothers and Sisters

The young Leo who has a baby brother and sister will still want to be as much in his parents' eyes as ever and may well tend to try to attract attention by showing off. There will be times when he'll act the clown and others when he may suddenly give a display of stormy temper, or simply make rather a lot of noise in order to get what he wants.

To counter this, parents should convey their enthusiasm for the new member of the family even before the birth. The Leo sister should be encouraged to sew or knit some tiny garment or perhaps make a soft toy or a very simple wooly ball for the expected baby, and the more Leo children of either sex can be involved in the necessary organization and arrangements, the better. They will get a great deal of fun from helping to paint the nursery, for instance, or perhaps restoring what was once their own cradle.

Leos make good, if rather bossy, older brothers or sisters. Interestingly, you will probably find that your child will respond very well to the birth, because on the whole young Leos are not aggressive even when at their most bossy! They will be excellent at teaching their younger brothers and sisters to crawl or walk, and their generosity will overflow when it comes to passing on books, games or any plaything that they have outgrown. Parents may need to be a little careful when Leo is involved in some very special interest; younger members of the family who interrupt or spill water over the painting in progress can expect short shrift — the Leo may be upset, and the interrupter will *certainly* be upset!

Fulfilling the role of brother or sister is in many ways ideal for this Zodiac group; it will encourage them to express some of their finest qualities. Their organizational ability will develop, as will their affectionate and warm natures; there should in theory be no question of jealousy, and if parents play their cards right it will be quite unnecessary for young Leos to waste precious time or emotional energy on such a negative feeling. Encouraging the Leo to set an example simply because he or she is older is an ideal way of countering jealousy even before it raises its head; most important of all, remember that there will be no need to be condescending to a Leo or treat him as a child — emphasize the fact that he is older and far more grownup than younger brothers and sisters and should always set an example, and you will see the desired result.

Every Leo aims to have his or her own 'kingdom'. It is important to allocate an area of space which is specifically their own; this gives Leo a sense of responsibility and of 'belonging somewhere'. Should the question arise of their sharing a room, it will be as well to call a family conference to decide just how things are going to be managed. They must not feel that a decision on such an important matter has been made without properly consulting their feelings. They will guard their own space with their lives, and heaven protect anyone who attempts to take it over. Allow them to decorate it in the way they want and make it their own in any way that occurs to them — posters and so on will stamp it with their individual personality.

If Leo is the younger child, you may need to be rather careful, because they may have the tendency to work to undermine the position of the older brother or sister. It will be all too easy for the young Leo girl to become a small glitzy moppet, putting an older, more reserved but perhaps more thoughtful sister in the shade either by showing off and always taking centre stage or by claiming that she must have special attention because she is younger. Remember too that the Leo child has a great sense of drama which might well be brought convincingly into play if young Leos do not get their way. It is vitally important not to spoil a Leo, especially when he or she is upset — otherwise the effectiveness of making a dramatic scene will convince them that they can always get away with murder.

Children with a Leo brother or sister in the same school will really have a protector who, if something goes wrong, will invariably spring into action as the avenger, coming down like a ton of bricks on the offender — not necessarily physically but with an air of superiority second only to that of the headmaster or mistress! If the evil-doer dares to repeat the offence, they really are asking for trouble.

## Leos as Parents

Above all else, Leo parents have a great desire to enjoy their children, and to make quite sure that this is possible, they should not start a family until they are in the right frame of mind to do so. They make excellent parents and are very eager that their children should have at least as good an opportunity for success in life as they had when they were young — and if possible, better.

They need to be careful, however, that in their enthusiasm for their children's progress they don't foist their own ideas too powerfully onto them. It is sometimes sadly the case that where a Leo has failed to succeed in a particular career, he or she will tend to push children in the same direction — for instance, the Leo mother who once had a strong desire to be a dancer but failed to make the grade can sometimes have her daughter in ballet school almost before she can walk and certainly before she can express a preference. Or a Leo father mad on a particular sport may force his son in that direction before he knows whether he likes it or not. The child may certainly succeed, but may also never forgive the parent!

You must be careful not to push your children; make an extra effort to consider what they say — their opinion is as important as yours even if it seems to be less well-founded. If their interests are completely different to your own, be grateful that they *have* interests and encourage them! The way forward is for you to make an effort to become interested in their preferences rather than forcing them to share yours.

You will probably get great pleasure from extending your children's horizons: taking them on expensive holidays to the Continent, showing them magnificent palaces and beautiful paintings, developing their sense of imagination and wonder. This — provided it is tactfully done — will increase their respect and admiration for you. When cash is short and you cannot afford expensive holidays, for your own sake as well as that of your children make a special effort to find out how you can satisfy those interests locally — and often free.

On the whole Leos tend to get on better with children over the age of six or seven than with infants. They find it fascinating to watch an individual mind developing, the personality emerging, but they can tend to expect too much of a three-year-old in the way of artistic appreciation and metaphysical speculation! If you become slightly bored with the very young one, remember that they will grow up, and the time will come when you will appreciate them as companion and friend, as well as your son or daughter. To encourage this friendship, you may need to take yourself down a peg or two. If they are continually presented with a vision of father or mother as centre of the known universe — chairman of this, president of that

— they may find it a little difficult to appreciate you as an ordinary human being with whom it is possible to have fun and sadly may tend to live in your shadow. So try to keep a sense of humour and not become too self-important. Your connection with your children's school is a case in point: you will enjoy the activities of the PTA, and may end up by chairing it, but try not to show off too much (and be very careful not to dress too flamboyantly on speech day; it could embarrass your child).

While we accept the fact that you will want to enjoy your children and expect a high standard in everything you do, realize that you might be a tough disciplinarian. Most of the time you will probably get the balance right, but remember two of the most prominent leonine faults are being dogmatic and being stubborn. Add to these your need for high standards and you could be a tyrant, crueller than you realize, in your attempt to produce absolutely ideal children always perfectly behaved and models of intelligence. You should also think about how conventional or unconventional you are and how easy or difficult it is for you to understand and accept the changing attitudes and opinions of people much younger than yourself. Some Leos find this very easy to do, while others, because they love traditional and accepted standards, find it difficult. If you are in the latter group, remember that especially when your children become adolescents you could have problems with the generation gap. All young people have, and should have, a rebellious streak, but there is the possibility that you could react badly to this if you are not sufficiently adaptable.

## Case Study

Ysanne - Sun in Leo, Mercury in Virgo, Venus in Cancer; Mercury Group 3, Venus Group 2.

From the Report: 'You do, I'm sure, really want to make something of yourself, and may well have a strong basic creative motivation. There is, all in all, a great deal of sheer positivity in your make-up which can be directed in many ways, for you are by no means lacking in organizational ability, and have a powerfully critical streak which is constructive rather than negative or carping towards others. If you want to go into conventional business, work in computers or accountancy might be a good idea. It would probably be pretty secure (financial security will be important to you) and I'm sure you could find a satisfying niche.

'It is important that you maintain your own singularity within any family circumstance (despite your enormous family loyalty, and indeed your very strong need to create your own family life and circle). It would not be a good thing for you to be under any man's thumb. Always preserve a feeling of independence and a sense of freedom. While you are very faithful and will (probably already do) have a terrific capacity to love really whole-heartedly, you must never ever feel cramped or suffocated by any relationship.'

Comment: Ysanne and her parents approached me for an analysis when she was nineteen and undecided about a career. At the same time she also consulted a vocational guidance organization. The findings were in many ways similar, but I was able to look more deeply into her psychological motivation. We agreed that a career in finance would be rewarding, but as you see from the above extract I also mentioned her maternal instincts. These have proved strong; she is a marvellous mother of two children, and as they reach school age she is beginning to do freelance accounting work, taking up again the profession she followed before marriage. She feels that greater financial independence will be rewarding, and the work will add a broader perspective to her life and the role of wife and mother. Ysanne is a creative dressmaker, but her basic creative motivation is seen in her role as home-maker.

## The Sun-sign and Its Rulerships

*Countries and areas*: Alaska, the South of France, Western Canada, Italy, Madagascar, Oregon, Rumania, the Pacific islands.

*Cities*: Bath, Bombay, Bristol, Chicago, Damascus, Los Angeles, Madrid, Philadelphia, Portsmouth, Prague, Rome, Syracuse.

*Trees*: bay, citrus trees, olive, palm, walnut.

*Flowers and herbs*: almonds, celandine, helianthus, juniper, laurel, marigold, mistletoe, passion flower, peppermint, pimpernel, rosemary, rue, saffron, sunflower.

*Food*: meat; vegetables with a high iron content; rice, honey, vines.

*Cell salts*: Mag. Phos., Nat. Mur.

*Animals*: big game, especially the cat family.

*Stone*: ruby.

*Metal*: gold.

*Colour*: the colours of the sun, from dawn to dusk.

# VIRGO

## (August 24 - September 22)

Note: Virgo is a feminine sign, so for the most
part I refer throughout to 'she', but most of my
comments refer also to boys.

## General Characteristics

The prim and proper child who never seems to get her clothes dirty and comes
home from school in the evening looking as tidy as when she left in the morning
will be a quintessential Virgo.

She will also be friendly and communicative, asking a never-ending stream of
questions about anything and everything that intrigues her lively mind. She can
be somewhat obsessed with detail and sometimes miss out on the broad perspective
of things; if you take her on a country outing she will tend to study one small flower
very closely, ignoring the thousands of others that cover the landscape. The same
thing will happen at school, where her general grasp of a subject may be less good
than her attention to detail.

Virgo will develop an extremely critical outlook on life, which will inform her
view not only of herself but of other people; it's quite important that you remember
that while this is part of her personality, she must also learn that just because people
are different from herself it doesn't necessarily mean that they are less admirable.
She will have high standards and could be depressed and disillusioned if she fails
to reach them; it will be at such times that her critical streak may centre too forcibly
on herself.

She is one of the world's workers but is not usually very good at organization;
to help her develop self-confidence (which is not always terribly strong in Virgoans)
it is well to remember that she will be at her best when she knows exactly what
is expected of her and when she has to do it. Her energy level is very high and
spiced with a tense nervous energy which must have plenty of positive, demanding
expression. If this is not the case, she will become very restless, nervous and twitchy,
finding it difficult to settle down to any task. Even if she is supposed to be sitting

still, reading or just watching television, she will be continually getting up and down fetching things for you or manufacturing little errands for herself, or at the very least constantly tapping her foot or snapping her fingers as though waiting for something to happen.

You will soon find powers of discrimination developing in your Virgoan child, who will analyse every aspect of every situation in which she finds herself, but it may well be up to you to teach her how to make definite decisions or reach conclusions, for there is a strong tendency in most people of this sign to underestimate themselves and their abilities. Even if they are clear in their own minds that a certain conclusion is the only one to draw, they are unable to convince themselves that they have been able to reach it unaided! Even when we praise them, they do not necessarily respond well — probably because of their inherent modesty, which will encourage them to believe you are just being polite. All that modesty is charming and delightful on occasion, but it can have a deeply inhibiting effect, and although Virgos work hard they often fail to recognize their full potential.

There is in every Virgo a need to serve others, which is marvellous if you are on the receiving end of it and a great help when it comes to helping to look after brothers and sisters. But you should try to keep the 'serving' motive under control, for it can tend to hold Virgoans back and inhibit their advancement in life.

Virgo belongs to the *earth* element and there is a strong practical streak in their nature; they are quite literally 'down-to-earth' people — reliable, bright and lively, and extremely talkative, but with an excellent balance between the extrovert and the introvert. Do what you can to bring this out, always bearing in mind of course their tendency to be over self-critical, modest, and self-denigrating.

It should not be too difficult to impress upon your young Virgoan the need to be wary of strangers. The chances are that if she is approached her natural scepticism and ability to look at people with that sharp, critical eye will overcome her equally natural friendly communicativeness. She has good powers of observation, and it might be a very good idea to help her develop them, so that should she become suspicious of someone she could give you a very detailed and vivid description of them.

As far as money is concerned, Ms Virgo will be naturally very careful; most Virgoans manage tremendously well, but sometimes because of their modesty they may find themselves receiving less than they are worth — or than another doing a comparable job. The very careful Virgoan attitude to money can sometimes border on meanness perhaps because they are too worried about that possible rainy day; this is something to watch for — while one does not want one's children becoming spendthrifts, squandering their pocket-money, or carrying a poor sense of financial values into adult life, Virgoans need to consider whether to give is not better than to recieve! Interestingly, as far as time and energy are concerned they are usually very generous, but there is often a hint of tight-fistedness in their personality. Your young Virgo will certainly want to put a certain amount of her pocket-money aside for holidays or save up for something special, and I would advise you to encourage her to plan for other people's birthday presents and — most importantly — for charity. One of the nicest things a young Virgo can do is become involved in some kind of charity work, for they are then positively expressing their natural love of service — especially if they are helping to care for less fortunate people, or perhaps for sick animals.

When one thinks of the image of young, out of school Virgo, the chances are that she will wear her school uniform with pride, especially if it is a dark shade of navy blue set off with a smart white blouse! On the whole, Virgoans are pretty conventional, and this usually shows quite strongly in their attitude to choice of clothes. In her teen-age years, though your idea of what is conventional and her's may differ, remember that in the context of her own generation she will probably be displaying a very modest image. Because she likes to be clean and tidy, she will enjoy wearing attractive smocks or overalls when working in the garden or about the house.

## The Three Ways of Thinking

Due to the influence of Mercury (see p.13) the Virgoan mind characteristically works in one of three ways. Because Mercury is the ruling planet of Virgo, its placing has also an important psychological influence.

★ The first group of Virgoans has a broad outlook on life, are self-confident, and often have considerable ability for creative work. Their critical acumen can be tinged with stubbornness and opinions can be dogmatic, but organizational ability is stronger than average with them.

★★ All the typical characteristics of Virgo will be emphasized for those of the second group; there is usually a high level of intelligence, but the tendency to be self-critical can inhibit the development of potential. Nervous energy is abundant, but it may be necessary to counter restlessness through physically demanding interests.

★★★ The third group contains those with the ability to see all sides of a question, and at decision making time may procrastinate. Sometimes lack of self-confidence will be disguised by feigned laziness. These Virgoans will tend to worry less than others, and may well be less prone to nervous tension.

## The Five Ways of Loving

Due to the influence of Venus (see p.13) Virgoans will tend to express their affection in one of five ways.

★ Members of the first group will express great love and affection, but the tendency to worry about their loved ones and to fuss over them like a clucking hen will become a dominant characteristic. There will be no lack of intuition, and their emotional level can be surprisingly high.

★★ Second comes a group of people who are less modest and more generous than the average Virgoan; they have enthusiasm for love and sex but will tend to expect too much from their partners. If they can curb their critical attitude, they will express their affection more positively.

★★★ A tendency to be over-modest may colour the attitude of the third group of Virgoans; attracted to someone their first thought will be 'But what could he/she see in me?' This can lead to procrastination, and these Virgoans are sometimes late to form a permanent relationship. They must learn to relax; they have more to offer than they realize.

★★★★ Those of the next group have a romantic attitude towards life and are more affectionate; they can even at times be in love with love, so it is good for them to learn not to ignore their critical attitude, especially when forming a new relationship.

★★★★★ When members of the final group fall in love, they will analyse the situation in great detail. They have a deeply passionate streak, but sometimes their attitude, especially towards the sexual side of the relationship, can be extremely clinical.

## Health and Diet

Virgoans vie with Cancerians for the Zodiac gold medal for worriers. This often ties in with the fact that the Virgoan body is area is the stomach, for slight stomach upsets can be the first sign for parents that a Virgoan child is worried about something.

I have already mentioned their high level of nervous energy and must underline here the fact that they really do need a lot of physical exercise. Getting out into the fresh air, taking long walks or cycle rides, is essential for their physical well-being. At the same time they will be developing their powers of observation, looking about them, and using up their nervous energy, thus keeping a balance essential for the health of their system.

You should bear in mind the fact that your Virgo child could easily be prone to headaches or even migraines, and that this is often related to worry, perhaps about a particular problem. Stress can also cause skin rashes or excema. At times when school problems catch up with young Virgo and you can see her becoming nervous and tense, I would strongly recommend a dose of Vitamin B complex, excellent for her nervous system. You will no doubt work out your own ways of calming her; always be on the watch for danger signals, for the sooner her worried brow can be soothed, the better!

There tend to be more vegetarians with a Virgo Sun-sign than any other — even at a time when there is a general trend in that direction. It is also an interesting fact that many of them fail to respond very well to conventional medicine, sometimes reacting badly to medically administered drugs — they can turn out to be allergic to antibiotics, for instance. On the contrary, however, they often make excellent progress, when ill, if they are given homoeopathic or natural herbal remedies. Those which calm their nerves and help them relax are especially beneficial.

It is good for all children to develop a regular sleep pattern, and some Virgoans may find this difficult, occasionally becoming hyperactive. Try gradually to quiet them down as bedtime approaches, perhaps with a warm drink or even some relaxing exercises. Again, homoeopathic remedies which promote calm, deep sleep can be very helpful and are absolutely safe and not habit-forming.

While it is unnecessary to distress ourselves with regular bowel movements, you should keep half an eye on this area for Virgoans, for whom there can be difficulties; diet is of course the chief factor and plenty of roughage is essential. I would recommend that your young Virgo is given packets of nuts or perhaps a banana as a between-meal snack.

Virgo's diet may turn out to be something of a problem in general, because Virgoans can be extremely 'picky' and critical where food is concerned — quite apart from what is on offer, you may even find them critical of your cooking! If Virgo seems to be eating only enough to keep a fly alive, try to encourage her to enjoy freshly-cooked root vegetables and salads — the more simply prepared food is, the nearer to its natural state, the better; she is much more likely to thrive on that than on elaborately prepared food — much less convenience food. At all times the devouring of junk food should be discouraged. Fresh fruit juices rather than sweet drinks should be preferred. With all this in mind, wholemeal bread, as opposed to white, is best.

When Virgo goes down with childish illnesses, I don't think you're likely to have a very easy time of it. Even when she is too young to put it into words, Virgo will be terribly cross with herself for getting ill in the first place, and that will put her in a fractious mood which will make her restless — she won't want to stay in bed even if she has a temperature and is feverish. One helpful thing is that Virgos love puzzles. If appeals to her patience and good sense fail, you could provide some new, interesting puzzle book, or maybe a jig-saw that she's not seen before, to keep her quiet and happy.

## The First Five Years

Don't be surprised if almost as soon as your young Virgo can toddle you find her imitating Mummy, sweeping, tidying up, and above all else doing a pile of washing! The chances are that you will find her, having stripped all her dolls' clothes from them, up to her elbows in soap-suds. Boys will imitate Dad and clear out the garage or workshop. Cleanliness is certainly next to godliness for Virgo. On the other hand she will also enjoy making mud pies in the garden, her natural affinity with the earth finding expression. You may also find her talking to the flowers — and that is likely to be a prelude to her developing green fingers when she is a little older.

Because she has a good intellect you should not have a great deal of trouble in encouraging Virgo to take an interest in books. She will like bright, cheerful illustrations and any book that stimulates her mind will be regarded as fun. Her first book could easily be an illustrated alphabet.

You could find that Virgo will want to learn to read long before she starts school. Some parents like to bring their children forward in this way; others prefer to leave it to the professionals. I personally think that Virgoans benefit enormously from this kind of encouragement. Similarly, she may be equally fascinated by numbers and helping her to develop basic mathematical skills could be great fun for both of you; besides which, if she's a little more advanced than the rest of the class when she starts nursery school, that will give her added self-confidence — especially important for our modest, often rather shy Virgoan.

When you first take her to play group she might become a little fractious, just because of apprehension and natural shyness. Fear of the unknown could prove something of a stumbling-block, and as with many children who tend to be shy it is as well to try to introduce her to some of the children already attending the group before you take her for the first time. Both at home and at the group she will enjoy being given helpful little tasks. This will give her life a structure, and will increase her sense of security.

She should find it easy and pleasant to be careful with her toys and to look after them properly. If you discover her treating toys aggressively — uncharacteristic for a Virgo — the chances will be that something is wrong somewhere. Don't hesitate to ask her a lot of detailed questions about how she's feeling — perhaps she will have been taking out some kind of anger on her Teddy Bear. Once she is confident in the presence of other children she will become extremely friendly and very talkative (that goes for her attitude to grown-ups, too). But it is essential that she should be able to trust her contemporaries and elders; once trust is established she will become a jolly, lively child with a bright smile and a positive expression. Remember that Virgoans may become overly domestic; while they will obviously enjoy helping out with the chores, you may sometimes need to encourage them to get on with school work — or even just with their play!

## School Years

Intellectually and logically, young Virgo will be very eager to start school — and always ready to do so. But emotionally, it may be a different story, and because of their natural lack of confidence and fear of the unknown you could find them quite reluctant to tear themselves away from home.

Once settled at school, they'll be basically friendly, but even at this very early age their critical sense will soon make its presence felt — 'Of course, Mummy, I do *like* MaryAnn, but you know, she's *terribly* lazy . . .' Comments of that sort will soon become commonplace.

Young Virgo will be neatness personified, and throughout her school days there will be a tendency for her to become something of a teacher's pet — not because she wants to curry favour, but simply because she is always eager to help in the running of the class; she will be the one to get to school ten minutes earlier than her friends to help give out books, and it will be most surprising if these qualities aren't noticed. As a result, while Virgoans are not particularly good organizers, because they are so useful (once they know what they have to do) there is a good chance of them becoming class monitors. Such a position will give them a great sense of responsibility, and that in itself will be of enormous benefit to them, developing their personality and helping them to prove to themselves that they are as good as anybody else.

Unfortunately this sometimes rebounds on them, and their classmates can see them as sucking up to teachers. They will not be slow to argue the matter, and they should easily be able to put their contemporaries in their place!

Being a member of as varied a group of friends as possible is an excellent thing for Virgo. Children from different ethnic groups and social backgrounds will stimulate her mind — she'll want to know all about how they live, their customs, their food, their different life styles. Encourage her to mix and leave her choice of companions to her — she will enjoy asking all the questions that occur to her.

It can be inferred from what I have said that Virgoans cope extremely well with reasonable discipline, and on the whole rather like it. They are not generally rebellious, and they can thrive on a set school routine. Their quick, lively minds are a great asset, and their thorough work will also stand them in good stead. Another point in their favour will be their neat presentation of their work; their exercise books and projects are tidily set out, and their handwriting can be clear, rounded and very readable — something else that is likely to endear them to their teachers. We must not forget that both boys and girls veer towards the conventional, and if you can choose for them a school which is run on somewhat traditional lines, they will probably thrive on its sensible and logical approach to its pupils. I have already mentioned the fact that Virgo will probably like wearing school uniform and take a pride in it; if there is any reluctance to starting school, perhaps you can encourage her by telling her how smart she will look in the uniform and what a great asset she will be to the school, having so much to contribute, not only through her neat appearance, but because she is bright and intelligent and most important of all willing to learn. And all those compliments will be entirely accurate!

The tension of being put to the test in examinations could undermine Virgoan self-confidence, so mysterious tummy pains may develop the night before. Worry will, from time to time, prevent them from doing their best. Thankfully, because of a new approach to education and examinations (at least in the UK) the end of term examinations are no longer a be-all and end-all, and Virgoans now have the benefit of being assessed over a reasonable period of time, which is very much in their favour. Try to point this out when exam time nears; it will help give Virgo's confidence a boost on the dreaded day. Parents should try to stop her swotting too intensively before examinations — unusual for young people but not entirely uncommon with Virgoans; if she shows signs of this, encourage her to relax and play a little.

When it comes to sport she should do well at athletics or any sport involving speedy movement which enables her to exercise quick thinking. Fast ball games will probably be enjoyed; cricket is popular (though Virgos may get a little bored while waiting to go in to bat!). Other outdoor activities which develop a sense of adventure — guiding and scouting, for example — are also good for them. Virgoans, perhaps more than the inhabitants of any other Zodiac Sun-sign, are from a very early age keen to be mobile, and almost as soon as she can walk she will drive you mad for a bicycle! Belonging to rambling groups, nature conservation groups, perhaps helping on a farm, are all excellent, and if they can involve close companionship with like-minded friends, they will make Virgo particularly happy.

## Out of School Activities

Virgoans have, over the years, gained the reputation of being particularly occupied with spare time recreation.

Make a suggestion and Virgo will follow it up! It is a particularly good thing for young Virgoans of both sexes to have a number of different hobbies, so encourage them to get involved one day in something that will occupy and stretch their minds, the next in something that will exercise their bodies. Contrast indoors with outdoors, movement with stillness, the practical with the intellectual, the artistic with the scientific. Ideally, young Virgo will be experimenting with her chemistry set in the morning and creating a new knitting pattern in the afternoon!

This group has an interesting affinity with natural materials, and like their Taurean and Capricornian brothers and sisters (the other earth signs) they have an instinct for working with wool, clay, and — for Virgoans in particular — wood.

Consistency of effort is sometimes lacking with people of this sign; so while there must be plenty of variety and change, when young Virgo says she's fed up, you should appeal to her practical element by suggesting she do something different — but insist that in due course she must also finish the task she has just put down.

It is a very good thing to encourage these youngsters to cultivate potted plants or part of the garden, if you have one. Watching things grow has a very special interest for them — it not only puts them in touch with nature but nurtures what is often a natural interest in botany.

Out-of-school activities that encourage self-confidence and develop a sense of adventure are essential: pony-trekking is ideal, and as already mentioned the more adventurous side of guiding and scouting should be considered and encouraged, especially as the young Virgoan nears adolescence. Many are naturally interested in health and hygiene, so Red Cross classes and membership of the St John's Ambulance movement are also to be recommended.

Here too are types sympathetic to conservation, and there are many groups formed to that end — preserving the countryside in general. Membership of the junior National Trust is also an excellent idea. Creativity often finds expression through all forms of craft work, and you should do everything you can to encourage your Virgoan daughter to sew, knit and crochet, and your son to learn a certain amount of carpentry or perhaps woodcarving. Both sexes will benefit from working with clay, modelling or making pottery, or perhaps weaving — and if Ms Virgo can put up a shelf and Master Virgo sew on a button, even better! If you think you have a budding writer in the family, then the very best present you can give is a prettily bound notebook and a family of felt-tipped pens! It is possible that we have an embryo media person here; why not get Virgo to write for the school magazine a report on her annual holiday, the school sports day, or perhaps a piece or poem about a family pet?

## Preparing for Life

There is a very good chance that Virgoans of both sexes will accept each other on their own terms, mixing in a natural, happy, friendly way, until puberty. But once the girls begin to develop and become aware that their bodies are changing, they often become self-conscious and shy of the opposite sex — and indeed of their own bodies. Virgoan modesty will blossom, and you can expect to a certain extent a return of the shyness you may have encountered when Virgo was much younger.

There is nothing more charming and delightful than natural modesty — and at its best it is a sweet quality expressed naturally by the young Virgoan. But alas it can often involve inhibition and become altogether too much of a good thing, so that we find Virgo almost not daring to move in the company of young men of her own age. Interestingly, the shyness will be covered up by talkativeness; words will come thick and fast, with the voice perhaps expressing tension in its high-pitched excitability — not altogether pleasant, and far from having the desired effect. It will be up to you to persuade Virgo to take things calmly and speak a few well-chosen sentences rather than thousands of hurried and garbled words.

Virgoan boys do not escape scot-free, either; their shyness will, perhaps even more obviously than with the girls, be expressed through volubility, and they will be also be specially prone to skin complaints, caused not only the hormonal changes of adolescence but because they are worried and tense. And the more worried and tense they get the more skin blemishes they discover, and so on, in a vicious circle. Both sexes' liking and need for cleanliness will be disturbed by this; have cleansing creams and treatments ready and encourage their use.

We must also consider the Virgoan's critical attitude; sometimes they will have a tendency to turn it on their boy-friends or girl-friends in a rather cruel and carping way. When they do, they should always ask themselves whether the nit-picking is not just an excuse for them to back out of any kind of emotional commitment.

Like the other Mercury-ruled sign, Gemini, they need a high level of intellectual rapport and real friendship within an emotional relationship — but that should be no excuse for holding back when the time comes for real love and emotional commitment, together with the development of a sexual relationship.

Both boys and girls may be intensely shy about their developing sexuality, and if they show signs of giggling embarrassment when you start to discuss sex with them, you should probably drop the subject, but make quite sure that they receive proper instruction at school. Sexual development can be rather slower than with many other signs, but refer to *The Five Ways of Loving* (p.119-120) and you may get a hint of how your child will react.

Parents should watch out for any tendency to cling to childhood — Virgoans may not want to grow up; they feel safe with well-established childish habits, which give them a sense of security. If they are attending a coeducational school, this will probably be less of a problem (and in any event it is not, of course, always the case). Fortunately Virgoans are well endowed with common sense, to which you can always appeal — together with their self-critical streak and their logicality — if you sense that it is beginning to happen.

In spite of their natural youthfulness and characteristic shyness, it is surprising just how well youngsters of this Sun-sign can cope with the outside world when it confronts them. They certainly won't suffer fools gladly — and in no way are they fools, themselves. Self-effacing they may be, but their natural scepticism and enormously practical and intellectual, analytical qualities make them sharp as needles — in spite of their liking for natural materials, no one will easily pull the wool over their eyes! They are certainly adept in argument and while they are not always good natural public speakers, they will be able to reach the root of all sorts of problems by shrewd questioning, and in one way or another they will make their conclusions and opinions known. The influence of Mercury doesn't go for nothing when it comes to Virgo — communication is one of their strongest points.

## Further Education

The young Virgo student, mentally astute, critical and quick-witted, is an ideal university entrant. She will certainly make the most of further education, but it may not be all that easy for her to settle into the very different life style with which she is presented.

Once she is encouraged to actually speak up and ask all the questions that spring to her mind during tutorials and lectures she will make very good progress. While her ideas are not perhaps of the most original, she is the sort of person to leave no stone unturned when researching her chosen subjects. She will make a lively member of quite a number of the societies and specialist groups available, and because she is reliable it is likely that she will find herself among the officers of at least one.

Virgoans, then, will make very careful and conscientious students. Their ability to cope with hard work is considerable. On the other hand worry and tension may cause the physical discomfort of headaches, especially if they are working under pressure as examination time comes round. This kind of problem could even build up when they have a relatively simple essay to complete for their tutor. I suggest that to counter the almost inevitable tension, you recommend that Virgo attend some form of relaxation class — yoga is especially good for this type, which seems to benefit enormously from its centring and calming philosophy and from the physical challenge of the exercises suggested. Remember that if they are eating in canteens, the slightly stodgy diet which is often on offer may not altogether agree with them; similarly if they are in digs or sharing a flat perhaps with other students, they should be encouraged not to eat junk foods — they really must pay some attention to their diet, for dietary imbalance often causes headaches, and they can add to the nervous strain of university or college life.

If she does not get into a university it might be as well for you to consider suggesting to the young Virgo that she attend business college, so that she can perhaps pursue a career in a large business organization, starting out in a fairly lowly office job and rising to a more important position; Virgoans make excellent secretaries and PAs. They are quick at learning business practices and computing skills, and training for business is ideal for them. But so is teachers' training college, for Virgoans also make lively teachers and lecturers. Home economics is also a possible subject for study, and those attracted to the land should be encouraged to follow up this interest by going to horticultural or agricultural college.

We must not forget that many Virgoans are attracted to the medical profession, so some may feel the inclination to attend medical school or become a student nurse. They respond well to the training, and indeed any profession in which they can help others suits them — as does any situation in which they can feel they are being of service to the community at large. Similarly, if there is a gap between the time Virgo leaves school and starts further education, but a disinclination to travel, any temporary work for charity or involving service to the community is to be recommended.

The urge to communicate should be considered when a career is being chosen and specialized training sought. If your Virgoan has a 'message', or is politically inclined, any course which may lead to work in the media will be beneficial.

While the grind of heavy machines could get on their nerves, on the whole Virgo can cope with working in a busy, bustling, noisy atmosphere. Varied work suits them, and if they have to spend part of the time moving around and then more time at a computer or typewriter in a large open office, they should thrive. They are willing to learn and will make good progress on training schemes, listening to what they are told and asking intelligent questions. Once they have decided on a trade or profession and their enthusiasm is ignited, they should stick with it — they are very good at practical work such as painting and decorating, carpentry, shop fitting. By the end of the course, they should be able to acquire the necessary diploma or qualification, and if they have been working with a particular firm they will stand a very good chance of being taken onto the permanent staff.

It may be that your Virgoan, while intelligent and extremely capable, seems somewhat lacking in ambition. Don't pressure her; remember that Virgoans are at their best when practising the skills they are learning rather than doing battle with rivals to reach the top! Encourage them to develop a good business sense, since they are not beyond making quite a lot of money — but it will be up to them to decide just how important financial success is, as opposed to real job satisfaction.

## Unemployment: Stresses and Strains

More than most Zodiac groups, Virgoans are vulnerable to nervous tension, and it is extremely difficult for them to learn to relax — often to the point that even when they seem to be relaxing, or claim to be, they are not, and you will find that in one way or another they will be busy burning off surplus nervous energy by fidgeting or flicking through a magazine without reading a word.

When life is running more or less according to plan this does not matter too much, for in many respects it is natural to them; however when worries pile up — and we must not forget that because they are worrying types this tends to happen quite often — the problem can become quite serious.

A young Virgo who has to cope with unemployment after leaving school or college must find some positive outlet for her nervous energy, otherwise it will build up and is certain to cause trouble. Ideally, she should devise as many practical things to do as possible — and all the better if they are geared to job-hunting. If she has done everything possible — written dozens of letters, scoured the newspaper advertisement columns — and still has time on her hands, she should be encouraged to keep busy in a simple way — finding perhaps a garden that needs tidying, doing voluntary work at a local hospital, or even getting busy at home with paint and paper.

The longer Virgo is on the dole the greater the loss of self-confidence, and she may all too easily loose her determination and eagerness to find a job. The will to work will still be there — by nature she is a hard worker — but the necessary positive attitude which bolsters assertiveness and would enable her to convince possible employers of her value to them may desert her, and it will be all too easy for her to say to herself 'Oh, I'm just not good enough — they won't want *me*.' Encourage her to approach the search for work as she would approach a job itself — working for herself just as effectively and conscientiously as she would strive for an employer. Objectivity will be a great help to her in this situation.

Virgoans have a good built-in resistence to drugs, and because she is health conscious she could well be low on the list of Zodiac types to succumb to drugs. Sadly, however, if she does succumb she is more likely to be completely destroyed — physically and emotionally — by the habit, and much sooner than most Zodiac types. There is a tendency for Virgoans to react badly even to medically administered drugs. If they can listen to the inner voice which so often makes them suspicious of quite respectable drugs, there is a good chance that they will steer clear of the dangerous ones — including tobacco and drink. One hint: beer seems to be specially bad for Virgoan males; apart from anything else they can put on weight spectacularly easily as a result of it!

Some form of negative escapism is almost certain to catch up with some of them, however, and their form of escapism may well be an attraction to religious cults; they should be very careful that if and when they develop such an interest, they do not lose their sense of balance and critical, analytical faculties. Parents can help; if a son or daughter begins to show an interest in religion, by far the best thing is to encourage them to channel this energy into the conventional churches, thus avoiding the emotional agony both for yourself and them, of their vanishing into some highly dubious and sometimes positively dangerous marginal cult.

## Interests and Spare Time Activities

Virgoans make good friends and generally have a fairly wide circle of them. They are naturally communicative and find it easy to engage others in light-hearted conversation and are themselves extremely chatty (they should guard their tongues, for they are sometimes rather prone to gossip!). They happily accept the opposite sex on equal terms, at least in the unemotional context of friendship or work; emotional ties are another story (see *Preparing for Life*).

They should be a little careful — and this really is something for which parents should keep an eye open — that their friends do not take advantage of them. Because they are so invariably willing to help it is all too easy, for instance, for them to agree to baby-sit for an older friend on an almost permanent basis, missing out on their own social life in oder to do so. Because Virgoans are fluent, they will easily convince their friends that they really don't mind missing the party — and it could be true, up to a point, especially if they're feeling rather shy that evening or if some member of the opposite sex is in pursuit and they are eager to avoid his or her attentions. But they should not make themselves entirely subservient to others and must be reminded that they can miss out on a lot of fun and experience of life if they never go their own way.

Virgoans fit in marvellously well if they are flat-sharing, but here again they could all too often find themselves regularly washing the kitchen floor, going to the supermarket, doing someone else's share of the chores, and taking the whole running of the place on their own slender shoulders, just because the others are lazy, unwilling, or out having fun. Virgoans of both sexes are Good Sorts, winning friends easily, but keeping them could be a little expensive of time and energy.

They make lively and certainly useful members of clubs and societies. They are very good at rationalizing situations and could well be in their element on a committee — at their best they are perfect honorary secretaries, giving up countless hours to attend to their voluntary duties; their motto: 'If you want anything done, do it yourself.' But, of course the same warning applies: they really should not aim to do *everything* themselves. Other people may always be ready to ask favours of them; they never seem to be ready to return the compliment. They should learn.

One of the most interesting things about being the parent of a Virgoan child is trying to keep abreast of their latest hobby. There is a good chance that by the time they reach adolescence they will already be hooked on a very wide variety of spare time interests which are essential to their well-being, both psychologically and physically; these help to keep a balance in their lives, burning up nervous and physical energy. Ideally, the young Virgoan should have one or two sporting interests — cycling or walking, for instance, would be ideal, as would games which combine speed of mind and speed of action — squash or tennis.

I have made much of the Virgo sympathy with natural materials, and involvement with and use of these should certainly play a part in their leisure time. Making items to decorate their homes or rooms can be particularly rewarding, and many a young Virgoan produces acres of patchwork, for instance. When involved in craft work, though they have a natural flair for detail they sometimes tend to cut corners, and they are constantly in a hurry, which can command and even weaken their technique. They make very good, wholesome cooks, and are often attracted to whole-food diets, making them excellent customers of good local health food shops. If they are vegetarians, a vegetarian cookery book would be a particularly useful present, enabling them to increase their repertoire of dishes. Maintaining their health, and indeed dragooning their friends into eating healthy food, can in itself become something of a hobby for a Virgoan.

Among the more conventional hobbies to which Virgoans often become addicted is sewing, which comes naturally to them; the girls in particular should be encouraged to make their own clothes, which they will enjoy. They are not terribly attentive to fashion, especially if the trends are somewhat extreme, but they will positively devour magazines (avidly reading articles on all sorts of subjects). They will certainly be aware of what is going on in the fashion world and should have no difficulty in selecting the styles that are right for their personalities. The designs of Laura Ashley are often favoured, for instance; friends might like to encourage them to be just a little more adventurous from time to time.

The main problem for a Virgoan who wants to keep a pet is that they are not always as clean and tidy as Virgo likes, and this should be kept in mind; a huge dog, shedding hair all over the carpet would probably be a bad idea — a smooth-coated cat might be better. Young Virgoans would probably enjoy keeping hamsters — almost as busy as themselves!

There is a sense in which this whole section is superfluous, for the problem will not be finding a hobby for a Virgoan, but stopping her from having too many. Try to encourage her not to be pathologically eager to pursue them *all*, but to take some time out for a real relaxation — to spend some time being busy doing nothing.

## Ideal Careers

The first essential for a working Virgoan is a clean and tidy environment. Uncongenial conditions — which means, for them, dirt and dust — will worry them so much that they will probably spend a great deal too much time and energy trying to remedy the situation by cleaning and polishing. Their own corner of an office or work place will always be squeaky clean, and the individual will often score high with superiors for that reason.

We must remember that Virgoans need to know just what they have to do, and when and where they have to do it. If they are PAs or secretaries they will be at their most confident when their boss has given them really comprehensive instructions, and they can busy themselves in carrying them out precisely as ordered. It is also encouraging for them to feel that they are making an important contribution to the progress of the firm which is employing them.

It is often the case that Virgoans will shun promotion because they lack the self-confidence to act independently; lacking instructions, they may not feel able to make decisions, much less act on them.

Careers in which a large percentage of Virgoans are to be found include the media (due to the powerful influence of Mercury, the planet of communication, which rules their sign). In contrast to people of their sister-sign, Gemini (also ruled by Mercury), they tend not to be the bringers of news or communicators of ideas, but will be at their best in work which allows them to express their strong critical acumen — for here are the critics of the Zodiac — the book, theatre, cinema reviewers, perhaps — while other Virgoans will find their niche as editors with magazines and newspapers or working behind the scenes in radio and television. Certain areas of the medical profession also attract them, whether as GPs or nurses. They make excellent neurologists, dieticians and physiotherapists.

The Virgoan analytical ability makes them wonderful researchers; this talent can be expressed both scientifically and in the media — they simply love 'finding out about things' — Sherlock Holmes was surely a Virgoan, with his admirable powers of deduction. These characteristics can be used in a career and many indeed be the basis on which one is chosen. They, and an acute sense of right and wrong, serve the Virgoan policeman or policewoman well — and like Holmes, they make good private detectives! Those with a strong humanitarian streak and loving and tender qualities (see *The Five Ways of Loving*, p.119-120) will make wonderful social service workers and will be successful in the caring professions.

Young Virgoans may very much enjoy mending things, and this could develop into a career in restoring antiques — china, furniture or pictures. Many are extremely bookish and will be positively in their element working in a first-rate bookshop or library (where their interest in restoration will be very useful). The latter should not be content simply to sit behind a counter stamping books but should take examinations in the subject and aim for executive posts.

If your young Virgoan has written successfully for school magazine, or entered and won essay competitions, it is worth remembering that there are a number of successful writers with this Sun-sign, and that while a sudden decision to be a professional writer (perhaps giving up a regular job to do so) is not a particularly good idea (most writers earn far below the average national wage), it will certainly be well for those showing an embryo talent in that direction to spend as much time as possible following it up. The chances are that it might develop into a spare time interest which could be profitable as well as enjoyable.

Virgoans love the fresh air and often have green fingers, so horticulture, or indeed agriculture can beckon. Work at plant nurseries or garden centres prove enormously rewarding and fulfilling for many of them. They can make real progress in such a career, perhaps becoming involved in plant breeding and the development of new species of foodstuffs; they may be able to in this way to satisfy a need to help others by contributing to research in new ways of helping to feed the third world.

# Travel

You may have a very worried youngster as you set off on holiday with your Virgoan son or daughter — will you succeed in catching the train? will the car get a puncture? will she be travel sick? will she like the holiday centre? the food, the people? And once you arrive, thoughts will focus on home — is the cat alright? did she remember to close her bedroom window? has her best friend got her address?

Well, that's Virgo for you, and you will have to put up with it! You should also take a more than usually complete medicine chest with you, for even a change of water, let alone a change of general diet, can upset the Virgoan digestion, and consternation about a new environment, new people, won't be any help at all.

But this of course is not to say that the holiday will be disaster from beginning to end, and there are certain precautions which will help to ensure that all goes smoothly. For instance, try to avoid extremes of temperature — though cold is probably more agreeable to the average Virgoan than heat; they will often enjoy a winter holiday. They must be able to get out and walk — in fact a walking holiday will be enjoyed by most Virgoans who have reached an age at which they can keep up comfortably with the adults in the party and enjoy the local countryside and scenery. They won't be keen on a very dry, arid countryside; lush, green fields through which a river winds is perhaps their idea of a really beautiful landscape. If this is not possible, try to ensure that they get plenty of exercise. And in case the weather closes in, take some indoor games or encourage them to get a book bag together to occupy that otherwise boring spare time which has to be spent indoors. Boredom can be a problem, and if you are spending more than a week or ten days away, a two-centre holiday may be a very good idea indeed. It is probably also a good idea to take your car or hire one, for the nervous streak in Virgoans often doesn't respond well to travelling on public transport — especially local buses.

Virgoans often like to be able to associate scenery and places with art or literature, so one of the Literary Companions to various countries or cities will be a welcome present for the older boy or girl. They enjoy finding out as much as possible about the new places they visit, and you could encourage them to spend their pocket-money on really detailed maps or good guidebooks. Otherwise you may well be driven mad by their incessant questioning. The money they have left will be carefully and well spent; shy they may be, but not too shy to bargain hotly with souvenir sellers or at market stalls (on a self-catering holiday they will be absolutely at their best at the street market getting the day's food supply).

# Virgos as Brothers and Sisters

The developing and enquiring Virgoan mind will focus strongly on a new brother and sister which she knows is about to arrive, and she will have all the questions on the tip of her tongue. They will spring from her natural logic, as opposed to her intuition or imagination, and the questions will go straight to the point: will it be a boy or a girl; *Why* don't you know? How did it *get* into mummy's tummy? When will it arrive? *Why* don't you know exactly when? And so on.

Virgo is not the type to want always to be the centre of attention, but after the family has been joined by a new member she will occasionally feel jealous. Sudden tantrums of any kind will be a sign of this, and at her worst she will be capable of spitefulness, both verbal and active. To counter this, encourage her to be of practical help; Virgoans are conscientious folk, and you can quite safely allow them to heat baby's bottle to the required temperature, or indeed to do almost any other task in which they express an interest. When the younger brother or sister gets a little older, one of the nicest things you can encourage Virgo to do is to read to them and perhaps play 'schools', passing on in a surprisingly mature way the vast experience of life even the youngest Virgo will have gathered and bolstering her own confidence. She will be very good, too, if her brother or sister is ill — playing nurse comes naturally to her, and she will come out with all sorts of bright suggestions for keeping the invalid happy and encouraging him or her to eat up or perhaps take the necessary medicine.

A tendency which can sometimes cause trouble is an occasional hypercritical attitude; if she turns this on her brother or sister it can be in the form of nagging, and I can't too strongly urge you to look out for this — once it takes a hold it is something that may last a Virgoan lifetime! The sharing of toys and the mending of broken favourites will be amusing to watch; the younger child will really be in trouble if a toy is damaged or made dirty.

If your children are at the same school, you may need to give the Virgoan a little extra encouragement — especially if the brother or sister ends the term in a higher position in form. Point out that Virgo has also done terribly well (even if it's not true), and underline their achievements (which will not be negligible); it may be that too much concentration on out of school interests has weakened their attention in class. They should not allow themselves to be worried or upset at such times, and as ever, a practical approach such as rescheduling homework so that it does not coincide with leisure activity will help with progress.

The younger Virgoan will either look up adoringly to an older brother or sister, and be very willing to serve them in any way, or will criticize their every move. Needless to say, either extreme is to be avoided — though that may not be easy, for at one end of the scale there is a possibility that the young Virgoan may make too many sacrifices, or even lose self-confidence because she feels she couldn't possibly do as well; at the other end, if the older child can do nothing right in the eyes of young Virgo, a sort of ongoing nagging argumentativeness will develop, at its worst disrupting the peace and quiet of family life — especially if the childrens' tastes are totally dissimilar. In both cases it is up to you to encourage compromise. You may find one way of achieving peace and quiet is to provide plenty of board games, or at any rate mildly intellectual games; Virgo will adore these and will be very good at introducing their brothers or sisters to them — whether they are interested or not!

This sort of situation would be at its worst were the children to have to share a room. You may find that in order to give the appearance of tidiness the busy Virgoan will hastily chuck her brother's or sister's toys into a box or under the bed, willy-nilly and without any consideration for the other child's feelings; this can result in a certain amount of chaos and disruption later, when things cannot be found!

Perhaps the most typical Virgoan child of all is Alice in Wonderland — a great sceptic who never stops asking questions but also has the capacity to enjoy herself. She even gets rather bored with her older sister! That sounds like a portrait of your typical Virgoan girl or boy.

## Virgoans as Parents

Family planning has never been much of a problem for Virgoans — in principle, at any rate — for they will be eager to start a family only when they feel absolutely ready to do so and will have made good provision for the child or children; the nursery will be impeccably decorated, a list of names will have been made and discussed, and the Virgoan mother will think very carefully indeed about the sort of conditions under which she wants to have her baby. The sign has a great sympathy for naturopathic and homoeopathic medicine, and the chances are that she will want as natural a childbirth as can possibly be arranged, subject of course to care and safety. In her anxiety that she and the child should, for instance, be free of unnecessary drugs, she should be careful not to ignore medical advice completely, especially if there is any possibility of complications.

Virgoan parents tend to have a somewhat clinical attitude to their children's upbringing, and it can be that they are a little over-concerned about keeping them clean and healthy. Keeping them healthy is, of course, fine, as long as it does not become a passion; should Mum get into a terrible state every time her child comes home looking even slightly mucky, it could in the long run have a bad effect on her nerves, making her tense and irritable — which is no help, should she be prone to headaches or migraine.

The very lively Virgoan mind responds extremely well to the role of parenthood; members of this Zodiac group are always keen to broaden their children's experience and outlook. There will be no lack of preschool teaching material and educational toys, and no country walk walk or outing to the shops — even if the parent is in a great hurry — will be devoid of interest, whether it involves pointing out a new species of butterfly or a new advertisement.

Virgoan parents must learn to relax *without their children*. Even before they are parents relaxation is something which is difficult enough to achieve, but once they have a family it becomes more of a problem. Before her young children come home from school, it is an excellent thing for any Virgoan mother to sit quiet for a while, perhaps doing some deep breathing exercises, or just listening to the radio or some favourite music. This may seem an idyllic impossibility — she will usually be busy getting tea and generally bustling around waiting for their arrival; but if she can organize her life so that she has a few minutes' peace — and I do mean peace — before the invasion, she will be much the better for it. Instead of the children arriving home to find Mummy fraught, worried and frowning, they'll find her relaxed and ready to listen to their stories of what they've been doing at school, and perhaps able to help them with some of their trickier homework.

When your children have settled into school life, you should not be shy of having your say in the running of the school; you will have much to offer at PTA meetings, and no doubt as has already happened in other areas, the chances are that you will become secretary.

I have already devoted much space to the Virgoan critical acumen, which is married unfortunately to the tendency to see little good in anything! Remember that many extrovert and lively children respond very negatively indeed to an over-critical reaction to their efforts. You should watch out for this; the children could lose their natural enthusiasm and be totally deflated if your reaction is always, 'Oh, well, yes, very nice. BUT . . .' Praise is more important than criticism, and encouragement to do better (if the attempt is really pretty miserable) will have much more positive results.

Spending time with your children should be a great joy to you, and the problem of expense — for many outings can now be horrendously expensive for parents with a young family — need not get in the way too much. You will find it easy to pass on your knowledge to them and will very much enjoy doing so. So walks around your neighbourhood, outings to museums or parks or to the country will be very effective in drawing you together as a family.

Although you are versatile and probably have a considerable range of interests, your children's hobbies could be totally different from your own. Sometimes Virgoan parents will fight this; it is much better, in the long run, to accept the fact that your children are not going to be clones of yourself and show an interest in *their* interests — it shouldn't be too difficult. Similarly, as they grow up, their opinions will also differ from yours; you are exactly the type to question them and to discover what they are really thinking — but try to keep an open mind, otherwise the generation gap will become a yawning chasm.

## Case Study

**Stephenia** - Sun and Mercury in Virgo, Venus in Libra; Mercury Group 2, Venus Group 4.

**From the Report**: 'I cannot too strongly urge you to be on the look out for a tendency to worry. This, like the possible build-up of tension, could be something needing a lot of guidance. You may find that when she is worried Stephenia will develop a tummy-ache or go off her food — a danger signal which may emerge before she consciously realizes that she is upset. It is absolutely no use to tell anyone to "stop worrying" — it only makes matters worse — but she will certainly be able to combat worry, and you can appeal to her logical mind: get her to write down all aspects of any problem and encourage her to reach a decision by consciously comparing all the contrasting apsects of a situation. She has a remarkably self-critical streak, and so can be very sensible and detached. Once having made a decision she will be able to move on to take positive action.

'In many ways she will be very romantic, though a modest charm will express itself when she is in love. This is an attractive trait, because it is perfectly natural; but looking at her attitude in another way, she has a strong need to relate in depth and could tend to jump the gun — tending, in spite of that modest quality, to fall in love quickly and often, swept along on a tide of romance. If you can help her to use her critical acumen — so good in other spheres of her life — by all means do so, but it won't be easy.'

Comment: Stephenia is only one year old at the time of writing, so it is a little early for many of her characteristics to emerge; I print this extract because the conflict described is very common indeed among Virgoans, especially if they have a Group 2 Mercury and a Group 4 Venus.

## The Sun-Sign and Its Rulerships

*Countries and areas*: Brazil, Crete, France, Greece, Hawaii, Iraq, Lower Silesia, Malawi, Switzerland, Syria, Turkey, Uruguay, the West Indies, Yugoslavia.

*Cities*: Athens, Boston, Brindisi, Corinth, Heidelberg, Jerusalem, Lyons, Paris, Reading, Strasburg, Toulouse; spas and health resorts.

*Trees*: nut-growing trees.

*Flowers and herbs*: similar to those of Gemini, especially those with bright yellow or blue flowers: aniseed, azalia, balm, bitter-sweet, bryony, caraway, elf-wort, fern, hare's-foot, lavender, lily-of-the-valley, maidenhair, myrtle.

*Food*: nuts (especially hazel and walnut), most vegetables (except cabbage).

*Cell salts*: Kali. Sulph., Ferr. Phos.

*Animals*: all domestic pets.

*Stone*: sardonyx.

*Metal*: mercury or nickel.

*Colour*: navy blue, dark grey, and brown.

# LIBRA

## (September 23 - October 23)

Note: Libra is a masculine sign, so for the most
part I refer throughout to 'he', but most of my
comments refer also to girls.

## General Characteristics

The first impression of a young Libran is of someone with a great deal of natural
charm, plenty of easy smiles, and a calm and relaxed attitude towards life. Very
little will seem to bother him, and sometimes you may be quite concerned because
it simply does not seem possible to hurry him. From a very early age, it's 'easy come,
easy go.'

But the personality is not that simple, and below the apparent calm he will always
be striving to achieve inner harmony and a well-balanced, secure life. Upsetting
quarrels within the family will be most disturbing to him, and even if they don't
centre around him he will still suffer from their effects and will need considerable
reassurance that not only was the quarrel nothing to do with him but that he remains
much-loved and wanted. You will see that emotional security and a balanced,
harmonious background to life is essential if the Libran is to progress and develop
his potential to the full.

The Libran, however, is no milk-sop; beneath the calm there is remarkable inner
strength, and it is very important that this should be developed. Make sure that
he always stands up for himself, and don't allow him to take the easy way out of
any tricky situation, for if this happens he could later in life tend to ride people.
His charm and the fact that he is so likeable often allows him to get away with murder.
But while every time you discipline him he will turn on the charm and smile sweetly
so that you may think your rebukes are streaming away like water off a duck's back,
he will in fact benefit a great deal from learning what is right and what is wrong.

It is important to remember that an essential part of the Libran personality is
the need to relate to others; if he has behaved selfishly — and this is something
for which you must constantly be on the look out — you will get the best results

from impressing upon him the fact that not only has he been selfish, but his behaviour has deeply hurt you and dented your relationship. There is also a Libran tendency to resentfulness, and even the very young will tend to bear grudges against their friends. Such reactions must be nipped in the bud if they are not to become boringly persistent in adult life.

At their best, Librans are extremely willing and helpful; they are kind, loving and affectionate, and perhaps their basic motivation is a great inner need to please their loved ones. When this is achieved, they will be very conscious indeed of the fact, for in positively expressing this delightful trait they will have become well-rounded and whole personalities. I cannot too strongly stress the fact that it is important to them to be able to balance the love and affection they give with the love and affection they receive; if that balance is not kept, problems of resentfulness will lead to general naughtiness and perhaps to displays of temper really directed at attracting attention. These may be quite difficult to resolve. The only way to treat them will be by gentle, firm discipline and correction.

It is very important that Libran physical energy is not allowed to stagnate; there is a tendency for Librans to take life a little too easily, and if you find your young Libran coming home from school and simply slumping in front of a TV set when there is homework to be done or he has a date at a sports club, he must be made to get moving! Similarly if he procrastinates about completing homework, you really must keep at him, for the easy life, which comes all too naturally to him, does not show him at his best.

Librans have a pleasantly carefree outlook on life, and their relaxed way with others enables them to bring the best out of most people with whom they come into contact. Remember that this delightful quality can lead them into danger when they are approached by strangers. Without frightening them or spoiling their warm, easy charm, you will have to point out to them very firmly that there are *some* unpleasant people around who can harm them.

Librans are very generous, and you will probably find that your young son or daughter will get through pocket-money within a couple of hours of receiving it! They will love luxury and appreciate all the creature comforts of home. The chances are that they will spend their money on more expensive things than they can really afford — being suckers, for instance, for beautifully wrapped sweets and chocolates. With a certain amount of encouragement you shouldn't find it too difficult to stretch their generosity when it comes to giving to charity; in fact they would rather give money than time — though because their energy level needs to be fully expressed, it is advisable to encourage them to take part in sponsored charity runs, cycle rides, swims, or whatever.

When they are a little older and can choose their own clothes the chances are that they will go for the romantic look — whatever that happens to be at the time. They will be bored to death by school uniforms; why not help them choose comfortable, attractive track suits in rather pale, pastel colours — making sure that they will wash well.

One of the most important areas of the Libran personality, one that needs careful development, is their capacity for decision making — or rather their incapacity, for they are notoriously indecisive and simply love sitting on the fence. From a fear of upsetting other people, they delay as long as possible coming down on one side or the other. They don't realize that this can annoy other people quite as much as any decision they may make! As early as possible in his life, train your young Libran to make his own decisions. You will find that even in very simple matters he will hesitate to make a choice, or ask you what *your* decision would be. Don't fall into the trap of telling him! Point out all the various possibilities, then leave it to him; even if he only chooses at the last second, you will have had a success — and if he makes mistakes he will learn from them. Better that than giving way and telling him what he should do — he would then always wait for other people to make up his mind for him, and this could lead to all sorts of problems when he is grown up.

## The Three Ways of Thinking

Due to the influence of Mercury (see p.13), the Libran mind works in one of three ways.

★ Those of the first group of Librans have clever analytical and critical minds with a strong rational attitude which can be appealed to if you find they are becoming indecisive or lackadaisical; there is a high level of intellectual energy which should be challenged. They have a tendency to worry.

★★ In the second group are those who though thoughtful and considerate of others will surely be indecisive; my comments above apply — try to develop the ability to make decisions. Beware of over-optimism, and help them to use their mental energy.

★★★ The third type of Libran has an incisive mind, and is extremely intuitive. The urge to find out about everything that is going on is married to considerable determination; an appeal to this group's innate ambition should have excellent results.

## The Five Ways of Loving

Due to the influence of Venus (see p.13), Librans will tend to express their affection in one of five ways; and because Venus rules Libra it has an additional psychological effect.

★ Those of the first group have a very great deal of love and affection to give; they are also extremely generous and sometimes rather showy, with a tendency to try to buy affection. They are excellent company and like to enjoy life.

★★ In the second group are Librans with a modest streak. Though romantic aspiration is present, there may be a tendency to think that partners do not find them attractive. Sometimes they are over-critical of their lovers and may tend to be discontent within a relationship.

★★★ The third group contains some of the most romantic types in the whole Zodiac, with a tendency always to be in love with love, over-glamourizing romance. It is essential to teach them to keep at least one foot on the ground; far from indecisive, in affairs of the heart they will rush in where angels fear to tread, and learn the hard way.

★★★★ Next, some Librans are very passionate with a strong sex drive and much emotional energy; jealousy and a certain amount of possessiveness can mar their relationships. It is essential they learn not to rock the boat because of emotions which may be wrongly based.

★★★★★ Finally, racy, light-hearted love is the prerogative of the fifth group; they will need freedom of expression and will certainly enjoy their relationships. But there can be difficulties, freedom not necessarily going hand in hand with domesticity.

## Health and Diet

You may well find that when young Libra starts feeding himself, he will be excruciatingly slow. This is just because he gets bored with the whole idea of filling the spoon and getting it to his mouth! Should you, however, take the plate away and exchange the meat dish for some delicacy such as ice-cream or a fluffy custard, the chances are that his energy will be restored and he will dive into it with glee. Do be careful, however, for it is all too easy for the Libran (like the Taurean, also ruled by Venus) to acquire a sweet tooth.

He should do well on light foods — salads in particular — and you could find that tomatoes, cooked or raw, will be popular. It is difficult to forget that this is the sign of the balances, and even when it comes to eating that keyword is particularly important: try to vary your Libran's diet as much as possible so that the essential balance is kept and he doesn't get too fond of sweet foods, which in the long run will not do much for his vitality or his figure. It is quite easy for Librans to eat every chocolate bar in sight; if you can encourage him to eat fresh fruit rather than sweet food at snack time — strawberries and raspberries, in season, are usually popular — that will be an excellent thing. On the whole, any fruit (provided it's reasonably sweet) will be a much healthier substitute to the chocolate bar. Biscuits and cakes should also be rationed.

Libra rules the kidneys, and any emotional disturbance can result in unpleasant headaches which may well have their root in a slight kidney problem — another reason why Libra's emotional life should be kept on an even keel. The parathyroids are also related to this sign, so food that builds the level of calcium in the body is to be recommended.

On the whole, young Libra should sleep pretty well, and like most of us it is only if he is worried about something that he will not be likely to enjoy a good night's rest. It should not be too difficult for you to get him to tell you when something has gone wrong with his life, but it is important that at such times he should not be allowed to be evasive but should tell you exactly what is disturbing him — whether it is his fault or someone else's — so that the problem can be cleared up completely and his anxiety-free nights restored.

Though few Librans will lose sleep because of worry, the influence of Mercury troubles one group in particular — you will soon know if your Libra belongs to it. The first signs of worry may well be when he complains of a tummy-ache; you will be able to use his very acute sense of rationality to deal with whatever problem is causing it.

Libran children are very friendly and like to be really close — physically — to those they love, but this makes them rather more susceptible than less forthcoming children to catching colds and childish illnesses. Short of keeping them out of the way of friends who are poorly, there is not a lot you can do about this — except that during the winter you might like to consider the occasional course of vitamins to increase their resistance.

In a way, young Librans will almost enjoy being ill — they will love the enforced comfort of soft pillows and warm beds and the extra attention, and because they are usually patient they will be no trouble to their nurse. To prevent boredom or perhaps sometimes real anger at having to miss out on what is going on in the world outside you should have some gripping story-books on hand through which they can escape into an imaginary world of demons, monsters and beautiful princesses.

Perhaps more than with most signs you should make sure your young Libran is getting enough exercise; the chances are that he will either be mad keen on sport or loathe it. If he loathes it and is unwilling to take part in it unless positively forced, you should find an alternative which will keep his energies moving. It may be that he will need to join some kind of action group because within his personality there is an element of the pioneer — something he inherits from his 'polar' or opposite Zodiac sign, Aries. Remember that he has a spirit of adventure, and this can help you devise ways of burning up his physical energy in enjoyable and fulfilling ways.

## The First Five Years

In many ways the early stages of bringing up a young Libran should be reasonably smooth, and there is a good chance that parents will enjoy the process! The easy-going characteristics of the sign usually make for a relaxed and happy child.

That is all very well, but it must be remembered that the stronger, more assertive side of the Libran personality needs nurturing and strengthening, not only for his own sake (he will eventually, after all, have to face up to life) but because charm, used to buy yourself out of trouble, can prove disastrous in the long run.

It is very easy to spoil young Libra, and to counter this tendency and get a positive response to your discipline and training, I suggest you be firm with yourself as well as young Libra and cultivate an iron hand in a velvet glove. In this way you will produce the very best of Librans who will be fair and diplomatic, without lacking inner strength and determination — who will have a fighting spirit and ability to cope when life becomes difficult.

It is very good for the young Libran to take on the responsibility for a regular task, especially if it concerns another's well-being. Feeding the goldfish or watering a pretty potted plant would be ideal; if he neglects his job, you can at once appeal to his conscience — he has been unkind to the fish or the flowers, and they are suffering as the result of his forgetfulness.

Get him involved with attractive picture-books as early as early as possible; you may find that building bricks are favourite toys — and either sex will probably enjoy playing with toy cars, fire engines or mechanical toys. Sometimes, the latter are rather limiting; don't forget that the Libran imagination, though not lacking, may need to be stirred up rather more than that of some other Zodiac types. Libra will certainly be a joy in the home, and it should not be difficult for him to smile happily when strangers visit. He will be a forthcoming and extrovert young child, and they will be amused at his consideration and his attractive antics.

It is very good for him to go to a play group as soon as this can be arranged; there he will relate to other children of his own age and the sooner the better. You could find that if there is any problem with other children, he may tend to shift the blame for it onto someone else. If he does so, have a detailed and searching discussion about it, for Librans don't like being in the wrong, and it is just possible that he could have been drawn into a cover up just because he does not want to make you angry. A vicious circle could develop. Get at the truth and let that iron hand gently but firmly persuade him into a nice, open apology to the child he has wronged. He may well be upset by all this, but it will be the best way of getting things over and done with and restoring his necessary sense of equilibrium.

He will enjoy the kind of television programme in which he can see other children at play, but he will enjoy it more if he can join in, taking part in games or songs, making things which he sees being made on the screen — though he may need some encouragement to do so. Once involved, he will realize that it is great fun to take an active rather than a passive role in anything which is going on.

## School Years

A structured framework to life is always necessary to a Libran, and a certain amount of sensible discipline is also necessary when he is young; even when he settles into his first nursery school he will take his best steps forward when this is the case. He will surely be popular with contemporaries and teachers, and probably from about the second day you will notice that he will want to take a favourite toy to school with him so that he can share his pleasure in it with his friends.

From the first, his attitude towards the other children will be one of wanting to be friends. He won't be shy or retiring, but should you notice him acting uncharacteristically the chances are that someone will have upset him. He may then become annoyed and even aggressive. You will find that if you discuss the reason for his anger he will be able to understand that it is not very productive; and if you point out that it is not *fair* for him to be permanently unfriendly to someone who has hurt him, and can persuade him to forgive and forget, the chances are he'll have a friend for life. At the same time he will have begun to learn a lot about other people — that they are not all the same as him, for instance, and that he must show consideration.

When Libra gets a little older he will inevitably be given homework to do. It is very likely indeed that he will underplay the fact, pretending that it isn't much, or that it doesn't have to be handed in for ages, and that he needn't do it until next week. The chances are that he will be saying this because he wants to watch a favourite TV programme, so look out for the situation and if necessary find out the truth from his notes or the school timetable — it may well be that he is slipping into a lazy, procrastinating behaviour pattern and, as a result, will make less good progress than he should. You could well find that he has rather a lot to do, and that it has to be given in next day. Firmness and determination on your part the first time you discover such a situation will prevent difficulties later.

The best type of school for a young Libran is one with a reasonably firm disciplinary code. Teachers who do not let their pupils get away with sloppy work or laziness will get the best out of a Libran, but at the same time young Libra will respond best to a sense of humour and to lively, kindly encouragement. A severe, cold, aloof and conventional teacher will not get good results.

Try to find a school with facilities which will offer the young Libran a chance to take part in some form of creative, perhaps artistic expression. We often find very talented designers (of fabric and fashion, in particular) among Librans; a well-equipped art room could be an excellent source of inspiration. The school choir or orchestra may also become important, but if your Libra has no real musical talent, do encourage him to lend a helping hand at such occasions as the school play or concert — he will be good at showing people to their seats and generally making them welcome.

It is interesting that in spite of the Libran's kind, generous, loving, and romantic nature, they have traditionally made excellent generals and explorers; beneath all the charm there is a certain degree of toughness, and you could well find that young Libra will become a keen and enthusiastic member of the football team. Encourage the interest, but in order that the balance does not tip too much towards aggression and assertiveness, try also to encourage appreciation of music, or perhaps the learning of a musical instrument — activities of that kind will act as an excellent balance to physical extroversion. (Incidentally, remember that the girls of this sign can come into this category too, sometimes tending to be rather tomboyish.)

When examination time approaches, young Libra is likely to try simply to ignore the fact, and if left to his own devices there is a distinct possibility that he will start to revise only hours before the examination begins. So if you are not very careful you will overhear him on the phone taking down a few notes from a more conscientious friend, blindly optimistic that he will get questions to fit the answers he has at his command! Encourage him to plan his revision like a well thought out battle campaign, and you may make an impression on him; even so, it could be necessary for you to stand over him to be sure he is actually doing the necessary work. You might even have to pretend that the television set has broken down and the phone been cut off!

Librans are often known as the peace-makers of the Zodiac, and your young Libran might well come home from school one day saying that he has sorted out a quarrel between friends; on the other hand on another occasion he may just as easily have had the most awful row with a friend and declare that they are enemies for ever. You'll know how serious the position is by his expression; if it is clouded, he will really be unhappy — but if it is still lively and bright, he has probably set up the quarrel just for the fun of making up!

## Out of School Activities

Perhaps the worst thing a Libran child can say is 'I haven't got anything to do', or 'I don't know what to do'. They will then curl contentedly up and drift off into dreamland. Daydreams are all very well, but may be an excuse for laziness.

Encourage your young Libran to be as active as possible outside school, getting him to join groups in which he can meet a lot of people and where the social life is an attractive added amenity. If he belongs to a sports club which organizes outings to interesting places — picnics, discos and so on — the chances are that your young Libran will get pleasure both from the games and the social activities. Actually, social activities are in themselves important to this Zodiac group, because later in life they will enjoy playing host or hostess and giving parties, so the sooner they get used to a varied social scene the better. This is worth bearing in mind when, say, you are going out for a meal, for young Librans very quickly learn how to order from the menu and how to behave in public.

When the Libran girl reaches her sub-teens, there is a tendency for her to become a little preoccupied with her increasing femininity. She'll be likely to arrange hair-dressing parties and maybe concentrate just a little too much on fashion, being rather too gullible about what she reads in magazines aimed at her age group. Of course it is good that she should develop a fashion sense, but sometimes such things tend to assume too great an importance, with the result that school work and sporting activities or creative interests might suffer. The boys are less prone to this tendency, though they may not care to admit it when they are suffering from puppy love.

Members of both sexes do well in scouting and guiding, and should be encouraged to go on camping trips and develop the spirit of adventure which is certainly a part of their psychological make-up, even if they may rather grandly claim that they couldn't care less about such things.

On the whole, Librans are not lacking in patience, so they may well be attracted to fairly long-term projects or hobbies that take some time to develop; if they can be bothered to put in the necessary practice time, they can do very well when learning a musical instrument, for instance; but on the whole such activities — and I include craft work — tend to keep them indoors, and as Libra is an air sign it is more important that they realize that they should actually spend quite a lot of time out in the fresh air, for as well as outdoor activities burning up their physical energy the fresh air itself will clear their minds and encourage them to think logically and use their astute and often remarkably intuitive minds in the best possible way. Having said that, activities which make intellectual demands on young Libra are also to be particularly encouraged. These might include games such as chess, or fast-moving sports in which mind and body must work in close co-ordination.

## Preparing for Life

As I have already hinted, love and romance are one for Libra and will hit them early in life.

Almost before you know where you are you will find your Libran starry-eyed and tending to mope around the place — in love for the very first time. Be sympathetic and above all don't tease. You can, however, point out that even if their heart is breaking because the loved one is taking no notice of them, life must go on, and Libra is most likely to succeed by finding out what the adored one is interested in and starting off being friendly rather than too obviously romatic. The youthful relationship can be fun and lively, as opposed to being too steamy.

At such times Libran indecision is not marked; you may discover that your teen-ager announces that he is getting married next week! This is because he is not only in love, but has a very strong psychological need for partnership — a deep relationship with another person is essential to the Libran's very being, and all too often they rush into total commitment before they are really ready for it; such partnerships can often end in heartbreak and disaster. It is not going to be easy for you to get this over to them, but it may be possible to appeal to the prospective partner — gaining their confidence and making him or her happy, comfortable, and unpressured in your home will encourage reason and good sense, and it may well be the partner who will be able to convince the over-romantic Libran to be more practical.

The more naturally boys and girls of this sign grow up together, the better. With this in mind, it will be advantageous, for your son or daughter to attend a coeducational school — the transformation from childhood boy and girl friendship to a more mature relationship will then be much easier, for the realization that it is possible to have good friendship as well as romance will be firmly planted from an early age, and this will help to stabilize young Libra's emotional self.

If your young Libran becomes deeply involved in a relationship while still at school, I suggest that in order that his work doesn't suffer he and his girl-friend should be encouraged to work together as much as possible. Projects, when completed, can then be praised, and the love-birds can flit off to their favourite disco and hopefully work off some physical energy!

Although many Librans need sexual involvement from quite an early age, it is sometimes the case that the girls especially want all the romance and colour without the sexual element. Sometimes there's a tendency for them to lead their men on then avoid a final commitment; this is unfair and the girl's mother should point out the fact that she should either learn to say no, or to be prepared to involve herself sexually; the middle course is a difficult one which may take more than a Libran sense of balance to achieve.

In the very early days of sexual awareness it is sometimes the case that the girls totally divorce sex from love, and live in a purely romantic, asexual fantasy world. Needless to say, guidance should be given, if possible within a sex education programme. Because of the influence of the air element of the sign Librans really need a high level of friendship within their relationships, and sometimes it is quite difficult to get them to understand when they are committed to a partner that life cannot be all moon-in-June. Though for a great deal of the time there must be intellectual rapport, there should also be romantic and sexual passion, and the skill is for them to achieve the right balance.

Parents of a young Libran should keep more than half an eye on their youngster when he is in love, for it may be that he will allow his partner to run his life. He knows that sharing is important, and deep down he will also know that it is not fair for one person to take all the decisions for another, but the desire to keep things sweet will persuade him to go along with every suggestion that is made, and the relationship could become one-sided. Find a way of encouraging him to stand his corner rather than being too lazy about putting up ideas about where to go on dates, what new shared interests should be developed, and so on.

# Further Education

Most young Librans will be eager to leave school in order to start work at univerity, or at least in some form of further education. They will feel more free, more adult, once the restriction and perhaps the boredom of having to wear a school uniform is a thing of the past.

The chances are that they will readily settle down into university life, and you will soon receive enthusiastic descriptions of their new friends and activities and all the parties they have attended.

Life will undoubtedly be wonderful, but let's face it, there is that little thing called work — and what of that? Well, if Libra has chosen his subject carefully he should discover that because of his new found free expression he will enjoy his studies and the discussion and argument that surround them. He will also enjoy lectures and debates and the consideration of every view of his subject, which he will put over well in all his study projects.

If his chosen subject only marginally interests him, however, his powers of concentration won't be terribly good, since his mind will more than likely centre on the social life of the university — sometimes to the point that a good degree will fail to materialize. If he can aim to work steadily, however, he should do well, for we must not underestimate his intellectual ability. I would advise parents to look back at *The Three Ways of Thinking* (p.139) and consider again which category their young Libran comes into — this will have a very important effect on his attitude to his studies, his powers of concentration and his critical faculties. He may be very good at research — perhaps his talents will lie in rational thinking — or perhaps his powers of intuition and the strong Libran sense of justice will make him someone to be reckoned with when it comes to putting himself on the line in political discussion.

Many Librans do well in the armed services; if they think of this they will benefit from specialized training at military colleges. Others who do not go to university and find themselves attracted to the visual arts could consider art school courses geared to fabric or fashion design. Librans have a natural sense of harmony and rhythm, and if they are not musical this often finds expression in drawing and the design of clothes or furniture.

Young Librans also do well to consider the beauty and luxury trades but should be properly trained — in, for instance, beauty treatment and therapy — rather than trying to wing it. These professions are particularly suitable for young Librans who have an interest in science but who are not so academically gifted as to be able to acquire a good science degree.

As is the case with all Zodiac types, it is up to the parents to be aware of the fact that their children's youthful hobbies can sometimes become successful and rewarding professions. If your young Libran has slogged away for hours on the sports field or the ice rink, or has done well in her ballet grades, do not reject this as mere exercise; sports or dance professions are of course chancy and demanding, but do think seriously about supporting them. And if the preoccupation has been with dress-making and dress-design, it is not impossible that you may well have a budding Zhandra Rhodes on your hands.

Because Libra is one of the financially generous signs of the Zodiac and likes a comfortable life-style, it is worth remembering that if they are to be happy they will need to make a lot of money — not just to spend but to give away. As part of their education it is essential that they learn how to handle money, especially if they are enterprising and think of starting their own business either very early or later in life. They can easily get bored with down-to-earth financial problems, and once they get going will really need someone to help with income tax, VAT, and so on. But teaching them to balance the books is a good start.

Similarly, if they are at university or college and receive a large financial grant at the beginning of term, they really should learn how to make it last — and should not be taken in by bank managers' offers to lend them large sums of money which they may tend to forget they will have to pay back.

## Unemployment: Stresses and Strains

When a young Libran cannot find work it is all too easy for him to slip into comfortable despair and a lackadaisical life-style, drifting from day to day and indefinitely postponing any action which could result in his getting a job — or at least putting it off until tomorrow. Sadly, in far too many cases tomorrow will never come, and he will gradually get lazier and lazier, spending more and more time in bed.

Taking the easy way out of difficult situations is bad for most people but absolutely fatal for him. It is quite possible that he will drift through the days making very little effort even to see what jobs are available; and when some are thrust right under his nose, but are not entirely appealing, he will not be at all ready to take them until something more suitable comes along.

It is obvious that Libra should have a good supply of copies of his c.v. to send off to prospective employers, and if you can motivate him thus far it might be enough to get his enthusiasm and energies moving in the right direction. Sadly, his staying power may not be terribly good, so you must do all you can to keep his spirits up and his energy flowing in the right direction. You can appeal to his sense of pride and his liking for the good life, but don't pamper him too much, for the cushier life is at home, the more good meals handed to him, the less he will be inclined to make a real effort. No matter how comfortably off you are, you should make life a bit difficult for him by demanding a reasonable proportion of his miserly social security payments as a contribution to the household bills.

It is essential that he take advantage of job training schemes which will give him work experience, and on the positive side it is well worth remembering that his natural charm and pleasing manner will make him attractive to a prospective employer. Provided he makes a reasonable effort to do what is expected of him on a work training scheme he will probably stand a good chance of a permanent position when it ends. Self-help is essential under such circumstances; indeed 'help yourself' should be his motto. 'On your bike' is not such bad advice to give a Libran!

Members of some signs of the Zodiac are more prone to negative escapism than others, and sadly it is often the case that Librans fall into this category. If your young Libran has been out of work for a long time, or has been deeply distressed by the breaking of an emotional relationship, do watch out for any subtle clue that he may be turning to hard drugs. Because he does not want to upset you, he will be more than usually discreet — not to say cunning — in concealing the habit if it does catch up with him, so it may be some time before you are aware of the problem. But there is no point in pretending that he could not easily get hooked, and once he is, he will find the habit very difficult to break.

Librans who turn to drugs are opting (again) for the 'easy way out' which is so attractive to them in difficult and demanding situations; it is hard for them to learn that the easy way out is often the harshest and most damaging. It is of course a matter of putting off the evil day — and the evil day, when they are on drugs, is the one on which reality and common sense break through, and they realize the extent of their problem. Appeal to their self-respect, and point out how deeply the habit is distressing their partners and loved ones — this will help them to withdraw, which will, again, sadly be perhaps more difficult for them than for members of most other signs.

## Interests and Spare Time Activities

While young Librans will have many friends of the same sex, enjoying ties of pure friendship with the opposite sex, as I have said, can be extremely difficult. Even if the boy and girl concerned share a common interest — membership of the same club, for instance — there is a pretty good chance that the Libran will have some romantic inclinations towards the other. So perfect friendship could be somewhat disturbed by the occasional sexual pass.

A lot depends on how Venus works for your individual Libran (see *The Five Ways of Loving*, p.139-40). Some can certainly view the opposite sex quite dispassionately and enjoy an intellectual rapport, and there is no reason not to encourage that, but others are such out-and-out romantics that they only see in the other person what they want to see — which is not a good basis for friendship — or for an emotional commitment, come to that.

But the Libran can readily adapt himself to life in the community as a whole and can usually cope with whatever circumstances he finds himself in — and he is good at adapting to various social circumstances, too. He may not enjoy being somewhere dirty or unpleasant, but has too many of the social graces to complain at the time and make other people uncomfortable. When he gets home, it will be quite another matter, and he will come out with a whole tirade about the dreadful things he has seen and put up with.

Libra is arguably the most social of all the signs, and a good social life is essential to him. It will probably indeed be his reason for becoming involved in all kinds of spare time interests and activities — and that is fair enough, for whatever his motives he will be an asset on the social level, provided he learns to contribute a certain amount of work towards the objectives and aims of the club. He does not make a very good committee member; he finds it very difficult to vote one way or the other when important issues are being discussed, seeing too keenly the pros and cons on each side; however, if we look at the Libran qualities in another context, we have in him the natural diplomat. So if he does end up on a committee, perhaps as chairman, his sense of balance will ensure that all sides of a question are heard and discussed — even if he is in dead trouble when he has to give a casting vote!

Giving parties is one of the things for which Librans were born. The guests will remember them for a very long time to come, for the host will have a good sense of occasion and his generosity will extend to the most lavish entertainment and the best of food and drink he can possibly afford — indeed he may break his purse-strings. Thinking of Libran hobbies, I would probably put entertaining and party-going at the top of the list, and the more prosperous the individual becomes the more they will want to be involved in such activities. Because he so loves entertaining, he may become very interested in cooking and may well spend a lot of time preparing some exciting and exotic dish which will delight and amaze his much-loved friends. If he takes the easy way out when cooking, and goes in for short cuts, they will almost inevitably work out well — it seems that the kitchen is the one area in which he can get away with such measures!

Fashion almost always interests Librans and may become a hobby in one way or another; many will while away a Saturday afternoon at a favourite boutique trying on each item, taking time in deciding what to buy. The girls should always be encouraged to sew, partly because it uses their creative instinct but also because it will enable them to enjoy clothes without necessarily spending a fortune on them.

The Libran image is not particularly outrageous within the context of their generation, and we usually find them looking attractive if at times somewhat sloppy. When romantic clothes are in fashion they will obviously be in their element.

Many Librans are extremely bookish and over the years will collect a large library, prominent in which will be stirring novels, family sagas and historical romances; they will also enjoy particularly well-produced and bound books, maybe of fashion, photography or landscape. We must not forget that Libra is one of the musical signs, and most are extremely appreciative of music — so in addition to shelves of books, there will probably be shelves of tapes and discs. Librans can tend to be passive rather than active people, appreciating things rather than making them, and it is important to keep a balance here. The ideal occupation for a musical Libran, for instance, will be accompanying a sympathetic singing friend on piano or guitar. It is also good for them to have a pet dog — one that is easy on the eye and knows how to relax, but one that readily demands walks (which will be good for both of them).

## Ideal Careers

Pleasant working conditions are important to many Zodiac types. For the Libran they are essential.

Occasionally, we find that the adventurous Libran — those attracted to the armed services, for instance — will cope extremely well in difficult and even dirty conditions, but for the most part they thrive best in harmonious surroundings which are comfortable and easy on the eye.

It is possible to pinpoint certain careers and professions as specially suitable for Librans. The diplomatic corps, for instance, is ideal; in it their ability to see eye to eye with other people, or at the very least to seek out fair means of agreement, comes into its own when they are working outside their home environment. It is also interesting to note that the Libran liking for a good social life can be satisfied in this career, and in fact is a positive asset in the diplomatic field.

When a Libran goes into business, it is essential that he does so in partnership. It may be that the Libran will want to use his financial flair while the partner is a front man involved in selling, but should the Libran be the more extrovert, creative partner, it is very likely that he will not be interested in keeping the books so he will need to work with someone who has experience in that area. If he is prepared to work hard, he will do extremely well, and will not find it difficult to attract the right sort of clients, who in their turn will like him; so the business should flourish provided Libra does not get too fed up with the hard work involved!

Many youngsters of this sign are attracted to careers in retailing, and if they are at all hesitant about choosing a job they should try working as a sales person in a large and glamorous department store; this will at the very least be good experience for them, but it may well be the case that they will make wonderful progress and be extremely happy and fulfilled in what can be a very glitzy atmosphere, in a job which is not, after all, a million miles away from being an actor!

There are other young Librans who make wonderful hairdressers and beauticians, so if yours has had a successful training along these lines, they should be encouraged to aim, eventually, to own their own salon. Their eye for beauty and for making people feel at ease will stand them in good stead as much as the certificates they have collected at the end of their course. Needless to say, my comments about partnership apply here, too. The same applies to the budding dress-designer — there is no reason why, once out of art school, Libra should not do extremely well. The rag trade is extremely competitive, and one needs plenty of contacts; so a few years working with some well-known designer label, getting to know the trade thoroughly, is probably essential.

Their sense of justice can sometimes attract the more academic Librans to the legal profession. They will have the tact and restraint to comply with all the rules of courtesy and protocol and, provided the individual is prepared to develop the more assertive and aggressive side of his personality in order to cope with court room argument, it's possible that he will enjoy a rewarding and successful career.

As a general clue to finding a good Libran career, any work involving making other people feel comfortable, happy and at ease will be suitable: a charming receptionist — especially perhaps in the hotel foyer — or a telephone operator (Librans often have very attractive voices which they can 'use' to great effect). In an entirely different vein we find many Librans are specially successful and talented engineers, sometimes working on large construction projects or contributing to the design of bridges, or perhaps heavy vehicles.

It may be that your youngster is attracted to pop music; if this is the case, I would advise you not to make it too easy for him — apart from the fact that it is a very competitive profession, he may feel that learning to strum a few chords on guitar or keyboard is enough to get him to number one in the hit parade. It is not! However, if as a child he has shown promise and gone through the mill of learning to play an instrument to a reasonable standard, it will be only fair to support and encourage him — the chances are his personality and dynamic charm will be a great asset if he has the chance to cut a disc or make a video.

# Travel

Librans seem to be even more pleased than the rest of humanity when holiday time comes round. In fact they'll probably have been hugging the thought to themselves for weeks or even months before the date of departure. They may not like all the fuss and bother of actually making arrangements, and you needn't expect them to join in the discussion about where to go — boring! But they will certainly be happy to set off.

It is sometimes seems to be no mere coincidence that Libra and lazy both start with the same letter; certainly when they relax, Librans aren't generally seen rushing about from Italian pillar to French post, from ski-slope to tennis-court. They, if anyone, will be happier spending a lazy day on the beach or the balcony, chatting with a few friends — rough and tumble games are probably not for them. But you'll probably have a lot of trouble if you try to get them to bed early, since they'll want long, romantic evenings at the disco almost as soon as they can walk. Getting them up in the morning will be an entirely different matter!

But even for a Libran that routine may pall somewhat after the first four or five days, and it is quite a good idea to encourage them to *use* their holiday a little rather than just living quietly through out. Adult Librans usually enjoy looking at buildings, paintings, sculpture — but often can't be bothered to search them out; the children have much the same attitude — they may grumble a bit about all the effort involved in climbing into the front seat of the coach when you've arranged an excursion, but they'll enjoy the scenery and probably be perfectly happy with whatever experience awaits them when the coach stops. They like savouring new atmospheres and are quite susceptible to them; you'll find that perhaps even more than you they'll end up with a real sense of what it's like to live in that Yugoslavian hill town, or that Scottish fishing village. But they may be a little embarrassed at some customs: they won't like having to bargain when buying souvenirs, for instance, and will probably end up paying a higher price rather than argue about it. They also like 'the best', so their souvenirs will be fewer, but more expensive, than anyone else's.

This is one of the signs that does not tolerate excessive temperatures at either end of the thermometer — seek out a moderate temperature if you want them to be really well — then they can sail around in their carefully chosen holiday clothes, impressing new young friends. You should not have to worry too much about their reactions to strange food — provided it is well presented and looks good on the plate. If this is the case, they won't be able to wait to try it, but if it is thrown together and looks rough and unpalatable, you may have a real problem, for Librans aren't good at roughing it — and that applies to the accommodation, too. In fact, despite Libra being an air sign, if one had to suggest an absolutely ideal holiday for them, it would probably be a luxury cruise! Nowhere much to go while afloat, so they could spend all their time happily lying on deck just occasionally dunking themselves in the swimming-pool while waiting for the next delicious meal and the well-organized excursion when in port.

## Librans as Brothers and Sisters

At best the young Libran makes a marvellously friendly, considerate and affectionate brother or sister.

When you tell him that the family is about to be joined by another boy or girl, you will find him sitting quietly with his head on one side (a common Libran gesture, by the way) and listening attentively to what you have to say about the prospect. He will cope with the gynaecological facts quite well, so you needn't be afraid to explain things fully. The only real problem may be that he might suspect that the arrival of a brother or sister will throw the family out of balance — that he will no longer get his fair share of love and attention. There can be a slight tendency to jealousy in some Librans, especially those with a highly emotional character, and this may be activated under such circumstances, so that the new baby does not get quite the welcome he or she deserves. In order to avoid the chance of jealousy developing, you should reassure Libra by stressing from the start the fact that when the time comes he will of course have to share everything — including your time — with the baby, but that there will be absolutely no question of your loving or caring for him less. And provided you are careful, later, to show him that this is true, the problem should not arise. Encourage your Libran to make something for the coming baby, or perhaps paint a picture for the nursery, thus involving him in the event.

Sharing is something every Libran will understand, because it is so obviously fair — and the Libran loves fairness and justice above all. But in the family, this preoccupation can of course lead to difficulties because it does mean that young Libra will keep an eye on everything around him to make sure that fair shares are given to all — and if a brother or sister gets a present too obviously more expensive or even in his eyes more desirable than his own, there will be trouble.

At school, the young Libran will be particularly good at standing up for his young brother or sister. You will find that even if it is the younger child who is the Libran, the tendency will still be for him to stand up for his brother or sister. His great sense of justice is always to the fore, and if he realizes that someone is being unkind to them, he will at once spring to their aid. He will also be quite good at sorting out the problem, though because he is close to his family the tendency will be for his scales of justice to tilt rather too enthusiastically towards them, which may not necessarily lead to peace in the playground.

At home, try to encourage your children to have joint interests. If the Libran is on the lazy side — and that is possible — he will be infected by the enthusiasm of his brother and sister. It is unlikely that he will altogether lack enthusiasm — it will be more a question of getting his energy going; once he's involved, he will get a lot of pleasure out of the shared interest. When you are choosing toys — especially creative toys such as chemistry or building sets or a sewing machine — think in these terms too, for the Libran often reacts best when led into a new interest by someone more enthusiastic than himself.

Sharing a room will be no problem as long as there is no possibility of Libra ever being give the excuse to cry 'It isn't *fair!*' — which is one of the major danger signals. The sharing brother or sister will find them obsessively concerned that everything should be carefully arranged so that they have equal space, toys of equal interest or value, beds which are equally comfortable, and so on. Even if there is a difference of several years between them, in extreme cases it might be as well for you to think of your children as twins when making arrangements or buying things, so that they get more or less identical treatment; this will alas mean that if you renew one bed you will have to renew both. The situation may seem rather hard on the older non-Libran, too, but if it keeps the peace, it will be well worthwhile.

It isn't difficult to persuade Librans to see reason, though sometimes stubbornness can get in the way. If this happens, you can usually pull them around to the realistic point of view by explaining that their behaviour isn't fair to you or to their brother or sister; the family should not always have to give in to Libra — their time will come when they are older.

## Librans as Parents

Once you are married or settled into a permanent relationship and the question of building a family arises, you will find that two possibilities could cloud the issue: one will be a tendency to find that you start your family before you have actually taken the decision to do so — possibly because you simply haven't bothered to take proper advice on family planning techniques; or you may simply procrastinate and postpone making the decision to have children until, one day, you discover it is too late. Do really listen to your partner, and be fair to him or her; make a definite decision at an early date about this vitally important matter — it is essential to remember that once you have started a family your life will never be the same again.

You will love your children very much and spend as much money as you can possibly afford on attractive clothes for them, and on making their room as pretty as can be; you will encourage them to enjoy many varied interests. But it is easy for you to spoil them, and they will soon recognize the fact and use you as a soft touch, wheedling you all too easily into giving them their way. Be careful: peace at any price is a motto that can lead to problems for Libran parents.

Consciously check yourself if you find that you are regularly buying them sweets and chocolate bars to bribe them into being quiet. Be aware of the fact, too, that when you become a parent your natural indecisiveness will encourage you to load every decision onto your partner! Try to remember that it is as much up to you to take family decisions as your partner. While joint decisions are always preferable, there will be many occasions when *you* really will have to make one for yourself — and if you do not do so, you will cause your children a considerable amount of annoyance and frustration just because you are not giving them the direction they need. Remember this even when they are grown up, otherwise they may find they are unable to make their own plans because of your indecisiveness.

You certainly make a wonderfully fun-loving parent, and as your children grow up they will collect a host of splendid memories of days out in the country or by the sea, all of which will have had the air of special occasions. You will probably create, in many ways, an idyllic childhood for them, but the tendency to seek over-easy solutions to problems, is, again, something which is difficult to resist. If you have read the paragraphs on *The Three Ways of Thinking* for those of your Sun-sign (see p.139), and have decided you fall into the first group, which will give you a decidedly critical streak, remember that you have a strong tendency to carp and perhaps even nag your children at times. Try to find a balancing logic and hold on to a sense of what is fair rather than simply expedient.

You are particularly good at devising joint activities with the children and your partner; allow your imagination free play where that is concerned, and plan those picnics, outings and holidays. Remember, spending as much time as possible with your children is one way of making a united family — provided you restrain yourself from expressing any hint of possessiveness. It is important too for you to take the trouble to find out about what your children's generation is really thinking and what their priorities are. It will not always be possible to glean this information from your own children, because they will simply express their own opinions. I suggest you do a little research, watching TV programmes and reading magazines aimed at their age group — in this way you will get a broader picture and will better understand your own children. Then you will be able to cope with any generation gap which seems to be developing.

I have already pointed out that Librans are high on the list of Zodiac groups when it comes to socializing and entertaining; this and your natural diplomacy, will stand you in good stead when your children are at school and you become involved in the PTA. You will be at your best helping to organize social occasions (perhaps in partnership with a lively, enthusiastic Leo) — and if you are elected to the committee maybe you could become a liaison officer or perhaps act as go-between, translating the teachers' opinions and needs to the parents and board of governors.

## Case Study

Kian - Sun in Libra, Mercury in Virgo, Venus in Scorpio; Mercury Group 1, Venus Group 4.

From the Report: 'Kian has terrific natural enthusiasm, and will respond in a delightfully enthusiastic way when ideas or suggestions are put to him. He may however tend to get bored at times, or rather quickly drift off a little from what is on hand. This, and the fact that he may not always want for any length of time to get on and do things for himself, is something you should perhaps watch in him; it is a tendency that could work negatively for him in the long run. I am sure that he has tremendous charm, and equally sure that he knows it — and can use it to full advantage! So he can all too easily get away with a great deal for which other children may suffer. Because of his charm he has the ability to get the better of you, and when he goes to school will find he can get the better of his teachers, too; so if, for instance, he has forgotten to bring a textbook or his football boots or a piece of homework, his explanations will be convincing and will probably be accepted.

'I think he is something of a fighter, and will certainly want to win. He will want to be "first", and you can easily appeal to this side of his personality: "You won't be top of the class if you don't work hard!" That is quite a good line to take, for he really will want to be top, to win at games or athletics; but his natural way is to use his delightful personality to full advantage rather than to make hard, dogged and consistent efforts.

'When he is a little older another element of his personality will come into play: I'm sure you will find that he has an extremely powerful critical streak. He can think critically and constructively, and because of his charm and the easygoing aspects of his personality, it is important that he should be taught as soon as possible to direct his criticism towards himself and his activities. Get him to analyse his attitudes — *why* he thinks in a particular way about a subject under discussion. This is important for Kian, for I think his critical acumen will help him enormously in life, mainly because there are such contrasting and powerful areas of his personality which need attention from the sound, down-to-earth critical side of him.'

Comment: Kian is eleven at the time of writing; his analysis was written just after his birth. His parents tell me that he does have great charm and is popular with his teachers — some people call him 'cute'. He certainly takes competitive sport very seriously, and it is in that area that his fighting spirit and need to win are positively expressed. These qualities very often emerge quite strongly in Sun-sign Librans and are particularly emphasized for Kian through the Libran polar sign, Aries (see p.14) which was rising at the time of his birth. Like many school age Librans he tends to get bored with some of his lessons and was slow to learn to read. His parents think his need for challenge will help him develop his self-critical streak.

I also mentioned, elsewhere in the report, that Kian could be naturally mechanically minded and might be attracted to the military; both these traits are developing fast.

## The Sun-sign and Its Rulerships

*Countries and areas*: Alsace, Argentina, Austria, Burma, China, Upper Egypt, Indo-China, minor islands of Japan, part of India, Manchuria, Siberia, some South Pacific islands, Tibet.

*Cities*: Antwerp, Charleston (U.S.A.), Copenhagen, Frankfurt, Freiburg, Johannesburg, Leeds, Lisbon, Nottingham, Vienna.

*Trees*: ash, cypress, all vines.

*Flowers and herbs*: those listed for Taurus, excluding those which are red or pink: alder, artichoke, asparagus, beans, brambles, cloves, columbine, daisy, elder, foxglove, marshmallow, mint, poppy, primula, rose, sorrel, violet. Also large flowers such as dahlias, rhododendron and magnolia.

*Food*: milk; apples; all cereals, especially wheat; all berries; grapes, pears; spices; sugar and strong alcohol excluded.

*Cell salts*: Nat. Phos. and Kali. Phos.

*Animals*: lizards and small reptiles.

*Stone*: sapphire.

*Metal*: copper, sometimes bronze.

*Colour*: pale blue and pink.

# SCORPIO

## (October 24 - November 22)

Note: Scorpio is a feminine sign, so for the most
part I refer throughout to 'she', but most of my
comments refer also to boys.

## General Characteristics

Popular descriptions of Scorpio will no doubt have given you the impression that
this sign has the highest sex-drive and that Scorpios can be preoccupied with sex.

Such statements are only partially true; more to the point is the fact that the
sign very definitely gives its subject the highest energy level of the twelve. The energy
is both physical and emotional, and there is a strong possibility that the emotional
force will be far and away the more potent. With this in mind, you can understand
that your Scorpio child has a great deal of potential — but potential that needs
very careful guidance and control if it is to be positively expressed to the full benefit
of the individual as she gets older. If direction is lacking it can be the case that Scorpios
stagnate, all their considerable resources turning sour and being wasted, the potentially
positive becoming negative in its expression so that we get someone moody, resentful
and jealous, caring little or nothing for what is going on around them.

It is essential that your young Scorpio be involved in all kinds of interests — indeed,
you cannot start too early attracting her attention to nature, things in shop windows,
pictures — anything you find beautiful and likely to hold her attention, even from
her pram!

She will be extremely intuitive and will probably pick up the prevailing atmosphere
in the home. As soon as she is able to hold a conversation she will start asking
searching questions well beyond her years: '*Why* aren't you talking to Daddy?'

You must be prepared for the occasional tantrum. When she is very young the
best approach will be to distract her attention by getting her involved in something
new — a toy or something different to eat. When she is older this may be more
difficult, for Scorpio types are on the whole rather complex people, and excuses
which will satisfy other signs will not work with them.

We must remember that their worst fault is jealousy. Do everything you can to avoid this negative and wasteful emotion taking over their lives and inhibiting some marvellously strong and positive characteristics. There is also a tendency to be deeply secretive. Again watch out for this from an early age; if you can overcome it while Scorpio is very young it will be less difficult for her to open out and discuss her problems freely with you — or indeed with a friend or a teacher when she is older and encounters a serious difficulty.

Like those of her polar or opposite sign, Taurus, she needs an above average amount of security, with perhaps the accent on emotional rather than material matters; she has a very natural business sense and the ability to make money, so material security should take care of itself in due course. Keep her very busy and in developing a steady, reasonably predictable routine all those powerful energy sources will find a positive outlet and this will form a good basis for your young Scorpio's personal development.

This is a Zodiac group which benefits enormously from learning to swim at a very early age. Along with the Cancerians and Pisceans, they should be taken to the local swimming pool for mother-and-baby sessions. Apart from the general advantage of being able to avoid drowning — and of course of using up some of that physical energy — the psychological effect of extended contact with water will help nurture and develop her emotional resources in an interesting and very subtle way.

When she is a little older and you have to warn her about not accepting sweets from strangers, it is reasonable to assume that her natural tendency to be somewhat suspicious will be something of a protection. By the time she is four or five her natural intuition will also be coming into play, and she should instinctively feel when all is not straightforward and well. Once you start explaining about things of this sort, or indeed any adult matters (and this applies to the earliest sex education), you should remember that she will not accept superficial answers, and if you are not well prepared the chances are that you will get into quite serious trouble when she starts questioning you.

It may be that from time to time young Scorpio will be found to take a rather pessimistic outlook on life — and it is likely that this will be because there isn't enough going on in her own life which really fascinates her; she needs some new interest — though it can also simply be the case that someone has said something to distress her. This will upset her whole being, and she'll often find it difficult to shake off. Try to get her to tell you just what is wrong.

She will certainly have very definite feelings — very strong likes and dislikes. When it comes to her favourite colours, for instance, she will probably choose a rich shade of crimson. However, in recent years I have seen many very young Scorpios going for the fashionable black — something we have all realized older Scorpios like. She will take a pride in any school uniform she has to wear, but she must be able to change into something realistically loose and unconventional for outside activities.

Scorpios have a wonderfully natural business sense, and in order to encourage her to develop it early, let her — or encourage her to — get involved in fund-raising for charity (especially if the sponsoring of some kind of endurance test is involved). This will be excellent for her in many ways, among them making her aware of world suffering. You will find she will manage her pocket-money well, perhaps secretly saving a few pennies here and there for important occasions. Remember she is extremely determined and can be very stubborn! Develop the determination, but maintain a balance between it and what can amount to bloody-mindedness. Her sense of purpose is second to none, and one of her best qualities is that she is a whole-hogger — once she has set her mind on something she will go all-out for it. She hates to waste a moment of life and loves enjoying everything that is going. When she is able to do this she will be at her best, all her intense energy consumed in a satisfying and fulfilling way.

## The Three Ways of Thinking

Due to the influence of Mercury (see p.13), the Scorpio mind characteristically works in one of three ways.

★ Scorpios in the first group, in spite of their natural ability to consider problems in depth, will have a tendency to be somewhat indecisive. They can see boths sides of any question but may tend to procrastinate. This should be countered; restlessness can otherwise occur, which leads to dissatisfaction.

★★ The second group contains those with a natural flair for careful planning; there is a strong ability here to think deeply. Here are the most intuitive but also the most stubborn of Scorpios, with detective-like minds and often a passion for research of all kinds. Sometimes a brooding moodiness is evident.

★★★ In the third group we find those who are able to take in the broad aspects of a problem or situation and consider it in detail. There is usually a sharp intelligence — a mind which will benefit from all intellectual challenge. Their outlook is more optimistic than that of most Scorpios.

## The Five Ways of Loving

Due to the influence of Venus (see p.13), Scorpios will tend to express their affection in one of five ways.

★ There is a tendency for the first group to be very critical of their loved ones, and sometimes a certain shyness can be seen. Parents should look out for this, for it can later inhibit the Scorpio need for and expression of a full and rewarding love and sex life. In the extreme, the attitude to sex can be clinical.

★★ In the second group are those with a great need for partnership and a rather over-romantic attitude to love. Care is necessary that they do not become too deeply involved in a relationship before they are mature enough to cope. Resentfulness can sometimes mar the love life; they must learn to forgive and forget.

★★★ The third group contains the most passionate Scorpios — and probably the most highly-sexed. Their strong emotions will be marvellously rewarding if positively expressed, and indeed if reciprocated. All too often however Scorpio jealousy and possessiveness becomes a serious problem.

★★★★ These Scorpios certainly have fun but need a certain amount of independence — a fairly light-hearted attitude to their partners makes life rather easier for them, though sometimes a tendency to be involved in more than one relationship at a time can cause problems. They can become quite jealous if they find their partners flirting!

★★★★★ The last group of Scorpios sets its sights high when choosing a partner, occasionally opting for money rather than, or at least as well as, love. They positively enjoy social climbing. They are often faithful, but in spite of their Scorpio passion sometimes lack real tenderness and can be somewhat cold.

## Health and Diet

Bearing in mind Scorpio's natural liking for the good life, there is a strong possibility that she will enjoy her food from the first solid mouthful, if not before.

As she grows up she may get a little too fond of food, in fact, and like Taurus, her partner across the Zodiac, she can be more than a mite greedy. If she is the type to put on weight, you really must watch her very carefully, for Scorpios never seem to be able to do anything by half-measures! Granted there are a great many who are extremely lean and wiry, but others can certainly become over-weight, especially if for some reason they are unhappy or their strong energy sources are not sufficiently used. If possible, encourage your Scorpio child to eat fresh plums or dried apricots or figs rather than chocolates, especially if they have heavy, rich fillings such as thick cream or liqueur — the kind of thing Scorpios positively adore!

Which leads us, of course, to exercise. I have already mentioned the connection with the water as being psychologically rewarding, and swimming will perhaps be specially enjoyed, but whatever the exercise, the great thing is to encourage consistency, taking it from the early days as a natural part of Scorpio's routine which hopefully they will want to carry on throughout their life.

If you find your Scorpio becoming lethargic, and if she seems to be moving considerably more slowly than her contemporaries, it will be as well to arrange for her to have a blood test; it is possible she may have a slightly inactive thyroid gland. Remember too that the young Scorpio might tend to worry rather more than you realize, and you will have cause for some concern if she becomes too quiet, introspective and reclusive, for then there is the possibility that she may be nursing some problem about which she is reluctant to talk. It is natural for her to keep problems to herself. You may find it difficult to persuade her to discuss them, but this secretiveness can lead to tension, which will almost inevitably affect her health. Stomachache, headache or constipation may be a sign. Sit quietly with her, and do everything possible to encourage her to talk; point out that just as she likes to have full information about everything that is going on and receive exhaustive answers to every question she asks, so do her parents — and they are there to help her, rather than leave her to cope with problems on her own.

When she catches the usual childish complaints she will probably be very patient. While she is abed, if and when she is up to it, concentrate on burning up her intellectual energy and keeping her mind active. Allow her, indeed encourage her, to read mystery and detective stories, and do complicated puzzles. That kind of thing will all being well prevent her from feeling too restless.

When she is well she should sleep deeply, and it is a particularly good thing for this intensely emotional type to develop good dream recall. She will probably have this, anyway, but talking about dreams and learning what they really mean (not, I underline, about the superstitions attached to them) will not only be intellectually interesting to Scorpios, the natural psychologists of the Zodiac, but will lead to a fuller understanding of her own personality. Both of you will benefit.

Scorpio diet should have plenty of fresh fruit and roughage; liquids to flush out her system are also important — there is a tendency that this may stagnate. When she is older she will definitely benfit from saunas and steam baths, which will help to rid her system of toxins which tend to build up in this particular Zodiac type. The body area emphasized by the sign is the genitals; any slight problem there should be investigated, and cleanliness should be particulary emphasized. It is well to remember, when they are babies, that what may only be a minor nappy rash could be something more serious: so check it out if it does not clear up in a day or so.

## The First Five Years

Almost as soon as young Scorpio can speak, you will be bombarded with a great many questions. While this is the case with many Zodiac types, Scorpios certainly head the list of those who want to know everything about the world, and to know about it thoroughly, so that one question leads to another, and another — and so on. You give one answer, and they demand another: 'Why?' — 'But *why?*'

Along with a searching mind, Scorpios need to be deeply involved in everything that is going on, and it is a good thing to give them toys which stimulate the imagination, for their imaginations are certainly very vivid, and will be of great help to them later in life. You will probably find your Scorpio the kind of child who is particularly fascinated by prehistoric monsters and has a feeling for slightly weird fairy stories (the tales of the brothers Grimm could be favourite reading).

Don't forget that she will have a lot of energy, and that it will be as well from as early an age as possible to establish a fairly demanding physical routine which will include energetic outdoor excursions where she can use this up. These should be balanced by equally strenuous demands on her intelligence; read to her as much as you can, get her interested in numbers — and indeed in anything that attracts her attention in the environment around her.

When the time comes for her to join a play group, she could be somewhat apprehensive and suspicious. Other people may get the impression that she is rather shy, but you will know better than that — it is more likely that she will be slightly inhibited by the unfamiliar surroundings, which will temporarily make her feel insecure. Taking her own toys with her will help, and you should make sure that she gets to know, as soon as possible, the other children attending the group — in fact if she can be introduced to them before she actually joins it, that will be big help.

The chances are that your Scorpio child has a very strong personality and will need fairly strict discipline — especially when she throws a tantrum or shows any hint of jealousy. If she seems to be stubborn you will have to use all your intuition and quick thinking to break her determination — perhaps entirely changing the subject and getting her involved in a different occupation will help. Then, later, maybe you can return to the problem and get her to see reason.

On the whole Scorpio has remarkably good powers of concentration, in advance of other children of her age. But though she has an instinctive need for in-depth knowledge, she may often tend — just when you think she is entirely involved in a game — to get suddenly fed up with it and cast it aside. This pattern, which emerges early in life, can be repeated from time to time throughout it, sometimes to the detriment of the career. Parents should watch out for this and question even a very young child about *why* she has suddenly thrown something down, and whether she has *really* exhausted her interest in it. Encourage her to finish what she starts.

## School Years

Before you know it, young Scorpio will be well and truly ready for full-time school; she may want to move on from her play group rather earlier than many of her contemporaries. (This is a particularly good thing if you also have a younger child to look after; Scorpios are a pretty demanding lot!)

If she was rather apprehensive about going to play school, and this problem seems to trouble her again when the time comes to move up a step, your best bet is to concentrate on explaining how much more exciting school will be — that there will be many more interesting, grown up things for her to discover there. In a way, Scorpio children are often rather old for their years; so you can appeal to that tendency too, especially if she has to wear a school uniform: 'Look how grown-up you are!' Her sense of pride will also come in useful as a persuader: 'Mummy and Daddy are so proud of you!' And the chances are that she *will* look grown-up, and that you *will* be proud of her! And finally, the naturally inquisitive Scorpio mind will draw her to a fresh pattern of life which will enable her to find out so many new things.

She should respond well to the discipline of school, which will give a solid structure to daily life; if discipline is not available to a Scorpio, if the school's atmosphere tends to be rather too relaxed, Scorpio can feel insecure and rather at a loss — she likes to know just what is expected of her, and in an undisciplined atmosphere her potential is unlikely to be fully stretched and developed. If you have a choice of schools, this is something to bear in mind.

She should become quite eager once she gets into the routine of study; she has the capacity to work extremely hard and to enjoy it. When examinations come round, indeed, she could work to breaking point — again something you should guard against. Try to persuade her not to let work projects pile up; if she is particularly busy or specially keen on one or two projects, she could neglect others and have to finish them in a burst of activity which might be too strenuous; a good sense of balance should ensure that she does well all round. In due course you will probably find out that she will want to specialize. This will give you a hint of her direction in future, if she goes on to polytechnic or university, and perhaps of an eventual career. Generally speaking Scorpios are capable of intricate, careful work; naturally adept with computers, they will take to these like a fish to water. There may well be mathematical and scientific talent, and research in that direction will be enhanced by intuition and imagination; they often have the ability to see a way through problems which may not occur to other people. Vivid imagination will be seen in the drawings and paintings of Scorpios who have an artistic bent, and such children should be encouraged to follow up the interest both in and out of school.

Young Scorpio has distinct likes and dislikes where people are concerned, and this applies particularly to teachers. She will work extremely hard for those she likes and continually test the others by asking searching questions (to some of which she will already know the answers) and be highly critical of the replies, provoking considerable argument if they do not measure up to her expectations. She will probably develop passionate crushes on favourite teachers — which is nothing to worry about — but if a fellow pupil becomes a rival for attention or affection, she could become jealous, which might become a problem. A sympathetic teacher for whom she cares will be able to steer her round many problems; if she shows signs of being uneasy, it may be because she has no teacher in whom she feels she can confide — and she has a tendency anyway to keep her concerns to herself (the more serious she feels them to be, the less she may want to discuss them). Try, in one way or another, always to be aware of what is going on in her mind and in her life, and to discuss a possible problem before it creates difficulty — that way you will be able to continue to discuss it, and to help if it becomes rather larger than either you or Scorpio expected.

Ties of friendship at school will be very strong and may last a lifetime. Disagreements, however, may be equally long-lasting, and there will be occasions when breaks in friendship seem likely to be irrevocable; in which case you might intervene, if the friendship seemed particularly worthwhile, and try to mend some fences. 'All or nothing' can be very much a Scorpio motto, and is not always a good thing, even if Scorpio thinks it is!

Heavy team games are excellent for both sexes; the competitive spirit, strong in Scorpio, is often married to aggression, and with their strong emotional force and high energy level can lead to excellent results on the sports field. They will get a great deal of pleasure from their success. As a water sign, Scorpio often makes its denizens good swimmers, and if they have not learned to swim before they go to school they will almost certainly want to do so when the possibility presents itself — and may go on to be good divers and underwater swimmers.

## Out of School Activities

You may think that when your young Scorpio is sitting doing nothing with a blank expression on her face, she is being lazy. It isn't necessarily so.

The chances are that she will be thinking very deeply about something — perhaps about some casual remark you or her teacher have made — or she may be planning some activity she and her friends have in mind. Scorpios are naturally secretive, and this can sometimes be a problem. The tendency can be positively used, however, if you encourage them to make secret plans for parties or for excursions for themselves and their friends or surprises for other people's birthdays. (Interestingly enough, they can also show an interest in 'magic' and conjuring — which of course requires a certain amount of positive deception!)

Membership of youth clubs or children's groups of various kinds is good for them, especially if some distinct purpose is involved; many young Scorpios enjoy playing doctors and nurses, so as soon as you like you can encourage them to be members of the junior Red Cross. If you live near the coast, they could become Sea Rangers, or train to be life guards. They don't mind hard work and have good powers of endurance; they enjoy adventure and have a strong element of bravery. Alas, they often have a somewhat cruel streak which can work negatively for some of them; it is an excellent thing to make them aware of the problem of cruelty to children or animals — let them help out at an animal shelter; it is always advisable to encourage the quality of sympathy in them, and encourage them to combat the effects of cruelty in others. Look out for any tendency on the part of young Scorpio to pull the wings off flies!

Perhaps the most important thing to encourage in any Scorpio who gets involved in an out of school interest or hobby is their will to succeed. If for instance she shows the desire to spend hours before dawn at the ice rink or a swimming pool, or if she slogs it out at the barre at ballet class after school, then believe me you really *will* have cause to be proud of her in due course; all the energy and strength of will of Scorpio will be being positively expressed. The chances of success will be high. Where you will have to be careful is if your child is not really involved in anything — for in that case her energy will be wasted. If she seems not to be keen on any of her school subjects and comes home from school and just sits around, you may be heading for trouble, since her positive qualities must be exercised; if she has no sense of direction she will end up being resentful of others' successes, and thoroughly discontented.

Scorpio enterprise is marked; it is excellent to encourage them to develop at least one hobby which can show a profit. When they are very little, they will enjoy playing shops and making a toy profit; they make formidable opponents at Monopoly! When they are older, they are usually eager to have some sort of a weekend job — helping out at the local hairdressing salon, taking a paper round, or doing farm work if they live in the country (Scorpios sometimes positively revel in the chance to get dirty).

## Preparing for Life

Up to a point, all children deserve a matter of fact approach to sex education, but because there is an added emphasis on sex for those born with a Scorpio Sun-sign, it is specially important for them.

It is very likely that your young Scorpio will reach puberty at an early age — perhaps earlier than you expect. His or her enquiring mind will be unrelenting when the time has come for full sexual education, and it is important that they receive really good and thorough instruction. Partial knowledge is particularly bad for them, and childish fairy tales about how babies arrive can do positive harm, for their vivid imaginations may get things wrong and their whole attitude to sex may get off on the wrong foot.

Coeducational schooling helps enormously in this area of a young Scorpio's life — though brothers or sisters of the opposite sex can also help to put things on a natural footing; anything should be avoided which gives sex a mysterious or forbidden glamour. The need to experiment sexually is perhaps likely to be keener for young Scorpio; apart from proper advice on contraception, it is of course vitally important that they should know about the health risks involved.

It is very likely that young Scorpio will at the earliest opportunity fall deeply and passionately in love. She will then either be overwhelmingly happy or in the depths of despair, depending on the reaction of the loved one. Her life will be excruciatingly miserable if the loved one is even seen talking to someone else; the green-eyed monster within most Scorpios will immediately start gnawing. In her early years you will, if you are wise, have been on the look out for any signs of jealousy, and she herself may by now be well aware that it is her primary fault. This does not however make it easier for her to control her earliest love relationships; together you and she will have to make a great effort to keep it under control, to keep reactions natural and easy and prevent her very powerful emotions from getting the better of her. A more realistic outlook can be encouraged by suggesting that she is over-dramatizing the situation (which may indeed be true). You could also point out that the boy-friend may be reacting to her own possessiveness or high expectations of him. It will be good for her to learn that many people — even some Scorpios — living in a permanent relationship with someone still need a certain amount of freedom. So she must learn to be logical and keep her strong feelings in rein.

You will find that Scorpio has a naturally strong need to explore relationships, perhaps with several different partners. It is not that they will flit thoughtlessly from one to the next; they simply seem to need to know how various people react to them, their personality, their sexuality. Once they have found someone to whom they can make a lasting commitment, they will do everything they can to make the relationship work, devoting all their physical and emotional energies to building it into something meaningful, worthwhile and hopefully permanent. Provided that by the time this happens they have recognized their tendency to be jealous and possessive, they make wonderful partners.

But if you can, encourage young Scorpio to have light-hearted fun with a group of like-minded friends of both sexes; if they become emotionally involved at too early an age they miss out on a very great deal of experience which makes those early to middle teen-age years enjoyable and memorable. If you find that Scorpio is rushing off with the gang to support a favourite team, or going on a day's outing to cheer a hero at a motorcycle scramble, you can be confident that he or she is really enjoying life. I'm not saying, however, that they will not make straight for the back seat of the coach with a favourite companion on the return journey.

If Scorpio has been reasonably disciplined at school and at home before adolescence, the training will have instilled a strong sense of right and wrong which will be extremely valuable; you should have no real cause for worry — added to which Scorpio instincts are quick to warn when anyone suggests something outside their private code, and common sense should prevail.

## Further Education

A Scorpio who goes into further education with a specific aim in view, and is entirely devoted to it, is likely to be more successful than almost any other Sun-sign subject.

This kind of Scorpio can cope with really extended study, and many of them are likely to carry on with that study for a lifetime.

Scorpios are generally extremely good at research, and they will not be content merely to make notes of what other people have thought or said, and think of ways of rephrasing them. They are not specially original, but following through accepted lines of thought they are good at resolving problems and exploring new avenues, adding their own conclusions.

They will at once see through tutors and lecturers who talk off the top of their heads and with an insufficient grounding in their subjects, and they will be very good at putting them on the spot, pointing out weaknesses in arguments and demanding hard evidence for statements they mistrust. Sarcasm and pretentiousness will cut no ice with Scorpio. Remember, the creature of the sign has a sting in its tail, and this can certainly be employed on occasion. In preparing essays it is sometimes necessary for Scorpio to recognize the fact that they can be long-winded, employing unnecessary long irrelvant quotations where a short, pithy statement would be better. They should continually ask themselves whether their work isn't becoming boring.

Although Scorpios are not unsociable, and will probably cope very well if they have to share a student flat, it is essential that they have a quiet place to study. If this has to be their bedroom, they will need a reasonable amount of desk area and good light. They are better working alone, uninterrupted by other people's chatter, and while they may well need their own kind of background noise to work to, if this is not what they themselves have chosen, it will cease to be a pleasure and become instead a mere distraction. A desk in a university library will perhaps be ideal; they will have all the tools of research at their elbow and a quiet and carefully controlled atmosphere in which to conduct it.

If your Scorpio is studying at home or has to work there during the evening, make sure that they have the environment they need and that they can work undisturbed, even if this means a certain amount of disruption of the home routine — you may find that on one day they'll happily skip supper altogether, while on the next they'll be knocking on the table demanding food an hour before it's ready.

They will certainly not live a solitary, isolated life at university; they will be determined to get as much out of the experience as possible, haunting their favourite cafes and wine bars to talk long into the night; and they will certainly be active members of the usual student bodies. There will be an accent on sport, and many will enjoy rowing, in particular, or canoeing — as well as the usual heavy team games.

In contrast to the physically demanding activities, they may find it beneficial to flirt with yoga, some contemplative discipline, or at least with a relaxation technique of some kind — especially if they are the sort of Scorpio prone to worry (see *The Three Ways of Thinking*, p.159). They must balance their lives if all their remarkable resources are to be evenly used. If they become low spirited or depressed, it may well be because they are concentrating on in-depth study for too long and intense a period. Question your young Scorpio about her diet — whether she is away at university or sharing a flat wth friends somewhere near you. If her friends are all slim and shapely but she puts on a few pounds, she may tend to indulge in a crash diet — and then celebrate because she's lost weight and start the cycle all over again. If you see a pattern of this sort developing, try to break it, otherwise her health and her powers of concentration will both suffer.

Balance really is necessary: Scorpios can, and should, work hard and play hard, but shouldn't let one area of their life suffer because the other has entirely taken them over.

## Unemployment: Stresses and Strains

Young Scorpios do not cope well with unemployment; apart from the usual frustrations they will readily become restless and sometimes lose their self-confidence.

If Scorpio becomes really angry because nobody seems to want her, it is in many ways a good sign — you can appeal to her fighting spirit to keep her up to the mark in searching for work. Encourage her to express her anger positively, and while she must not spoil her chances by trying rudely to bludgeon her way into employment, she can become effectively assertive, and when she attends interviews her natural dynamism and keenness will come to the fore. Ruthlessness — or what appears to be that — must be controlled. She will be very willing and ready to work, and this will stand her in good stead and increase her chances of being engaged. The young girls of the sign may, when job-hunting, become a little daring and want to try out their powers of seduction on a would-be employer; keep your eye on the outfit they wear for interviews — a neckline near the ground does not always impress!

If she gets depressed and frustrated, you may well have quite a difficult battle to keep her interested — even if she has good qualifications, she may tend to feel that the battle is simply not worth so much effort. In that case, perhaps you could suggest to her that she develop her own enterprising skills. Why not encourage her to go in for a little buying and selling? Could she, for instance, gather some junk together and try her luck, perhaps with some like-minded friend, at a stall in the local market? Has she any creative skills she has failed so far to exploit? Could she get help from an enterprise scheme or trust fund? Perhaps she has a scheme which could impress a bank manager, and attract a small loan. I say this because not unlike many Taureans and Capricorns there are plenty of Scorpios who have succeeded in building wonderful business empires from extremely modest beginnings.

When she is compiling her c.v., it won't be difficult to appeal to her business sense, and she should take quite a lot of pleasure in making sure that it is really accurate and looks good.

There is no denying the need to escape from boredom or frustration, together with the desire to experience every aspect of life, are dangers for young Scorpios should they be offered drugs. There is a leaning towards excess, especially when life is real and earnest, or they have perhaps suffered a broken relationship. They will then eat and drink too much, possibly smoke too much, and even — should the situation be really unpleasant — turn to drugs. Alas, they will not be content with half-measures; even within one evening, the situation could get really heavy — and once hooked, they will find it difficult to pull back.

Once they decide they want to kick the habit they will announce that they're quitting, cold turkey, and may even succeed in doing so — for a day or two. But unless life has become a great deal better and the original cause of the calamity has been removed their determination may not be strong enough to overcome the horrors of withdrawal. This problem is so difficult for them that you are unlikely to be able to be of much help. Encourage them to seek professional therapy; they will find it in a perverse way fascinating to explore the real reasons for their own downfall, and once they understand them will find it easier to come to terms with the problem and make slow, steady progress towards recovery. Once they have managed this, they will be able to be a great deal of help to those still stricken, for no one will be better able to sympathize and understand.

## Interests and Spare Time Activities

Scorpio's friends will be of various ages and various backgrounds; it is just as likely for a Scorpio girl to befriend some lonely old man as some tiny child. Expect her to bring home people of every race, colour and creed.

This is a particularly good thing for Scorpios; they will learn about humanity and love doing so. If she seems to have too few friends, she may be obsessive about them — and in the long run that can prove detrimental, for she will want their entire lives to centre around her own, and they may find that just a little tedious, more than they bargained for when they accepted that first invitation to tea. It is far better for the net to be thrown wide to catch fish of every size and description. Scorpio will find them all fascinating, though she can sometimes make friends without thinking too carefully about what they have in common — especially if they are of the opposite sex, and this can lead to disappointment and frustration.

Simple friendship between people of the opposite sex can be easier for some signs than others, and it is certainly rather difficult for Scorpio, who even with the best will in the world tends to get emotionally involved. One of the few things that will defuse the situation is a passionate interest in a mutual hobby.

Scorpios should never forget that they need regular exercise. This often takes care of itself when they are at school or university, but later he or she should make sure they exercise at least three times a week; membership of a health club is highly recommended, if it is financially possible — aerobic classes and weight training are specially recommended; both boys and girls will benefit from courses in karate or some other means of self-defence. Judo often attracts Scorpios. The boys in particular will go on playing team games for many years but should be careful they don't go on too long after their bodies begin seriously to protest and, when they do stop, should adjust their diet if they do not want to put on an undue amount of weight.

When it comes to hobbies, it is often fun for them to express their natural inquisitiveness — perhaps in researching in detail some aspect of local history, or following any kind of trail. Many enjoy industrial archaeology. Pluto, the ruling planet of this sign, is said to bring things out into the open, and that has its special appeal to Scorpios. Solving mysteries of any kind delights them. Ghost-hunting could attract them, for many Scorpios are fascinated by the occult, and some are definitely gifted in that respect. But if they feel this attraction, or think they are clairvoyant and wish to develop the talent, they should be careful to obtain proper instruction. Whatever one thinks about occult powers, there is ample evidence that they can be dangerous if misused and misdirected, and the amateur can easily suffer psychological damage.

Many splendid photographers are found in this group — perhaps professional, but certainly amateur; a cheap camera will probably have been in her pocket almost since birth, but many Scorpios will be delighted to find a friend who has a dark-room, or will rig up her own, and either teach herself to develop and print her films, or look for someone who can teach her.

Scorpios can look very smart indeed; they will tend to go for a fashion look which enhances their sexuality, and when they are young can dazzle — leather and shiny fabrics do a lot for them, though sometimes (especially recent years) they can wear too much black. A little light relief does no harm, adding interest and sparkle.

They are certainly able to play their part in improving the life of the community; they are keen to chase up anything which seems to be socially wrong and see that justice is done. They are also usually willing to contribute time and energy generously to schemes which will improve the environment or help the less fortunate. Elected to a committee of any kind and finding the overall attitude somewhat complacent, they will not waste time before stirring things up; their determination will make its mark, but if they become chairperson their stubbornness and conviction that they are right could upset their colleagues.

Scorpios love good living and are lavish entertainers. They will use bottles of wine and pints of cream in the kitchen, and their meals are memorable. Unlikely to take short cuts, they will spend hours in the kitchen; if they have no time to prepare what they think of as a reasonably good meal, they will spend more than they can afford on entertaining their loved ones or friends at restaurants.

Perhaps more cat than dog people, if they choose the former they will be elegant — Burmese or Siamese, perhaps. Sometimes Scorpios tend to own slightly unusual pets.

## Ideal Careers

It is very important that however Scorpios choose to spend their working hours, there should be a considerable amount of emotional involvement in the job.

If the individual is bored and uninterested there will be a lack of inner fulfilment, and this is particularly negative for Scorpios, for when it occurs their emotional energy is not being expressed in a powerful or rewarding way, and in time this can lead to serious discontent, and the energy itself tends to stagnate; the result is that the Scorpio concerned becomes bad tempered and very stressed.

It is often the case that those of this sign will get enough inner satisfaction from making money — and that's fine up to a point; even so, if the actual work holds no real interest for them they should really make a point of directing their emotional energies towards some compelling spare time interest, to counter the boredom of the working day. Very often Scorpios have a marvellous flair for making money and are strong and decisive business people — so if they are building their own business there will most certainly be considerable inner satisfaction. The same satisfaction can be found if they work for a large firm, provided they have a personal involvement (perhaps as shareholder or partner).

However, Scorpios are at their best when the work itself is rewarding, and they are able to spend their days involved in something they have wanted to do since childhood.

Thinking of their natural ability for research and delving into all kinds of problems, we find that many rise to high positions in the police force or become successful private detectives, while others are fascinated by the workings of the human mind and strive and study for many years to become psychiatrists or psychologists. Yet others, drawn to the medical professions, become eminent surgeons. Elsewhere, we find the same kind of ability and motivation expressed in the butchery trade, for instance, while in a completely different area, mining and engineering are also popular and extremely rewarding. Those who favour the life-style of the armed services will often rise through the ranks in the Navy, and sometimes in the Army.

Not unlike the people of their polar or opposite sign, Taurus, we must never forget that Scorpios need considerable financial security; perhaps this is one reason why they are so good in business. They are brave and will take calculated risks, but only when they are as sure as possible of their ground. Work in banks and large finance corporations, in insurance, and the Stock Exchange is rewarding and worthwhile for those of this sign.

Remembering that they enjoy good living (and are sometimes more than slightly self-indulgent), they make excellent connoisseurs of wine; importing and selling it, or perhaps writing about it for a newspaper or journal, is something a Scorpio might consider when deciding on a career.

Along with Virgos, Scorpios enjoy research of all kinds, whether scientific or artistic; if a job entails a certain amount of this, the chances are that Scorpio will find it rewarding and do well at it. They have good powers of concentration and plenty of patience, which is obviously an asset; they can cope with long-term programmes of work.

There is something about which I must warn you: Scorpio will work long and hard but will sometimes decide for their own very private reasons to give everything up to make a drastic change — perhaps when he or she is just in sight of the very peak of an ambition. This can happen to Scorpio at almost any age; it seems almost natural to them to make change for change's sake — sometimes they need to do this (for all kinds of deep-rooted psychological reasons), but there are times when, without a second thought, they throw the baby out with the bath water and start again from scratch. This does not always work out as well as they think; as parents you can only be on the look out for such situations and at least make sure that they understand the consequences of their actions. The will to succeed, however, is always present, and there is no lack of potential; once your young Scorpio has decided on a line of action, you should do everything in your power to help her stick to it and make it to the very top.

## Travel

A nice, quiet, relaxed holiday, with early nights and long hours of sleep, is not going to suit a Scorpio child.

Scorpios take their holidays seriously, and scarcely will one be over than Scorpio will be planning the next, deciding where they want to go and what they want to do, piling up things to take, cajoling parents into falling in with their plans. They won't mind too much where they go as long as there's lots to occupy them — sea sports, of course, but also games of all kinds, and perhaps more than a sniff of adventure within reach.

Actually, though they enjoy planning, they will also like being surprised — both by an unusual holiday in an unusual place, and perhaps by slightly unusual means of getting there. They will specially enjoy colourful and exotic countries where life is as different as possible from their familiar surroundings: north Africa, for instance, or the Far East, or, nearer home, Spain and Italy — but the quiet, inland places rather than the crowded coastline — though beaches where there are mysterious rock pools, caves or grottos will be fascinating to them.

More than perhaps any other sign, Scorpios will relish adventure holidays, and they are tough enough to be able to cope, even at a very young age: grazed knees will be ignored, bruises laughed away, as they struggle along through the sun or the snow — they can put up with high or low temperatures. Remember, though, to provide plenty of liquid if it is really hot, because they tend to dehydrate — and make them wear a sun-hat (they won't like it, though dark glasses will be popular, giving them an air of mystery!) and dab on sun cream because their skin can be sensitive to the sun and burn more easily than they may realize.

Apart from physical action the Scorpio's imagination must be stimulated if they are not to be bored. They enjoy a good mystery, so a holiday which hinges perhaps on a trail of some kind will capture their enthusiasm; they'll also enjoy caving or scuba diving to mysterious depths (when they're old enough). They'd be happy with a telescope in the banks of Loch Ness, waiting for the monster to emerge so that they can snap it with their camera — and a Scorpio will always want a camera to record the holiday, though some may prefer their own sketch-book. One can't get away from the fact that even at best Scorpios have a slightly cruel side to their nature, and a visit to a castle with a dungeon full of implements of torture will bring up some enjoyable goose-pimples; they'll spend ages climing the ramparts and examining the arms and armour. As soon as they're through the door of Madame Taussaud's they make straight for the chambers of horrors, and a visit to HMS Belfast, with all her guns and protective armour, would make a splendid Scorpionic excursion.

There should be no difficulty about food — they'll dive into great bowls of shellfish, paella spaghetti, *moussaka* or eel pie with every sign of enjoyment, though they may live to regret not being a little more cautious on the first evening of the holiday!

## Scorpio as Brother and Sister

With a Scorpio child, I'm afraid you must face up to the fact that if you decide to have another baby she is almost bound — more keenly than most — to feel the pangs of jealousy.

There will be times when she will probably make a fuss and show off to attract attention, and she will occasionally display dramatic tantrums for very little real reason. That's the bad news. The good news is that she will be so fascinated by every stage of your pregnancy and delivery that you shouldn't be surprised if she asks if she can be present with Daddy at the birth.

Remember that she enjoys secrets and surprises, and you can certainly involve her in yours! You can treat the arrival of the new baby as a very special intrigue, talking to her a great deal about whether it is likely to be a brother or sister. Once the baby has arrived you should watch out very carefully for any trace of reclusiveness or reluctance to talk to you about her feelings — it's easy for Scorpios to bottle up their worries, whether they are four or forty, and if they do so when they are little it is very likely that they will continue to do so in adult life. This is not a good thing, especially for people of this sign.

Make a very special effort to tell your young Scorpio everything you can about the baby: when he's cutting his first tooth or eating his first solid meal. Perhaps she can give him a spoonful now and again, for everything which involves her with him will help to counter any jealous tendencies. Without wanting to spread alarm, I should say that very occasionally, and in the most extreme cases, jealousy can actually give rise to physical cruelty; so it really is very important to make Scorpio understand that the new arrival does not in the least weaken your love for her. If she is very little, cuddling her and the baby at the same time will also help. Remembering that she has lots of energy and is able to work hard, I see no reason why you should not also alot her some specific chore to help involve her even more in the life of the family. Encourage her to be particularly gentle with the baby. It will be good for her to develop a sense of responsibility, especially if she is the older child, and if at any point along the way she should fail in her duty, make a strong appeal to her conscience; she is unlikely to forget the incident, and certainly unlikely to repeat her negligence.

When Scorpio is the younger child, she will probably grow up quite quickly, and you will find her imitating her older brothers and sisters at a very early age, giving them a very good run for their money. Her determination to keep pace with them will be a considerable source of amusement. She may tend to dramatize some situations, but you will soon get to know when that is happening and make allowances.

When your children are at the same school there is a good chance that Scorpio will bravely see to it that her brother or sister is properly treated, especially by other classmates. If any problem arises, she could get pretty angry with the offender, and, if the occasion justifies, won't be beyond sending the enemy home with a bloody nose! If, on examining the situation, you find she has over-reacted it is one hundred per cent essential that she is made to apologize; never allow Scorpios to get away with unjustified violence, whether physical or verbal! You must also be on the look out for any slightly sneaky behaviour; when she has to share a room with a brother or sister, for instance, and she doesn't have enough space for all her toys, she may tend to throw out some of theirs, and some much-loved teddy bear may unexpectedly go missing. (I suggest you look in the dustbin — or is the loo blocked?) In spite of all the negative facets of the Scorpio character, there will usually be a tremendously deep bond between brothers and sisters, and once she has come to terms with the presence of another child within the family, she will be extremely loyal and willing to spend a lot of her natural energies enjoying their company, and she will be keen to share in the hard work of looking after them. Sharing common interests will ensure that Scorpio encourages younger siblings to improve skills and knowledge, but I must say she will also see to it that she stays out in front!

## Scorpios as Parents

You will no doubt be thoroughly enjoying a very fulfilling sex life with your partner, but I don't think you are likely to take unnecessary risks, and it seems unlikely that you will enter upon parenthood without having thoroughly discussed the matter beforehand, making quite sure in your own mind that you absolutely want children and are really ready to start a family. Since you enjoy research, no doubt you will have read a lot about the role of parenthood, and neither the various stages of pregnancy nor the early years of child rearing should hold any mystery or horrors for you.

Although it is always good to keep children busily occupied with all kinds of interesting projects, you should be careful that you don't push them just a little too hard!

Of course it is wonderful for any child to be deeply involved in a great variety of activities and have parents who encourage them. Apart from anything else they can then make an early choice of what fascinates them most and build a good foundation for a rewarding leisure life. But you should remember that it isn't everyone who has such a high energy level as yourself, and it is just possible that you may be expecting a little too much of them, especially if you are encouraging them in an area in which you were involved when you were young but were frustrated. Because Scorpios are Scorpios, you, along with some other Zodiac types, may tend to try to superimpose your own image on that of your children, trying to produce little clones of yourself. In all sorts of ways this is wholly unwise; do not expect them to be interested in your interests or fascinated by your preoccupations.

No parent will be more delighted than you when you learn that your children are desperately interested in or have a talent, a gift, for something — almost anything! You will encourage them to develop it to the full, whatever it is, and will make sure there is enough money to pay for clothes, travel, extra tuition. The chances of the child succeeding in the chosen interest are very much enhanced by your enthusiasm.

You may have a tendency to want to find out more about your child's private life than he or she wants to reveal. When she is very young you will need to know what is going on in her life; that may be true when they are older, but you must learn to respect your youngster's privacy. Your natural intuition will always stand you in good stead; rely on it. But you may need to keep check on your equally natural inquisitiveness. If this gets out of hand and you start spying on your child, reading her diary perhaps, that will be the time to remember that you also have a tendency to over-react and may well need to curb it!

It is important to remember that no matter how young you are, times have changed considerably since *you* were small, and though you may have a first-rate relationship with your children, you and they are not of the same generation. It is important that you should try to understand their priorities and listen to their views, which could be very different to your own.

Though always keen to make money, partly in order that your children can enjoy all the good things of life, do aim to keep a balance between work and spending time with them. The hours you spend together will be well spent, and because you enjoy life, you will get no greater pleasure than seeing them catching your enthusiasm and becoming involved in a great many activities.

When your children go to school, try to set some time aside to involve yourself in the PTA; you can use your best Scorpio qualities to detect what is wrong and bring it out into the open. Don't be afraid to air your views, and if you are elected to the committee, you will probably do well as treasurer, helping to raise money and balance the books.

One final word or warning: remember that you sometimes care so strongly about discipline that you may go too far — Scorpios can be very strict indeed. You can also be stubborn to the point that your children will see you as utterly intractable, whether you are in the right or in the wrong. If any of the family accuses you of stubbornness or of not caring to go to the centre of a situation, or listen to their argument, they will probably be right. So try to keep it in mind that flexibility and compromise are in no way a sign of weakness.

## Case Study

Carolyn - Sun and Mercury in Scorpio, Venus in Sagittarius; Mercury Group 2, Venus Group 4.

From the Report: 'Carolyn has hidden depths, and if she is questioned about something she may at times try to fob you off with rather a casual or offhand remark, keeping what she really thinks strictly to herself. This tendency to secretiveness, to keep her true feelings hidden, may be something you will have to accept: quite honestly, I do not think there is very much you can do about it. She herself will be aware of it and will have to come to terms with it in her own way. This could prove a conflict for her, as it is an area of her personality which doesn't quite fit in with her other characteristics. She may therefore find it puzzling, saying to herself "I don't know why I reacted in that way — I just did!"

'While at times she may show twinges of jealousy, she herself needs to feel free, and this is something she and a prospective partner will very definitely have to sort out, for her demands in this sphere of her life will be pretty high. She will probably be highly sexed, but at the same time will like to have men as friends. I think there is a lively and fun-loving side to her nature which will be most endearing to those who come into contact with her when she is older; perhaps this is emerging already.'

Comment: Carolyn's mother requested her analysis when her daughter was twelve and she herself in the throes of a divorce. She could see Carolyn's powerful Scorpio characteristics emerging, and certainly recognized that she had inherited her own somewhat complex needs in emotional relationships. In reading the report she also learned quite a lot about herself.

## The Sun-sign and Its Rulerships

*Countries and areas*: Algeria, Bavaria, North China, Korea, Morocco, Norway,

Paraguay, Queensland (Australia), Syria, the Transvaal, Uruguay.

*Cities*: Baltimore, Cincinnati, Dover, Fez, Halifax, Hull, Liverpool, Milwaukee, Newcastle upon Tyne, New Orleans, St John's (Newfoundland), Stockport, Valencia, Washington D.C., Worthing.

*Trees*: the blackthorn and all bushy trees.

*Flowers and herbs*: in particular dark red flowers; arnica, bayberry, bryony, broom, capers, cayenne pepper, furze, geranium, honeysuckle, hops, juniper, leeks, mustard, nettles, onions, peppermint, rhubarb, tobacco, witch-hazel.

*Food*: all fish; cereals, especially wheat; onions, tomatoes, and leeks; beer.

*Cell salts*: Calc. Sulph., Nat. Sulph.

*Animals*: crustaceans, most insects.

*Stone*: opal.

*Metal*: steel or iron.

*Colour*: Dark red, maroon.

# SAGITTARIUS

## (November 23 - December 21)

Note: Sagittarius is a masculine sign, so for the most part I refer throughout to 'he', but most of my comments refer also to girls.

## General Characteristics

Your Sagittarian child will be enthusiastic, lively, open, and uncomplicated. He will not be difficult to understand.

Sometimes his zest for life will lead him into scrapes, for he likes to take risks, and if someone else dares him to do something he will be unable to resist the challenge. These basic characteristics will emerge when he is really quite young, and you will probably find that they will outline a pattern followed throughout his whole life — the need for challenge and the desire to accept it without question is very much an integral part of the Sagittarian personality.

He will be an energetic child, and it's likely that he will start to move around from a very early age. He'll be daring, and here is a Zodiac type you'll need to protect from hazards in the home, for he will be continually exploring; but it is important not to curtail his freedom so much that you dampen his spirit of adventure. Keeping the balance between allowing him to move about unhindered and warning him about dangers, will not be particularly easy. His open manner will lead him to trust everyone, and here is another area in which care must be taken — you will have to explain very carefully to him the dangers of trusting strangers too completely at first sight, for he will tend to accept gestures of friendship in the spirit in which he thinks they are offered, and may be somewhat at risk.

He should start talking at a very early age and will have good powers of communication. The questions he will ask will have a remarkably adult flavour, and you should not be afraid to stretch his mind when you answer him.

There is something very coltish about the movement of young Sagittarians, and they can be extremely daredevil. They may tend to care too passionately about sport; if you can, persuade them to cultivate a balance between their need for physical exercise and their intellectual interests. The wild young Sagittarian will more than likely eventually develop into a well-rounded, well-educated and highly intelligent man or woman.

The worst fault of this Zodiac group is restlessness. Remember that like those of their opposite sign, Gemini, they are extremely versatile; it is important for them, again like Geminians, to complete each task they start. If they get fed up with what they are doing they will inevitably turn to something else, but the new occupation may not be entirely engrossing either; encouragement of consistency in a wide range of activities is highly desirable so that the Sagittarian's broad potential will develop and restlessness is less likely to take hold.

It's very easy for the young Sagittarian to exaggerate. If he comes home from school in a particularly excited state, bursting to tell you something, it might just be that his tendency to embroider the truth will get the better of him. To counter this possibility I suggest you question him in-depth and pull him up pretty vigorously if you discover any exaggerations or loop holes in his story. If you do not do this when he is young, it could become something of a problem later in life, especially since it could encourage boastfulness.

Sagittarius is known as a most adaptable sign, and should you have to move to another district the move itself should not affect your son or daughter too much, even if they have to change schools — you will find their routine will be far less upset than that of more sensitive Zodiac types. You will probably discover that he will be very generous; you may have to be fairly strict when it comes to doling out the pocket-money. When the time comes to increase it, it will be a very good idea to link it to some achievement, in or out of school, so that he will feel that he has actually earned it rather than that it has dropped upon him from the sky.

There is a natural kindness and charity about most Sagittarians, and you will find that he will be in the van when charity fund raising is under way. It will be particularly good if he can use his love of sport to raise money; he will enjoy the challenge of being sponsored and may well surprise his sponsors by his powers of endurance.

Here we have one of the most informal of all twelve Zodiac types; the men of the sign, for instance, simply hate wearing neckties. Both sexes usually hate formal dress, so make sure your Sagittarian children have plenty of colourful track suits, and more especially some nice polo-neck sweaters; Sagittarians love these — lightweight in the summer, heavier in the winter. However, despite the fact that they dislike the uniformity of school clothes, you may well be amused to discover that much later in life your Sagittarian will continue to wear his school or college scarf with pride, even when university days are long since over. No Sagittarian's winter kit is complete without a big, chunky anorak and boots.

If there is a balance to be kept, it is in the use of their physical and intellectual energy. You may find that your individual Sagittarian is either predominantly physical or intellectual in interests; balancing the time given to study and time spent on the sports field is crucial to his development. You will probably be able to catch a hint of the direction in which young Sagittarius will go by the kind of toys to which he is attracted; if he is crazy about batting a ball about then it is fairly obvious that he will be the sporting type. If, on the contrary, he loves his picture-books he will probably lean more to the intellectual side of life. But I suggest that whether your Sagittarian is colt or filly, you make sure that there are several soft, cuddly animals at the foot of the bed — children of this sign are noted for their love of animals, which may start this way and will soon go on to a demand for real, live pets.

Sagittarians are among the most independent of all Zodiac groups, and along with Arians are extremely adventurous. Also like Arians, they tend to be somewhat reckless, and there's an above-average chance that they will receive more of their fair share of grazed knees and bruises. Watch out for injuries, but don't attempt to crush their spirit.

## The Three Ways of Thinking

Due to the influence of Mercury (see p.13) the Sagittarian mind characteristically works in one of three ways.

★ In the first group are those Sagittarians who are capable of deep, incisive thought; they have sleuth-like minds and are among the most cautious people of the sign. They have good memories and are particularly intuitive; sometimes they can be uncharacteristically secretive.

★★ Among the second group are those extremely optimistic, fun-loving Sagittarians whose sense of humour tends to be boisterous. There will be a remarkable capacity for study, and if the mind is properly controlled, conscientious effort will hone the intellect.

★★★ The third type is capable of logical, rational thought but intellectually may be slow to develop at first. These people are ambitious, good at planning, and couple breadth of vision with a certain natural caution. Optimistic with a practical outlook.

## The Five Ways of Loving

Due to the influence of Venus (see p.13), Sagittarians will tend to express their affection in one of five ways.

★ Those of the first group will have a delightfully romantic side to them and will express their affection with warmth and charm. They have a flirtatious tendency which is pleasantly expressed in their natural charm but can lead them into difficulties.

★★ The second group comprises passionate and highly-sexed Sagittarians who must be aware that possessiveness and jealousy can mar their relationships. They must understand that many people need a certain freedom within a relationship (as they themselves do) and cannot be kept locked up in too intense a partnership.

★★★ Some Sagittarians take a great deal of sheer fun and pleasure in their emotional relationships and may sometimes have more than one partner at a time, which can obviously lead to complications. Intellectual rapport is essential.

★★★★ In the fourth group are the most faithful of Sagittarians; sometimes there is a tendency to marry for money or position and an element of cold aloofness can mar the expression of true emotion, but they will take great pride in their partners.

★★★★★ The final group contains those who need their independence; this can cause conflict when the time comes to deepen a relationship. Freedom of expression within the relationship is essential; possessiveness is not tolerated.

## Health and Diet

Generally speaking, the Sagittarian constitution is robust. There is no lack of physical energy and strong emotion. Provided the energies are kept in balance, you should find that your Sagittarian child is healthy, happy, and very good company.

Sagittarians thrive on challenge, and it is not difficult to relate this to their health and diet. They need a lot of exercise, so to prevent them from stagnating I suggest that even when they are very young you set them little challenges — set them a target for how far they should walk one day, then set it a little further the next; skip fifty times today, sixty-five tomorrow, and so on. That sort of pattern will be fun for them and should also have a very positive psychological effect, encouraging them to set goals for themselves throughout their lives — not only of course in sport and exercise but in other more important areas.

They are very low on the list of Zodiac worriers, so this should not be a particular trouble, and problems should not preoccupy them too greatly. It is very rare for a Sagittarian to shut up like a clam when something is wrong. Should you notice a clouded expression creeping over his face, however, and he becomes a little quieter than usual, encourage him to talk — if he does not the chances are that he has a problem which seems to him to be unusually difficult.

He will have a very healthy appetite and, in due course, will enjoy really hearty food such as rich, meaty casseroles; but never forget that Sagittarius rules the liver, which for him can easily be upset. Watch out for signs of liverishness, especially after your young Sagittarian has attended his first adult party, or has been eating unusual food (see Travel). The body area for Sagittarius covers the hips and thighs, and many of this sign tend to put on weight in spite of healthy exercise. This is not likely to happen when they are very young but it is something to look out for (especially in the girls) at puppy fat time, as they approach puberty. Later, the only way to control fat in these areas will be with a fairly careful diet or at least a well-regulated mealtime routine. Thigh muscles and hamstrings tend to be vulnerable in sport or exercise.

Sagittarius is somewhat accident prone, and because he will love to gallop over the countryside on his real or imaginary pony, climbing, seeing how far he can jump, and such country matters, he will probably get more than his fair share of cut knees.; This is very typical of the fire signs, of which he is one (see p.15). It is not going to be particularly easy to encourage him to be careful, unless you have reason to believe that he belongs to the first group in The Three Ways of Thinking.

You will run into considerable difficulties when he suffers from the usual childish illnesses, for he is not going to be a very good patient. Unless he is really most unwell, it will be practically impossible to keep him in bed — so all I can suggest is that you make sure his room is at precisely the right temperature (don't forget he needs fresh air!) to allow him to scamper about in a very light-weight but warm jacket, rather than staying in bed all the time (provided, of course, the doctor will allow it). When he's well, he'll never want to go to sleep — but when he does, he will sleep well.

When young Sagittarius wants to take something to school to nibble at between meals, he will benefit most from dried fruit and nuts (perhaps covered in yoghurt); so encourage him to call in at the health store rather than the sweet-shop — if that's possible. They will certainly have an eye for large, gooey cakes and pastries, especially those that are rather spicy as opposed to rich in sweet cream, but these are equally fattening — a measure of dried fruit is probably the best alternative, though you may have some difficulty in 'selling' it!

In theory you are very fortunate to have a Sagittarian child, for his or her health shouldn't concern you too much; they are less prone to illness than many other signs, especially illness provoked by tension or worry, and the tendency to psychosomatic illness is negligible. The only serious problem may arise as a result of their tendency to take risks.

## The First Five Years

Your young Sagittarian will start to sit up and take notice from a very early age; you can expect that first beaming smile at least a week before it's due, and before you know where you are he'll be crawling, then walking.

Remember he is by nature adventurous and, as with some other Zodiac types, it is specially important to guard against accidents. All good parents have fire-guards and gates at dangerous places, but I strongly advise you to get this kind of thing thoroughly organized some time before it actually seems necessary.

Sometimes, Sagittarians are hyperactive; though they don't have problems with tension, they find it very difficult to relax, and at birthdays, Christmas and other festivals, try to get loving grandparents and aunts to give them interesting and demanding toys which will fully engage their attention and help them burn up some of that tremendous nervous and physical energy.

The lively Sagittarian mind must also be kept active; here is a group of children who want to read before they go to nursery school. Don't be afraid to teach him his alphabet and numbers as soon as his attention span seems sufficient. ABC books and picture books will be specially popular with him, and because he is an affectionate and loving child, remember my allusion to cuddly toys — especially woolly animals.

The play pattern can be rather erratic; watch out for this — boredom and restlessness can often become quite serious problems later on. Sagittarius is an extremely versatile sign, and you may find that young Sagittarius will be involved in more than one interest at a time. This is not altogether a bad thing, but even from these early days, if he says he is fed up he really *will* be fed up — and that will be the time at which to divert his attention, perhaps to some physically demanding activity or, if he has been running around, to something quieter and more cerebral.

When he asks questions, he won't demand an obsessively detailed answer — he'll accept what you say but will then go about investigating the matter himself, adding to his knowledge through his own efforts. Of course this is highly desirable, and you should encourage it — and encourage discussion which will stretch his intellectual potential (which should be excellent).

He will be more than ready and indeed very eager to join a play group; it will be fun, and once he has settled in — which will probably be about five minutes after he goes through the door — you will see him approaching other children and probably making them laugh as his somewhat broad sense of humour will emerge early in his life. When you must discipline him, appeal to his sense of logic; if he's naughty, it will probably be through thoughtlessness rather than vindictiveness; you can correct him in a nice, simply, straightforward way, for he is basically honest. Always come straight to the point, and if you make a threat be sure to carry it out if he errs again.

## School Years

As with any other aspect of life, your young Sagittarian will be excited at the prospect of going to school.

He will be more likely to enjoy school than children of most other signs; if you have a problem it will be that he may not take things sufficiently seriously. From time to time, disappointment may set in simply because he gets bored with lessons, which he will expect to be lively and entertaining. When and if this does occur it won't be so much his fault as the teacher's, who will probably be unstimulating. Young Sagittarius will simply not be sufficiently challenged in the classroom, and his mind will not be stretched. If there is little you can do about this at school, try to make up for it at home.

The transition from the play group to nursery school should be easy enough, but you could well have a problem if you have to put your young Sagittarian into uniform — especially after the initial pride of being more grown up has worn off! Both sexes tend to dislike conformity and regimentation and will not be happy to look just like everyone else; the moment they get home from school they will dash upstairs and fling their uniform off, being particularly careful *not* to untie their tie. The knot should last the whole term.

One thing Sagittarians will hate is a claustrophobic schoolroom; they will get very fractious in a stuffy, crowded atmosphere. They will simply have to learn to accept the fact that such conditions are sometimes unavoidable, and that they must try to forget the physical circumstances and concentrate on the subjects being taught and the freedom with which their minds can range, within these.

When examination time approaches, it will be a great temptation for Sagittarians to ignore the whole business — and very often the gods are with them; if, on one occasion, they study hard the night before the examination and the questions just happen to be on the subject they've swotted up, they will accept this as an immutable law of school life, and it may well be that they will have to learn the hard way that it is not! If you can encourage your Sagittarian to put extra time aside, well in advance, for revision, by all means do so — but it may not be particularly easy.

One of the most interesting talents Sagittarians possess is a flair for languages: do encourage this at the earliest age — if you go abroad on holiday when he has only just learned to speak, it will be a step in the right direction to teach him to say 'please' and 'thank you' in the language of the country you're visiting. It may well be enough to ignite his interest and is something you and he should consider as a possible specialization, later.

A love of literature and considerable flair for writing essays, compositions, and sometimes poetry, may show itself. There is a tendency for children of this sign to veer more to the arts than the scientific side of school study. The exception is if your child belongs to the third group in *The Three Ways of Thinking* (p.179). His imagination will be colourful, and you will certainly see it emerge if he writes short stories. When he paints, there is a good chance that his pictures will also be highly colourful, with bright flowers and with the Sun in the centre, perhaps with rolling landscape below. (It is an interesting psychological fact that when children omit the sun from their paintings, it can often be a sign that they are unhappy about something; this is especially true of Sagittarians and Leos.)

Their need for challenge can result in a quite competitive spirit, but it is the process of achieving rather than the achievement itself that preoccupies them. Once a goal has been reached, there is very little chance of Sagittarius sitting about resting on his laurels. His attitude will rather be 'I've done that — so what's next?' He will get a lot of this kind of satisfaction if he is involved in athletics rather than heavier team games, though I don't say that he won't enjoy those just as much.

As with all children, his attitude to school will be very much coloured by the attitudes of the teachers he encounters there; he won't hesitate to criticize them if he thinks that he is being taken for a ride intellectually — and he'll certainly tell you if he thinks there is something lacking in a particular teacher. Perhaps more than most children, he will move ahead in leaps and bounds when he is able to work with sympathetic and inspiring teachers; likewise he will be entirely bored and very restless if he has no rapport with them.

Here are Zodiac characters who are open and honest; if Sagittarius is accused of some misdoing, you will be able to get at the truth. Personally, I don't think that you need have any qualms about accepting whatever he tells you — the tendency to exaggerate apart. If you hit a tricky situation when his story conflicts with that of other people, you can probably confidently believe him.

## Out of School Activities

It is difficult to conjure up a picture of a young Sagittarian sitting doing nothing, once school is over — unless, that is, the TV is on and he is watching a programme about wildlife, far off countries, or some intriguing historical or Western drama — in which case, he's not *really* doing nothing, for he'll be taking it all in, feeling that he's actually taking part, experiencing what he sees.

It is good for him if you restrict viewing hours in order that he doesn't spend too long sitting still. It is necessary to encourage inaction with some children, for it can help them relax; with Sagittarians the best relaxation is a change of activity. I have mentioned their dislike of claustrophobic rooms; while they may not complain about having to be indoors for long periods of time, remember that it is particularly good for them to be out in the fresh air, even in unpleasant weather. Provided they are well wrapped up they are unlikely to catch colds or chills, for on the whole they have a pretty robust physique and can cope with the outdoor life.

The Sagittarian sense of adventure will benefit from all kinds of outdoor expeditions — either with you or with youth or scouting groups. There will be times when you will be bound to worry about him — a natural tendency in parents — and yes, his sense of daring will get him into scrapes, but his instinct will distinguish between the just-dangerous-enough and the too-dangerous-to-try. When he has his first bicycle, do everything you can to encourage him to enjoy maintaining it; provided he does not get so intrigued that he takes it entirely to pieces and can't get it back together again, such an interest will make him aware of the necessity to maintain safety standards. Needless to say, protective clothing should be provided for the various sports he gets involved in; if this is expensive, then encourage him to ask for it as part of his birthday or Christmas presents.

If you have in the past read descriptions of the various characteristics of Sagittarius, you will no doubt have found that many astrologers say that Sagittarians love horses and riding, and this is perfectly true with many of them; should your young Sagittarian son or daughter come to love ponies, you should realize that such a passion will be very important to them, and while riding lessons are often very expensive, I would suggest that you do everything you can to arrange some for him or her. It might be possible for them to pay for lessons in part by helping out at the stables, and they can get other part-time jobs to enable them to buy the kit they will need.

Sagittarians are not particularly patient, and the hobbies they enjoy should on the whole show quick results: you will be doing your Sagittarian a service if you encourage him, in at least a few of his activities, to slow down and take more care — his tendency will be to ignore detail.

## Preparing for Life

In no area will the Sagittarian desire for challenge be more relevant than when he reaches the age of puberty and realizes for the first time just how attractive some other human beings are!

He will think of sex as a voyage of exploration and will be very keen to relate his conquests and experiences to his friends. His natural optimism will persuade him that he will always be able to capture the girl of his choice, and when he realizes that this isn't necessarily so, he will be able to shrug his shoulders resignedly and turn his eyes elsewhere. After all, the grass is always greener over the hedge (the motto is very apt for Sagittarians, and particularly so when it comes to the question of their love life).

As soon as you like, you can encourage him to enjoy the company of the opposite sex; it will help him to realize that there is more to life than sex. It may be that when he really falls in love for the first time, he will neglect his studies — nothing unusual about that, but the chances are that he will be more likely to listen to warnings from his girl-friend, when examination time approaches, than from you; so maybe you should cultivate her! If she has worked harder and gets better grades than he, his need for challenge will be renewed, and he will want to regain the ascendancy; the battle will be fun to watch. All this applies, of course, to Sagittarian girls, too — but on the whole girls tend to be more conscientious than boys, so the situation is perhaps less likely to arise.

Young Sagittarians will happily accept sex education and are well able to take it in their stride; they will not be afraid to ask frank and searching questions. It seems unlikely that they will be heavily obsessed with the subject at any stage of their development; their attitude should be very well balanced — like their whole straightforward attitude to life in general. They will want to experiment, like every other growing boy or girl, but they will not take early relationships too seriously. Sometimes it may be necessary for you to point out to them that other people are far more sensitive than them, and that whether they mean to or not (probably not) they can upset partners more than they realize, perhaps just by some casual remark which seemed innocuous to them but has hit their partners hard.

Growing up is an entirely natural process for the Sagittarian who has been to a coeducational school; you will find that the change from child to young adult will be perfectly straightforward. Both sexes will be intrigued but not frightened by the changes in their bodies, though your Sagittarian daughter may need to be reassured that the nuisance of her periods and perhaps the necessity to wear a bra need not cramp her style — especially as there is a distinct possiblity that through her childhood she may have been somewhat tomboyish. If this is the case, you should encourage her to take pride in her developing figure and point out to her that her sporting interests should not suffer — indeed keeping fit is part of being an adult.

Sagittarians are gregarious by nature, so it is very likely that even when they make their first dates they will tend to go round in groups. This should suit them very well, for it presents an additional challenge of friendship as well as bonding — and they will always expect to have more fun in a crowd. After all, if you're out for the day with other couples, you can always split up once you reach your destination.

You may feel that from time to time all your warnings about the various dangers and pitfalls of life have fallen on deaf ears, and certainly you may have to be cruel to be kind — for there is a recklessness about people of this Sun-sign, and it is not always easy to appeal to their common sense. But never underestimate their powers of reason and logic; these may not always be apparent, but one serious mistake or family upset can usually put them back on the straight and narrow for the future.

## Further Education

Astrologers always claim that Sagittarians are *the* students of the Zodiac — eternal students, in fact.

Ask an adult Sagittarian his plans for the autumn, and they will almost certainly include a course of study in one subject or another, and when your young Sagittarian leaves school you can be quite sure that if he goes on to university or technical college or takes some kind of specialized training, he will not only enjoy every moment but will gain a great deal from his study and leisure hours; in fact his time in further education will make a deeper impression on him than on most other people.

Even if he has to leave school and is fortunate enough to go straight into work it might be as well for you to suggest that he take some evening course or other which could lead to an extra qualification that will be of advantage in his new job. Under such circumstances the ever-present need for challenge will be satisfied, and even if the course is a rather expensive one it should certainly prove to be very worthwhile in the long run.

Sagittarian open-mindedness and breadth of vision are well suited to university life. All through student years this type will challenge his teachers with an excellent grasp of the overall concept of his chosen subject. However, where he will have to work harder than most is in absorbing boring facts and details; there is a tendency with Sagittarians not to retain facts terribly easily and to hate to be bothered with what they too often see as unnecessary detail. The intellectual capacity however is excellent, and the more it is stimulated the greater the achievement of the student.

I must however warn you as parents that if your Sagittarian is particularly keen on sport and manages to obtain a university place, there is a high probability that he will vanish into one team or another and all too rarely be seen in the lecture room. Sometimes this is less detrimental than it might seem — there is a considerable cachet, still, in being an Oxford or Cambridge blue, but this does not take the place of a good degree, and Sagittarians when young are sometimes on the wild side and their examination results disappointing. When this is the case it usually indicates that they are learning their lessons the hard way; they will generally make up for lost time after university.

Another astrological tradition insists that young Sagittarians who are especially wild in their youth often become wise philosophers in age, when their intellectual side eventually dominates over the physical.

When Sagittarius first gets to university he will lose no time in getting involved in the various groups and societies available. Because he likes to live every day to the full you can rest assured that even if he tends to neglect certain aspects of his work, he will still derive great benefit from it.

Although you may have managed to persuade him, while he was at school, to do some constructive revision before examinations, you may find that all your efforts go by the board when he is at university. He really is very much the type to revise at the last minute. Nevertheless, he is often capable of producing a brilliant paper when the time comes — so try not to be too concerned if you hear that he is still dashing from party to party, from sports field to theatre, the week before his finals.

It is possible that the Sagittarian natural flair for languages will emerge while he is still at school; as a subject for a degree course they have a lot to be said for them. Many Sagittarians collect good English degrees and many read law. There is also a strong link between this sign and religious studies, so we also find a fairly high number of Sagittarians reading theology.

Overall, despite the attractions of the sports field, this seems to be the ideal sign if you are a student! My best advice to parents of a Sagittarian is to go on encouraging him, whether he is attending university, teachers' training college or polytechnic, or simply on a youth employment scheme, resting assured that he will take advantage of everything he is taught. Sit back and await results!

## Unemployment: Stresses and Strains

It is as well that Sagittarians are optimists — sometimes, they can indeed become blindly optimistic.

Of all Zodiac types they are least likely to be unduly disheartened while unable to find work. Hope springs eternal for them, and provided they keep up the pressure on prospective employers, attending interviews and scouring the newspapers for advertised opportunities, they should be able to remain reasonably buoyant and positive.

There will almost inevitably come a time when Sagittarius has been out of work for a longer time than seems reasonable, and he may well then falter a little. Should this happen, there is a good chance that your encouragement and support will help him enormously, but remembering his capacity for and enjoyment of study surely, the very best thing he can do is devote his spare time to gaining more knowledge which will bring him new qualifications, or perhaps to study something which will fill his time with a pleasurable new hobby. It would be particularly enjoyable for him to take a course of driving lessons — or advanced driving lessons if he has already passed his test. These are often surprisingly inexpensive and are especially good for Sagittarians, who tend to take risks.

Charity field work can also appeal, and if it enables the young Sagittarius to travel abroad, so much the better. He will also find particularly enjoyable and worthwhile any odd jobs he can grab which entail working with overseas visitors.

You may need to check the appearance of your Sagittarian's c.v. and the letters of application he writes to prospective employers; they could give the wrong impression, for they do not pay attention to detail and can also be rather sloppy about presentation. The same thing applies to attendance at interviews; Sagittarians do not always care to bother about 'inessentials' like looking smart and neat, forgetting that not everyone would agree with them. Even when there is a large number of applicants for one coveted position, however, his wonderful, enthusiastic manner and lively expression will stand him in good stead.

It is fair to say that although Sagittarians are eager for new experiences they would have to be in a very desperate position indeed before they would start to experiment with drugs. Yes, they may well smoke too much, and perhaps take a little too much wine or beer — but somehow (perhaps because of their inherent zest for life) the notion of drug-taking is particularly abhorrent to them.

If Sagittarians get involved with drugs, they will unfortunately find it very difficult to give them up — they are so open to new experience that the idea of closing the door on something which on the face of it at first offers a new technicolor world of sensation is unthinkable. However, it is certainly true that once their attention is drawn to the results of drug addiction they will fully recognize their horror; the idea that their intelligence is being blunted will particularly distress them. They will probably have been very keen athletes or sportspeople, too, and will hate the idea of the damage drugs do to the body. Likewise, they are unlikely to take steroids to improve their performance. The best way to help them will be to convince them that there is still a brave, bright world waiting for them outside, once they have kicked the habit; renew their optimism and hope, and they will be well on the way to withdrawal.

## Interests and Spare Time Activities

Generally speaking the young Sagittarian has no problem about enjoying ties of friendship with the opposite sex; the tendency to go round with a group of friends will cling to them rather longer than to many Zodiac types — besides which there is a very strong element of friendship in every Sagittarian love affair, a lively intellectual rapport being important in a Sagittarian partnership.

He will fill every spare hour with a variety of interests ranging from sport to the arts and intellectual pursuits. In the past there was said to be a strong connection between Sagittarius and hunting, and certainly the hunting instinct is present — but today is usually expressed in hunting down bargains, almost making it a part of his regular routine to visit junk and charity shops! We must not forget either, that similar hunting instincts are expressed in pursuit of the opposite sex — and in affairs of the heart the chase is for the Sagittarian just as exciting as the eventual conquest.

Many Sagittarians are very bookish, and those visits to junk shops often result in a large and very tatty collection of second-hand books, with volumes on foreign travel, translations, and stories of high adventure among them.

Some Sagittarians have a flair for restoration and will work happily to set ancient clocks in order or make broken toys work again. Some like working on vintage cars or motorcycles — but in such cases the individual Sagittarian will have to learn to be patient and to work in rather more detail than usually comes naturally to them.

We must not forget that the outdoor life is of great importance to this sign; many will get special pleasure from working with animals, perhaps on a farm or nature reserve. Going on safari and studying the habits of wild animals will also give them enormous pleasure. If they do not have the opportunity for that, any connection with animals is probably a good substitute — they would very much enjoy breeding dogs, for instance.

The young Sagittarian will benefit particularly from taking a year out between school and university, to travel as extensively as possible at that age. Don't be apprehensive if he says he wants to do so; what he gains from the experience will make any worry of yours worthwhile, for he will win more knowledge and experience than he is likely to gain from his formal education.

It is just possible that your young Sagittarian could become involved in a weird religious cult; do watch out for any signs of this, for it could be dangerous — though he does not lack common sense or strength of character, he might find it difficult to return to the family fold even when he realizes his mistake.

Generally speaking Sagittarians are not over-concerned with their image; it will certainly be a very casual one. But should your young daughter say she has to attend a formal function and needs an evening dress, encourage her to choose one which is soft and comfortable and in a style which will not hamper her movements — boned bodices and straight skirts are not for Sagittarians, whereas a full, pure silk skirt with a soft blouse or chemise top will do much for her, and she will be *comfortable*. If for some reason Sagittarius has to wear formal clothes, you will at least be able to say quite truthfully that they look splendid in them.

It is likely that young Sagittarius will involve himself in the running of a club or society; he will be a volatile member of the committee, and because his enthusiasm is infectious he will certainly get things done and spur other committee members into positive action. He has a good overall sense of justice and fairness, so if he becomes chairman his popularity will be no means diminish. He will however need a willing work-horse of a secretary to deal with the fussy correspondence and storms in teacups which always seem to occur!

It may be that he will enjoy going to the races, or perhaps to casinos. A day out on a race-track in the company of good friends can of course be great fun — but should you find he is making a habit of it, or perhaps of slipping into the local betting shop a little too often, I cannot too strongly urge you to do everything you can to distract and discourage him. There is a very strong gambling instinct in Sagittarians, and from time to time this can become quite a serious problem. They enjoy the risks involved and seem not to be conscious of their losses, finding it difficult to stop even when their luck has very obviously deserted them. Happily, for the most part the instinct lies dormant, but for those who get hooked it really can become a serious obsession and a major problem.

## Ideal Careers

We find Sagittarians in all walks of life, and the list of careers which particularly suit them is a spectacularly long and varied one.

There are traditional links between this sign and the law, and certainly many Sagittarians enjoy working as solicitors and barristers. Because of their love of language, many become successful publishers, and others are well satisfied working in the teaching profession (the centaur of the sign was a teacher and sage). These often work best with older pupils, either at senior school level or in further education — they expect a very great deal of their pupils, and are not always particularly patient in coping with younger age groups. The Sagittarian professor lecturing his intelligent young students in a dramatic and witty manner will surely be enjoying himself and is Sagittarius at his best.

Another tradition links this sign with animals, and there are a great many Sagittarian veterinary surgeons; it is certainly a profession your young Sagittarian might like to consider, especially if he has a natural way with animals and is interested in their welfare. The connection with foreign countries also makes its presence felt — many Sagittarians work in the travel industry as couriers and guides; others spend several years living and working overseas and many are preoccupied with exports and work in the export divisions of firms.

I cannot too strongly underline the fact that it is important for members of this lively sign to have a good grasp of foreign languages; this is almost certain to come in very useful indeed at some time or another in their life, often in their jobs. It is frequently the case that the Sagittarian will choose an occupation simply because it will give him the opportunity to see places overseas. They should think very carefully before taking work just on that basis, especially if for instance they are thinking of working as an air steward or on a cruise ship; yes, they will of course travel, but may well end up seeing only the interior of hotel rooms or their cabins and tiny glimpses of foreign places through windows.

It is often said that Sagittarians are *the* philosophers of the Zodiac, and certainly no matter in what circles they move they often develop an admirably balanced view of life; this can stand them in particularly good stead when they have to deal with difficult situations or with superiors who are less intelligent than themselves or who satisfy their ego by throwing their weight about.

It will often be the case that because he learns so much from every experience of life, the Sagittarian will become wise before his years; quite early in his career his opinions will be sought by those who are older and apparently more knowledgeable than he, and they will be heard and respected. From time to time this will probably be a source of surprise and amusement to the Sagittarian, who will probably tend to shrug the whole thing off as if it were nothing very important. But as his parents you will inevitably feel considerable pride at his progress.

It is vital that once Sagittarians have made something of themselves they should be able to go on to further achievements; if they are in a job in which they can only progress to a certain point and no further, they will be bored and restless even before that point is reached — the all-important challenge must be present in their lives if they are to make the best of their potential.

They have a liking for change, and sometimes (rather like their Zodiac neighbours, the Scorpios) will make a change of direction just for the hell of it. They must be careful about this, since they could in the long-term spoil their chances because they have thrown away good opportunities. Sometimes we have to encourage our Sagittarian friends and loved ones to be a little patient, especially if they don't think they are making as much progress in their careers as they should.

If they are self-employed, their enthusiasm for their business will certainly get it off to a splendid start, and because they are good communicators they will not find it too difficult to get their ideas over to their prospective customers or to get easy publicity and put the business on the map. But because of their tendency to take financial risks there is always a chance that they may over-invest or perhaps borrow too much money and start in too big a way. It is therefore a good idea for them to work with a slower, steadier and more practical business partner.

## Travel

Sagittarius is a sign traditionally strongly associated with travel, and it is rare to find a member of this sign who is not delighted to go anywhere for any reason!

Your Sagittarian child will probably start going off on little organized sorties of his own, possibly with friends, at a very early age. If his school announces an organized trip to the country, or better still abroad, they will be the first to plead to be allowed to join it, and will nag away (in the nicest possible way) until you agree. You needn't worry about whether he will cope; he will — the pleasure of travelling will enable him to put up with rough conditions, if he must; he will positively prefer long camping holidays in the most rudimentary tent to short holidays in luxurious hotels. (He can deal with almost any extreme of climate, too).

He will be so delighted at the changing scene that he may be careless — not specially of life and limb but certainly of bag and baggage; he is just the sort to rush to the train window leaving his passport on a seat to be picked up by some passing crook!

It is a very good idea to allow Sagittarius to help you choose holiday destinations and join in all the planning of routes. He will absolutely love juggling the plane and boat timetables to get you where you want to go just when you need to be there. If you take your car on a motoring holiday, announce the fact in plenty of time so that he can spend as many evenings as possible with maps of Spain or France spread over the kitchen table, measuring distances with his school dividers and working out just how you get from Dunkirk to the Swiss border without having to negotiate the Paris ring road! Make sure however that you double-check the route, for once you are in the car and moving, he may well start calling out instructions for short cuts from the back seat and lead you down one-way streets or halfway up mountains; eagerness is not always balanced by consideration and careful thought!

You may find that when your journey has ended and you are safely ensconced in your holiday hotel, the journey seems just to have started for Sagittarius, who will now start planning all sorts of journeys around the area. Let him get on with it, but make it quite clear that he's on his own (if, of course, he's old enough to cope). If you try to keep him under control and tethered to your apron strings there will almost certainly be a row; he will get very restless indeed if he's not allowed to move about, particularly if 'there isn't anything to *do*'. A holiday with a restless Sagittarian is no fun for anybody unless you can learn to relax and let him get on with amusing himself in his own way — which means a sort of perpetual motion!

It is a very good idea to encourage him to learn something of the language of the country in which you're holidaying — if only so that he can ask the way when he's out on his hired bike, or enquire where and when he's to change local buses.

## Sagittarians as Brothers and Sisters

As soon as a younger brother or sister is able to sit up and take notice, your Sagittarian child will assume the role of teacher, teaching them how to count, showing them picture books and games.

Because he is unresentful, broadminded, and straightforward, there is very little chance of your other children suffering too many jealous tantrums or unkind behaviour from Sagittarius. You will probably find that while some children with baby brothers and sisters tend to revert to earlier behaviour patterns, your young Sagittarian will more than likely do the reverse, appearing older than his years because he will find coping with a younger brother and sister a challenge, a good reason for enthusiasm and excitement.

You should be very careful when leaving your children alone together, however, for it will be very easy for the young Sagittarian to assume that baby can do all the things *he* can — so he might lift her out of her pram and start encouraging her to crawl or walk long before she is ready to do so. Needless to say, such a situation could be hazardous — not only to the baby but to Sagittarius himself, who may attempt to lift her and strain himself in the process.

Because he has a good mind, he should cope very well with the news that a brother or sister is to arrive; when you decide to break the news is a matter for you, but remember that he is not particularly patient, and once he knows he will expect you to deliver there and then! — so possibly the longer you leave it the better. He is frank and open-minded, and you can expect him to pass on the news to other members of the family, or to friends, before you may want them to know; perhaps another good reason for delaying.

When Sagittarius is the younger child, he will no doubt goad his older brother or sister into action, and should that older child be somewhat shy and retiring you may conceivably have some problems, because the strong extrovert Sagittarian qualities could tend to make him overshadow a quieter, more introspective member of the family. But Sagittarians are not selfish and will always listen logically to reason, so he should understand when you explain just how different people are, and encourage him to be gentler and to make allowances for his less extrovert brother or sister.

I think you will find that your Sagittarian will enjoy having a brother or sister in the same school as himself. It is possible that quite a lot of friendly rivalry will build up between them, especially if they are in different houses or excel in different subjects. This could spur both children into action, but here again it is really important to point out that we are all very different, and subjects that may seem boring to Sagittarius can be fascinating to the brother or sister — so there is no need for him to scorn her because she is fascinated by algebra while he considers it meaningless nonsense. You may also have to point out that people work at different rates, and that he should not be impatient if brother or sister takes longer than he with homework — or completes it in half the time.

When it comes to room sharing, you may have to go in for a lot of encouragement where tidiness is concerned; Sagittarians do tend to believe that the right place for everything is the floor, where it can easily be found! I suggest that you work out a careful rota which will make it clear who tidies the room on which day; if the place still looks like a pigsty after young Sagittarius is supposed to have had his turn, both you and his brother or sister should come down on him like a ton of bricks!

It is particularly good for Sagittarians to share an interest in a household pet — but he may get very fed up with having to care for it, so the operative word is 'sharing'. There will be little point in getting him a hamster unless you are ready to clean out the cage from time to time — on the other hand, a family pet can be a splendid way of helping to cement a relationship between him and his brother and sister, for while from time to time there will be lively arguments as to whose turn it is as to walk the dog or change the fish's water, his natural sense of justice and ability to see reason should be developed, as will his consideration for his siblings.

## Sagittarians as Parents

Watch it! You are optimistic, devil-may-care, and enjoy a lively sex life, and you may tend at such times to throw caution to the wind. If you've bought this book you're presumably about to become parents or already have children — but if you didn't really plan them, at least you can carefully plan the next, or encourage your partner to take the responsibility.

You make wonderful parents, however, and are as enthusiastic and optimistic about parenthood as about everything else in life. But there is a golden rule that applies especially to Sagittarian women, and I cannot too strongly urge you to think about it: because you have a good mind and need challenge — and setting aside the fact that bringing up a child is in itself of course interesting and demanding — it is one hundred per cent essential that you have at least a few hours a week right away from your children; if you don't you will become stagnant, and Sagittarian restlessness will become a problem. As your children reach the toddler stage, in spite of the fact that you love them dearly and want them to develop quickly, you will find that their limited conversation will bore and frustrate you. That is why contact with the outside world, preferably outside the home, is so essential for you; you really must be involved in something that fascinates you and stimulates your mind — perhaps a lifelong interest, perhaps a new study course. Provided you have this outlet for your intellectual aspirations, you will rank among the best Zodiac people where good parenthood is concerned. Generally speaking, that particular problem is less likely to arise where Sagittarian fathers are concerned, but the same rule would of course apply if you happen to be a father bringing up children alone, or if you are perhaps out of work and have reversed roles, mother being out for most of the day while you look after the children.

Sagittarians have a spendidly constructive attitude towards their children, treating them on equal terms and not finding it difficult to become involved in their interests. This is because the sign is adaptable by nature. The generation gap too, should be no serious problem, for you will thoroughly enjoy discovering what your children and their contemporaries are thinking and doing. Because you have a wide variety of interests, you will from time to time almost dazzle your children with new ideas; remember not to expect them to fall with equal enthusiasm upon all of them — don't be impatient if their progress isn't as speedy as you would wish. Not everyone's mind works at the pace of yours! To help them in the best possible way, you might well have to go in for rather more detailed explanations and develop greater patience than you perhaps at first realized.

Provided Sagittarian mother manages to keep up her own interests, both she and the Sagittarian father will enjoy the leisure time they spend with their children. They won't lack ideas for outings picnics, days out — perhaps at leisure parks or sporting events. Try to achieve a balance, arranging visits too to galleries, museums and places of historic interest — for your sake as well as the children's. Your fascination should be infectious, and the greater variety of entertainment you can offer them, the quicker you will find out where their real interests lie; you can then in due course be more selective and specialist.

You will probably spend more time discussing the best type of school to which you send your children than most people (and see *School Years*, p.182). Should you spend your hard-earned money on private education? or opt for state education and spend the cash on specialist out of school training? or save for mind-expanding holidays abroad? It may well be that you will decide on the latter. But once your children are settled at school, your involvement in its organization — via the PTA — will be above average. At social occasions many Sagittarians will enjoy running side shows and won't be beyond making fools of themselves to raise some extra money. You will also enjoy organizing school visits, or additional treats for the children during the school holidays.

# Case Study

**Robert** – Sun and Mercury in Sagittarius, Venus in Capricorn; Mercury Group 2, Venus Group 4.

From the Report: 'I think you have a considerable potential for accountancy, which will be well directed and used in that career, but there is a great deal more to say about your career potential than just that. Perhaps in the very long run accountancy could possibly be a means to an end: while it is certainly a career you will enjoy, it may well be that you will, over the years, move on to other perhaps broader areas of work, using accountancy as a good solid background but aiming rather higher at a career which may allow broader scope.

'I think you may well find that your career will never be static for long. Without being too dogmatic or at all fatalistic, I can say that you will also find that you are likely to make some fairly important changes of direction during your working life, and it is not beyond possibility that some of them could be pretty drastic. This is very much part and parcel of your life pattern — and it is a positive indication. Still, I should warn you that there is a part of you that may always suspect that the grass is greener on the other side of whatever fence you are working near! Challenge is vitally important to you, and you could well feel tremendously attracted to new projects, always looking forward to what you feel you want to do next, where you go from here . . .

'Should you allow that area of your personality to dominate your decisions and emotions, you might quite possibly find yourself making changes for the sake of doing so, which would definitely not be a positive use of your excellent progressive potential.'

Comment: When I wrote this report for Robert he was about to go to a 'crammer' to improve his A-level maths. The quotation speaks for itself. Any Sagittarian who is planning (for want of a better word!) a conventional and predictable career must consider whether it offers enough challenge, and whether once settled in it, restlessness and dissatisfaction may not bother them. In this case Robert's flair for business and finance was emphasized by his Group 4 Venus (Venus in Capricorn) and other elements of his individual birth-chart.

## The Sun-sign and Its Rulerships

Countries and areas: Arabia, Australia, Chile, Hungary, Madagascar, Pakistan, Provence, Spain, Tuscany, Yugoslavia, the Vatican City.

Cities: Avignon, Budapest, Bradford, Cologne, Naples, Nottingham, Ohio, Sheffield, Singapore, Stuttgart, Toledo (both Spain and U.S.), Toronto.

Trees: lime, birch, mulberry, chestnut, ash, oak.

Flowers and herbs: balm, bilberry, borage, cinnamon, dandelion, dock, mosses, pinks, sage, thistles; carnations.

Food: asparagus, tomatoes, onions, leeks.

Cell salts: Silica, Kali Mor.

Animals: horses, animals that are hunted.

*Stone*: topaz.

*Metal*: tin.

*Colour*: dark blue, royal purple.

# CAPRICORN

## (December 22 - January 20)

Note: Capricorn is a feminine sign, so for the
most part I refer throughout to 'she', but most of
my comments refer also to boys.

## General Characteristics

It is likely that from a very early age life will be real and earnest for your Capricornian
child, who will tend to take herself extremely seriously; she will not, for instance,
simply be childishly inquisitive but will have her own very important reasons for
every question she asks.

You may well find that even when she is very young indeed she will be remarkably
grown up — what used to be called an 'old-fashioned' child — giving the impression
that she learned a great deal about life before she was born. There will be times
when she may tend to take herself far too seriously, and if you find this to be the
case it will be important to appeal to her naturally off-beat sense of humour — one
of Capricorn's most delightful characteristics which, like the serious outlook on life,
will emerge when she is very young.

She will be a very matter-of-fact kind of child and will store her knowledge in
an extremely logical and practical way. She will probably have a very good memory,
and there will be little need for you to tell her anything more than once.

Most Capricorns are conventional, and certainly like everyone to behave primly
and properly — to the point at which it may be necessary to explain from time
to time that life cannot be lived always and entirely by the book.

You will find that she will accept discipline well and often without comment,
but if *she* disapproves of something you can be quite sure that *you* will hear about
it — Capricorn grumbling, at all ages, is notorious.

Having said all that, we must not forget that Capricornians can also be giddy
mountain goats, who particularly enjoy their own achievements and love life and
are enormously ambitious. High on the list of Zodiac hard workers, many start from
modest beginnings and go on to great things.

It may well be that your young Capricorn will lack self-confidence. Interestingly, she has the capacity to be very self-confident indeed, but this positive side of her nature needs careful nurturing; she will feel disgusted with herself if she fails a test, for instance, and her outlook could become pessimistic — in such a case do remind her of her past achievements, exaggerating a little if necessary. The best kind of progress she can make will be slow and steady; try not to force her and think of the whole process as one of gently but firmly walking behind her, encouraging her every step but allowing her to take it for herself.

She will be extremely reliable and will like her life to be lived within a steady routine — this will satisfy her need for security. She could become somewhat addicted to routine, and I think it is always good for a Capricorn to be suddenly jolted off the rails from time to time; start the process when she is quite young by springing unexpected surprises on her. She may not always appreciate this, or enjoy it much, but after all life isn't always entirely predictable, and she must be made aware of the fact.

It will probably be the case that you are very modern in outlook; maybe you have opinions about the way you want to bring up your child which are ahead of current thinking. But when your child is a Capricorn there are some difficulties in the situation, for she will almost certainly be very conventional in outlook, and her attitude to life could be very different to yours. Do take this into consideration when, during her early years, you have to make important decisions on her behalf.

It is very important that Capricornians keep moving; sometimes their physical energy can fall almost to nil — their metabolism occasionally tends to be slow, or to become slow. A good long walk to school will do no Capricorn any harm at all.

On the whole those of this sign are 'careful' with money; if you notice any hint of over-caution or meanness, do counter it immediately — encourage your young Capricorn to give to children's charities, thus setting a pattern which will hopefully help to prevent her being too close with her money when she is grown up. She should have a good business sense, which is fine, but you may need to teach her that hard earned money is to be enjoyed as well as manipulated or just kept in a bank.

I don't think you should have too much trouble when it comes to warning her of the danger of talking to strangers; by nature she may seem distant and aloof even to relatives and potential friends, but she will respond very well to your well-chosen words.

Because she is conventional she will probably take great pride in wearing school uniform — indeed she may well not want to change out of it after school! You will find she will look terrific in rather dark colours, but you could also encourage her to relax in some of the softer pastel colours — perhaps pale blue or green. The boys of the sign should also look good in and enjoy wearing wool sweaters in those softer shades.

Perhaps one of the most important things to consider when bringing up a young Capricorn is their tendency either to be extraordinarily ambitious or to seem over-cautious about anything that sounds remotely difficult. It should not be too hard to discover into which category your individual Capricorn falls: if she is of the ambitious sort, you will be well away. Your role as a parent will be exciting — and who knows, at times you may even have to hold her back a little. But if she is the fearful kind, and just wants to coast along without making too much effort, do realize that it is not because she is lazy but because she lacks that essential confidence in herself and her powers.

The emotional level of people with a Capricorn Sun-sign is not likely to be very high (though see *The Five Ways of Loving* below, because their expression of affection can vary). Generally it is the case that they are on the whole undemonstrative and reluctant to show their feelings. Obviously this is not very helpful in any area of life, and it will be a good thing for you to try to encourage your Capricornian to say what she really feels from her very early years, and not bottle up her worries and problems no matter how unimportant they seem to her to be. Encourage her to enjoy life and have fun, and if she is at all uptight remember that it is important that she learn to let her hair down from time to time.

## The Three Ways of Thinking

Due to the influence of Mercury (see p.13), the Capricornian mind characteristically works in one of three ways.

★ The first group will undoubtedly have an uncharacteristic optimism and enthusiasm to their nature. They will enjoy challenge, and their Capricorn ambition will be imbued with a positive outlook and breadth of vision.

★★ In the second group we have the serious, constructive thinkers. Children in this category are often slow starters at school. They must be allowed to develop at their own pace and should be encouraged rather than pushed. Considerable mathematical and scientific ability is often present.

★★★ The final group comprises remarkably original Capricorns, but there is sometimes conflict between expression of the conventional self and a desire to act in a very unconventional manner. Intraction can be a problem. Here again, scientific prowess is also present.

## The Five Ways of Loving

Due to the influence of Venus (see p.13), Capricornians will tend to express their affection in one of five ways.

★ The first group has a high emotional content and considerable passion; those Capricornians will love very deeply — though sometimes jealousy can mar their relationships. They must learn not to suppress their emotions or for reasons of their own inhibit their sexual expression.

★★ There is a remarkably jovial, flirtatious streak in the second group of Capricornians. They will enjoy many relationships and perhaps be somewhat less faithful than most Capricorns. Generally they will get much pleasure from life and are unlikely to be mean with money.

★★★ Those in the third group are extremely loyal and faithful to their partners, many having one great love in their lives. Sometimes it is a little difficult for them to express their true feelings, and this can come between them and deep fulfilment in a loving relationship. An older partner is sometimes favoured.

★★★★ In the fourth group are people to whom independence is extremely important. Often dynamically and magneticaly attractive to the opposite sex, they will develop an individual life-style and often be very reluctant to sacrifice it for marriage or a permanent relationship.

★★★★★ In the final group are those who have some wonderfully kind, loving and affectionate qualities. Their emotional level is high, but they may tend to think that they have little to offer a prospective partner. They need to develop self-confidence in this sphere of their lives and know they have much to offer.

# Health and Diet

The sign rules the knees and shins, so when your young Capricorn starts to get mobile, be prepared for her to bruise and cut her knees more than most children of her age.

Capricorn usually have strong, wiry bodies, but it is very important that they keep moving, for their joints are also traditionally ruled by this sign, and there is an undeniably greater tendency for them to suffer — in age — from rheumatism and arthritis; even young Capricorns are not exempt, and sometimes complain of aching legs and pains in the joints.

With this in mind one would think that they would not do particularly well in cold weather, but usually the reverse is true — they thrive in it and often flag when it is too warm or humid.

Capricorn is quite high on the list of Zodiac worriers, so that you may discover that your Capricorn is not always as optimistic in outlook as you would like. When she is worried her expression will change and she'll probably become quiet. It may be that she lacks confidence in herself, and that in itself can cause tension and the eventual outcome might well be digestive problems or some weird untraceable tummy aches. These are most likely to occur during term-time — when the real reason will more than likely be concern over some exercise or study project.

On the whole, Capricorn children should thrive on a well-rounded, simple diet. You should find that she will like fairly hearty stews and casseroles, and perhaps fish dishes. Like her personality, her taste in food will be somewhat conventional, and you may have some difficulty in persuading her to try new dishes or unusual food of any kind. If she is at all picky about her food, try to encourage her to eat nuts and cereals, for it will be particularly good for her to have food high in fibre, calcium, and protein to help to build and maintain her energy level.

It will be very worthwhile for you to encourage your young Capricorn to take care of her skin. This should be fine-textured, and she should from an early age get into the routine of using a light moisturizer. Fine skin is an asset to any girl, and her careful grooming will preserve it against the ageing process. The skin will probably be particularly sensitive (in boys as well as girls) and the sun might treat it badly. Cleansing the skin properly is particularly important for both sexes, especially at puberty, when there could be more than usual trouble with spots and other blemishes. Of course you will take your children to the dentist regularly, and this is particularly important for Capricorns, who either have superb teeth (in which case the dentist will reassure you and them), or there will be an above average number of problems, in which case the earlier they are discovered and treated, the better. With this in mind it is fair to say that it is vital that Capricorn children in particular should eat as little chocolate and sweet, sticky food as possible. They should enjoy roasted peanuts and fresh fruit, apples, pears and bananas — even the occasional raw carrot or some other vegetable — at snack time.

In some respects your young Capricorn may quite enjoy the process of having to stay in bed when she suffers from one of the common childish illnesses — the extra attention will make her feel important, and as she is naturally patient there should be no prospect of boredom making her too restless. Picture-books, if she is young, and good long story-books when she is older, will pass the time.

If she goes through a period when she does not sleep well, it is more likely to be caused by worry than anything else, and you should always keep this in mind even if she does not talk about her problem. Maybe a classmate or a teacher has wounded her sense of pride, or she has been unjustly chastised. Have you put her nose out of joint in some way? You must get at the root of the problem, perhaps going in for a little extra cossetting in order to restore her confidence and allow her to sleep peacefully once more.

Finally, make sure that she has regular exercise and regular meals — with Capricorns, routine solves any number of problems.

## The First Five Years

It is likely that a young Capricorn child will take life very seriously and have a remarkably mature outlook.

In many ways she will be quite a paragon, accepting discipline and enjoying carrying out any regular task you care to set her. It is particularly good to make her responsible for something specific quite early on in her life, for this will increase her self-confidence and prove to you that she is extremely reliable and trustworthy. It will also encourage her natural ambition if when she does well you praise her and recommend that she try something a little more difficult.

Because she is basically rather a serious child, it is quite important that you develop her sense of fun and pleasure. While for many Zodiac types it's necessary to restrict trivial occupations such as watching cartoon films on TV, this is probably quite a good thing for young Capricorns, especially if you watch them together, and she sees that light-heartedness and a sense of fun are not a waste of time.

It is never too early to give young Capricorns books and toy musical instruments; they love reading, so the sooner you can involve them in the printed page the better. Let her early books stir her imagination rather than satisfy her practical knowledge — the practical side of her personality will be automatically satisfied, while her imagination will benefit from a little prompting. Rather than books containing run-of-the mill illustrations of everyday things and events, she should be provided with more adventurous picture-books with imaginative illustrations — perhaps some of the wonderful Arthur Rackham pictures of elves, fairies and the supernatural. It is as well to bear her imagination in mind when deciding what regular task you should give her; watering a fast-growing plant, for instance, would be ideal, for she could see it changing and developing.

Capricorn is an earth sign (see p.15), and you should remember that those of this element sometimes tend to be literally too down-to-earth, too practical. To counter this, it is good, especially during the early formative years, to encourage an appreciation of the lighter side of life, and to stimulate the imagination. In other words, do what you can to invigorate what can sometimes be a slightly stuffy personality.

When it's time for Capricorn to go to her first play group, you may find her taking a backward step in her development for a few weeks. This will be because of the change in her routine, and maybe some slight feelings of insecurity as a result of being away from home for the first time. Don't give in to your instinct to take her away immediately; play group is just what she needs — and you can certainly stress the 'fun' side of the experience — and the fact that she will have bigger and possibly grander playthings there. As is always wise with children who are apprehensive about their first experience with other children, you might try to arrange that she meet them before she first goes to the play group.

## School Years

It will certainly have been to your young Capricorn's advantage if you have been able to take her to attend a play group, for then, when she starts nursery school, she will already have had the experience of being away from you for set periods of time and will know what it is like to be with other children and under the care of a virtual stranger.

You will probably find that she will tend to be something of a loner. Don't worry too much about this; remember that Capricornians are very loyal, and once a tie of friendship is formed there is a very good chance of it lasting for a long time. As this is true of the adult, so it is true of the child.

While in many respects she will feel secure and thrive in a conventional school with a reasonably strict code of discipline, it can happen that she becomes almost too concerned with morality — with what's right and what's wrong; while the background of a conventional school is excellent, she may sometimes need to let her hair down (or have it released for her!) and go a little wild. You will find that she will get great pleasure from athletics and sports which allow her to express her naturally competitive spirit; that is an excellent area in which to encourage her to relax, providing a balance to her more serious preoccupations.

You can expect her progress at school to be gradual rather than brilliant, for she is by nature a plodder rather than a leaper. She will take school work very seriously, and her exercise-books will probably be a model of neatness. If by chance she hits a period when she says she 'doesn't care' or 'can't be bothered' or is simply fed up, it is very likely that she will have some problem which she may be reluctant to disclose. Her attitude towards difficulties at school will probably be coloured by the influence of Mercury (see p.199); your line of approach should be geared to her own attitude — try to decide which group she belongs to. Whatever this is, you should be on the look out for any loss of self-confidence; she is probably more sensitive than you realize, and you may have to go in for quite a bit of reassurance in order to set her back on an even keel. It is also worth remembering that Capricorns really do enjoy the occasional grumble, and that while you should take her seriously, there will be times when she'll actually be grumbling about nothing!

I don't think you will have much difficulty in persuading her to do sufficient revision before examinations; in her methodical Capricornian way she will have worked out just what she needs to do, and although she may be somewhat apprehensive at the thought of the examination itself, she will be extremely ambitious. Provided she is reasonably confident her ambitious streak will be a great spur to success. If she is very academic and studious it will probably be a very good thing to encourage her to have a little break from time to time, perhaps organizing some small diversion (a visit to a cinema or a concert) in order that she does not cram too much. At times she may find it quite difficult to relax and will need help if she is not to have difficulty sleeping — or simply read far into the night.

You can be pleased if, at the end of each term, you find she has risen two or three places in her form; such steady progress means that she will be gaining in self-confidence and applying what she has learned in just the right way for her. You should give her a treat of some kind as reward for a good school report — even if you are slightly disappointed that her results aren't rather better. And don't forget that during the holiday she should be encouraged to relax and enjoy some light-hearted fun — perhaps, too, a change of scene.

If the question of boarding-school arises, it will not be altogether a disadvantage to her, though she may not find it easy to be cooped up permanently with a large group of girls. Problems may stem from a lack of privacy, for she is probably a self-contained person who will not always want to be with other people. However, the boarding-school atmosphere will bring her out of herself, and once she has settled in she could well develop into a giddy mountain goat, helping to organize midnight feasts in the dorm and being an extremely useful member of the school hockey team or orchestra.

Because she can take responsibility, she may well rise to be head girl of her school, or at least a prefect. She will certainly fulfil this role well, but in some respects it can set a distance between her and her contemporaries, which is not a specially good thing for her. Capricornians can cope perhaps better than members of any other sign with a lonely senior post, and in an authoritative position she must always be encouraged to use her wonderful sense of humour, especially when she has to exercise her authority — otherwise she will almost certainly lose friends, and eventually respect, because she may tend to be thought of as remote and unapproachable.

## Out of School Activities

When considering how your young Capricorn should spend her leisure hours, two things are important: she should be encouraged to take part in activities that involve a lot of physical movement, and what she does should involve her sense of ambition and allow the opportunity for achievement — challenge and the accomplishment of objectives are important to her.

Ideally she should belong to some kind of sports club — whether to play a team game or to go on expeditions of some sort (perhaps rock-climbing); the choice will be hers. When she is a little older, she may well appreciate the opportunity to learn to ski; many Capricorns enjoy winter sports. If her school offers some kind of expedition which would take her into remote areas of a foreign country, it would really be an excellent idea for her to join it; though these trips are expensive, the expense would be justified.

You may find that she is a natural musician, and if she asks for music lessons you should not automatically dismiss the idea as a temporary craze; people of this sign rate high in the musical Zodiac. She will benefit enormously from membership of a youth choir or orchestra; if this is not connected with the school, it will be even more valuable, for she will then be meeting unfamiliar children from widely different backgrounds. In passing it is only fair to say that Capricornians tend to be social climbers, and sometimes an element of snobbery can be seen. Watch out for this unlovely characteristic when she is very young, and try if you can to counter it — perhaps by making sure she meets children less fortunate than herself (one of the reasons why it is excellent for her to join an organization with a very catholic membership).

Even if your Capricorn shows no interest in performing, it is likely that she will appreciate music, and you can encourage her to develop the broadest possible tastes — she will probably take classical and pop music with equal pleasure.

When it comes to craftwork, the 'earth' element makes it presence felt once more: many Capricorns love gardening and looking after plants; sometimes they like to grow exotic vegetables, so you may find you have a fine regular supply of asparagus to hand. If there is any chance of her helping out at a local garden centre or market garden, this will be most enjoyable for her, and perhaps also lucrative. Like members of their fellow earth-signs Taurus and Virgo, Capricorns find it psychologically rewarding to work with natural materials — so here we have potential potters, weavers, sculptors and wood-carvers. Model-making, too, can be popular and rewarding.

You may find your young Capricorn deep in a copy of the *Financial Times* or some company report — and if they are, the chances are that they are already in imagination chairperson of some big business. Fine! Obviously she is ambitious and heading straight for the top. You might encourage a loving grandparent to present her with a little capital, in order that she can, in a very small way, start to play the stock exchange — some shares can be bought in small quantities for a few pennies.

## Preparing for Life

Although many young Capricorns show considerable intellectual and behavioural maturity at an early age, they are often slow to develop, emotionally.

Sometimes increasing awareness of their physical development and sexual needs can be somewhat frightening to them, and they may need an above-average amount of help and guidance throughout puberty. It will be worth your reading *The Five Ways of Loving* (p.199-200), and considering in what way you think your particular Capricorn will express his or her love, for each type will need a rather different kind of guidance.

In general, once they fall in love, they fall very hard and make wonderfully faithful partners. Their attitude to sex is extremely responsible, and they will respond well to sex education — though when they come to put their knowledge to practical use it is very probably that some inhibition and shyness will betray itself and somewhat cramp their style. It may be that it will take rather longer with them than with members of some other Zodiac signs to achieve full expression and satisfaction within an emotional and sexual relationship.

The Capricorn attitude to growing up is most interesting: from childhood they have probably never felt anything other than mature. On the surface, dating should come entirely naturally to them, and when Ms Capricorn goes off on her first date she will give the impression that she is an experienced woman of the world; underneath, however, she will be a vulnerable girl. It will be easier for her to accept the opposite sex on her own terms if she has attended a coeducational school — but that may turn out to be a mixed blessing, for she will then be so used to coping with boys as friends that the step from friendship to love and sex could seem to her to be almost impossible.

For various reasons she may find a first boy-friend when she is fifteen or sixteen and somehow convince herself that she must be faithful to him well into her seventies — discovering too late that it is quite a good thing to have a fairly wider experience before making a lifetime commitment. It is an excellent thing if she can be encouraged to go round in a group of half a dozen or so friends. That will help counter her tendency to be a loner and if she is part of a group there is a very good chance that she may gain experience with more than one partner.

She will always have a tendency to want to look up to her partners. This is good, because if he is more academically inclined than she — or if he makes more money — she will naturally want to reach at least the standard he sets. But you may well have to dole out not only a lot of advice but a lot of serious plain speaking if she chooses a partner who is considerably older than she — something this Zodiac type tends to do. (Remember here that I am not simply speaking about the women — the men are equally likely to seek maturity in their partners.) No doubt they will claim that age does not matter; it may not, at first, but problems do tend to develop later.

It is likely that your Capricorn son or daughter will demand a high level of friendship within their emotional relationships — it is not just a question of needing a good *rapport* with a partner; they should work together to build themselves a good life. There is often a strong accent on material success, so there can be a joint working relationship within marriage, and this is usually successful. If Capricorn's prospective partner is unambitious, she must learn to instil him with all her forward-looking aspirations and give him every encouragement to make as much of himself and his potential as possible — and she must understand it will be no good her becoming deeply involved with a stick-in-the-mud, for the chances are that should that happen the relationship will swiftly pall and her tendency to grumble will become a constant moan (perhaps not without good reason, but it will not contribute to happiness in the home). When choosing a partner she should always ask herself 'Has he good potential?' If she can honestly say yes, then from a practical, sound beginning will grow trust and loyalty which will eventually lead to a full and faithful expression of love.

# Further Education

A Capricorn who has worked steadily and well during school years will probably go on to work in the same way at university or polytechnic.

You may think that this is the case with all Zodiac types, but that is not necessarily true — many youngsters are so delighted to leave school that they look on life at college as a blessed release from the obligation to work. Some Capricorns are in danger of taking an over-serious atittude to university life, but hopefully as they settle into the new routine they will be encouraged to get involved in the social side of student life, so leavening study with a certain amount of fun — perhaps more than they anticipated.

Ms Capricorn will probably be a conscientious student, then, and will certainly work hard on essays or research, but at lectures and discussions there may be times when she feels she has little or nothing to contribute, and she could be somewhat reluctant to join in debate and argument. However, as her confidence grows you may well see a considerable turnabout in her attitude, and if for instance she is anything of a political animal her skill in debate will be well-employed, and will be something to be reckoned with. Her extremely off-beat sense of humour will be an advantage here, and you could find her involved in university theatricals — maybe writing satirical sketches and even taking part in them.

In theory, she should be very good at budgeting her grant — but we must never forget the Capricorn tendency to go social climbing, and there will be times when she will want to show off a little and might spend rather too much on entertaining people who matter to her, or students from a different social background with which she identifies. Needless to say this can be an expensive occupation, and is rarely as rewarding in any sense as Capricorn expects; if she complains that she has spent all her money and is living on junk food, the reason will probably be that she has over-spent for what may be rather silly reasons.

As I have said (see *School Years*), her attitude to examinations and revision for them is probably pretty sound, and it will not be too difficult for her to make time for study by cutting herself off from more exciting diversions. Her lecturers and teachers will either make or break her — her progress will be linked to their attitude towards her. If she has a healthy sense of her own value and has an instructor who is bitter and sarcastic, she will know precisely how to hit back at him — and the clash could spur her on to considerable progress; but if she is the apprehensive or nervous type his effect on her could be quite damaging, and she will have to look elsewhere for inspiration. If she is living at home and working from there, do try to ensure that she is taking some time out for pleasure as well as spending her life studying; it could go either way, with too much work and too little play, or — if she particularly enjoys the social scene — the other way around, with a somewhat devil-may-care attitude to study. The chances are that she will learn the hard way; failure and poor examination results will damage her sense of pride.

It may well be that throughout her school years Capricorn has been very much involved in some extramural study, perhaps in an all-engrossing hobby. If she shows real devotion to it, it is very likely that she will make a go of it as a profession. For instance, if she spends years studying the flute and has achieved good grades, the opportunity to go on to music college should not be automatically dismissed, even if music does not seem on the face of it a job for an ambitious Capricorn. She would be quite likely to find a position with a symphony orchestra when her training is complete, and perhaps even go on to be a soloist. It is particularly good for Capricorns to follow through a pattern of this kind; it is another very important way in which they can express natural faithfulness and loyalty — in this case to a theme or preoccupation rather than a person — which will eventually lead to a permanent relationship and the achievement of an ambition. What more could any Capricorn want?

## Unemployment: Stresses and Strains

Young unemployed Capricorns should be encouraged to treat their situation in a completely rational and businesslike way.

All along the line you should give them a great deal of moral support, for as time goes on, and there is little or no response from prospective employers, despondency will set in more firmly than with most other Zodiac signs. 'I'm no good at *anything*', will become a constant complaint.

Past achievements mean a lot to Capricorns, and they are always heartened to remember them. So make sure that your young Capricorn includes every past triumph in her c.v. — even if some of them seem insignificant. It may be that she will take the view that some things are not worth including, that no employer would be interested in them, but she must be convinced that this is not the case — and, indeed, it is not. Apart from which, seeing her past achievements set out like battle honours she will be reassured that she has already made a mark in life, and this will cushion her against dispondency.

If Capricorn can be persuaded to be assertive and forthcoming, her chance of impressing employers at interviews will be enhanced, for they will see her practicality, the logical and sensible way in which her mind works; generally speaking, you need not fear, when she goes for an interview, that she will not see to it that her image is just right for the occasion. Doing things properly is important to every Capricorn.

Bearing in mind the fact that Capricorns are quite prone to worry, she could find it difficult to relax; make sure she doesn't begin to lose interest in any of her hobbies or spare time occupations — she must keep up her sporting activities and exercise regimes; she must also have a bit of peace and quiet — however she likes to achieve it. She is among the Zodiac characters who could tend to want to cut out when she feels that things are going really badly; spur her into keeping up regular action and job-hunting, specially if you find that she is rising later and later in the morning — bed can represent a psychological retreat from her problem. The right attitude to that problem will mean that she will adopt a regular, steady routine of tackling it. There will be times for visiting the library and going through the advertisement columns, times for writing letters, times for relaxation, and so on.

In many ways Capricorns are less likely than people of most other signs to slip into the drug habit — apart from anything else, they will be outraged at the enormous sums of money that have to be paid for the stuff! Surely, she will tell herself, there are other more productive ways of throwing money away than this? Should you suspect that she has turned to drugs, however, take advice on how to cope with the problem. It may, sadly, mean reporting to the authorities and getting medical help. This may seem an unpleasant step to take, but Capricorn reacts best to a considerable shock. The sudden appearance of a doctor or a social worker or even the police might in itself be sufficient to snap her out of the habit, which she will only have adopted in extremity and as the result of a complete loss of self-confidence. Remember that her family is very important to her, and the fact that she is letting you down badly and behaving disloyally will, if you can bring it home to her vividly enough, make a strong impression.

If there is someone within your circle for whom she has a great regard, you might appeal to that person for help — there is a very good chance that they will be able to work wonders, especially if they happen to be of a much older generation.

## Interests and Spare Time Activities

All work and no play makes Capricorn a dull girl — something you may have to remind your youngster about at times, especially if she so enjoys her work that she finds it difficult to put it down, even after business hours.

Hopefully, she will realize that life is to be enjoyed as much as it is to be used for profit, and at least at times be a typical Capricorn giddy goat. She, like all the Zodiac signs, must keep a good balance between work and play.

It is fairly unlikely that her circle of friends will be enormous, and she will certainly make a clear distinction between real friends and mere acquaintances. When she is very young, she will not be very likely to come up to you in a park and say 'Oh, mummy, this is my new friend . . . I've just met her!' It is part of the Capricorn pattern to develop ties of friendship with great caution, whether with a man or woman; but — perhaps as a result of that initial caution — once a friendship is cemented it will last for life.

If Ms Capricorn has had musical interests during her school years, either creative or appreciative, she is very likely to continue to enjoy them throughout the rest of her lifetime. Indeed, whenever she considers starting a new hobby or taking a study course of some sort she might like to consider lessons on a new instrument, or a music appreciation course. Of course she will realize that she will find it rather more difficult to start to play an entirely unfamiliar instrument in her teens or twenties, but she will nevertheless undoubtedly get a lot of pleasure from it.

Outdoor activities should form part of her life out of school or work. She might enjoy belonging to a group of ramblers, for Capricorns enjoy walking, and we must not forget that like the creature of their sign most of them enjoy the mountains, both as scenery and as objects to climb; rock-climbing and mountaineering are among the Capricorn's favourite hobbies. Capricorn must not forget the natural affinity with the earth and natural materials. If she did well in school pottery or craft classes, here are worthwhile areas to explore later.

When it comes to fashion, Capricorns of both sexes seem to look their best in formal clothes — whatever 'formal' means to their generation. The women of the sign are noted for well-shaped legs, so the neat black suit with a skirt clipped around the knee level will often look particularly dashing and elegant on a young Capricorn, especially for an interview or if she is working in banking, the law, a big city institution, or anywhere where such dress is *de rigeur*. The young men of the sign also look good in formal suits. In leisure hours, both sexes probably feel most comfortable in garments made of natural fibres — wool in particular. Interestingly, an amusing status symbol for this Zodiac group is a beautifully made, and no doubt very expensive, cashmere sweater (cashmere is goats' wool!)

Capricorns usually enjoy an active interest in community matters, sometimes involving themselves in local government; they will put up for election to the council, or at least give support in local elections or on advisory committees devised for the general welfare of the community. Indeed, they quite enjoy committee work, and if they belong to a group or society which meets to support one of their interests, time and energy spent serving on the committee or a sub-committee will be worthwhile for them and their efforts will not go unnoticed. Along with Leos, Capricorns tend to be prominent in such situations, often becoming chairperson or president.

Sometimes we should tease our Capricorn friends a little because of their enjoyment of the social scene, which is linked to their keenness to climb the social ladder. If one is entertained to dinner by them, there is a good chance of finding their boss or their boss's son or daughter in attendance; some of the guests are also likely to have rather more money than their host! No doubt a good time will be had by all, and it is on such occasions that Capricorn will trot out the best wines and spend a lot on the menu. On other occasions, Capricorn in the kitchen will normally be happiest spending time rather than money, buying perhaps cheaper cuts of meat but spending ages preparing and cooking them.

The Capricorn choosing a pet won't be moved by its bright, appealing eyes or fluffy coat. She will rather want a pet from the top drawer — something slim, smart and elegant, no doubt; which is not to say she will not care for it and, in a Capricornian way, love it. A mutual understanding will develop between them; she is unlikely to become over-sentimental or gushingly affectionate, but a special bond will centre on trust, loyalty, friendship and understanding. Psychologically, especially if Capricorn lives alone, it is excellent for her to have a pet; it will subtly help to counter the inclination to solitude. If she has long working hours, a cat would obviously be most convenient.

## Ideal Careers

For Capricorns either the world is their oyster — or they seem to be unable to achieve anything at all!

It can be the case that even the most successful Capricorn will sometimes fall into a negative frame of mind; it is likely that they will have come a long way on the road to success but have perhaps suddenly hit a plateau — and they will then forget all about their progress and feel entirely discontented, incapable of accepting what success they have.

Security is important to them, and they feel most confident in professions which seem least susceptible to redundancy, bankruptcy, or complicated take overs.

They can cope satisfactorily with a busy, working atmosphere, so sharing a group office should be no problem — they have the ability to cut themselves off from their surroundings. As I suggested (see *School Years*), their best way forward is a steady climb; if they are ambitious they will take promotion in their stride, and they are very capable of coping with the kind of top job which may cut them off from colleagues and friends, putting them in a position where the decisions are theirs alone. They never mind looking squarely at the buck if it stops at their desk. Responsibility is good for them, though very often they see it as a heavy burden they could well do without; their partners can only share their burdens by giving tactful encouragement.

When a Capricorn is working with a group of other people, she will certainly pull her weight, and the team as a whole will make good progress. But should she be promoted she may tend not to listen too carefully to the views of subordinates — there is a tendency for her to be autocratic. She should always guard against this, remembering that she is very conventional and while it may be a very good thing not to accept new ideas at the drop of a hat, she could tend to ignore what may well turn out to be innovative and progressive suggestions — the results of which could be beneficial.

Many Capricorns are to be found in the Civil Service, or as town planners, estate agents and estate managers. Agriculture, too, is sometimes attractive. Those of a scientific bent may find that higher mathematics in some way accompany their working hours, and they can be successful teachers of geography and lecturers in geology. The building profession and its subsidiaries provide enjoyable Capricornian occupations.

Many Capricorns find themselves tied to jobs which are somewhat boring and repetitive; some will be inclined to say, 'If only I had the opportunity to get out . . .' But work which is secure is, alas, often somewhat boring — and may also carry just the responsibilities which on the whole suit the Capricornian temperament. Finding themselves in that sort of situation, they should make sure that their spare time is spent in ways which they find specially rewarding, aiming perhaps to be creative or involved in some philosophical or esoteric interest; then their minds and personalities will not stagnate under the strain of a dull daily grind.

Those Capricorns who become teachers often find themselves, in due course, appointed headmaster or headmistress. This usually involves a great deal of administrative work and less actual teaching. In such a situation the individual Capricorn has to decide whether personal ambition and the need for additional security actually outweighs the pleasure of teaching. The decision will not be easy, but it may help to know that while Capricorn will inevitably be missed by her pupils, her attitude to the school and her ability to shoulder responsibility will stand her in good stead if she decides to accept the appointment.

If a Capricorn is attracted to medicine, areas that could be particularly rewarding are dentistry, physiotherapy, orthopaedics and osteopathy. The study of rheumatic and arthritic conditions will also be particularly engrossing.

We have already talked about the possibility of a Capricornian starting a business from scratch and building it up into a going concern. The image of the self-made man or woman is particularly Capricornian. They can become somewhat obsessed with work, to the exclusion of all else, and for the ambitious Capricorn the sky is very definitely the limit. With ambition we can link power. Unfortunately some Capricorns find a position of power attractive just for itself; they may then be extremely ruthless. Though these are in a minority, it is important that all successful Capricorns remember what life was like in the early days when they were at the bottom of the heap; they will then be able to identify with those who have yet to make the grade.

# Travel

It is as well to prepare your young Capricorn well in advance of her holiday, for she will probably be a little apprehensive about travel and leaving her familiar surroundings.

I think you will find nevertheless that provided you take her into your confidence, show her the brochures of the hotel and pictures of the place for which you are heading, she will become intrigued and less fearful of what might be in store for her there.

She will probably catch your enthusiasm, and the foreplanning you have to do will be reflected in her own preparations. Encourage her to make definite decisions about what she wants to take with her: a good, long storybook will be ideal — especially if there is a longish, boring plane journey; a notebook or sketchbook; her diary, if she keeps one — a good opportunity to encourage her to start? — and a small draw-string bag in which to put her souvenirs and keepsakes. You may well find that she will collect stones and seashells, or other valueless but meaningful things. The bag is essential, for she will collect so many things that otherwise your luggage will be full of them!

Without any doubt at all Capricorn will enjoy lakes and mountain scenery, so countries where these are in profusion will be ideal for her. Her fine Capricorn skin may take the sun rather badly — something her Cancerian partners in the Zodiac are also prone to — so do take a good sun-screen block, even if she has a very dark skin. Be careful, too, that she does not get over-heated, for she may well suffer rather more easily from heat exhaustion than some children.

A new and unusual diet should not worry her once she has been persuaded to try any strange-looking dish put before her, and she will perhaps particularly enjoy fish dishes; but don't be hard on her if she says she simply doesn't like the look of a meal, because her intuition can stand her in good stead, especially when it comes to food.

Incidentally, taking Ms Capricorn away on holiday provides you with a good opportunity to encourage her to increase her self-confidence, for though in general she may be somewhat shy with other children, she will certain enjoy telling them all about her holiday when she comes back, especially if it has been rather unusual. We must not forget that if she has one or two very special friends, she may miss them when she is away — so while she is normally rather wary about approaching people she doesn't know, if you can encourage her to do so while she is on holiday it may be somewhat easier for her.

Capricorns love tradition and the past, so visits to large cathedrals, palaces and exciting ruins or archaeological sites will usually engross her, especially if you can regale her with the legends of the area and stories of any historical events that took place there. A seaside holiday will give her a good opportunity to improve her swimming skills.

## Capricorns as Brothers and Sisters

When a young Capricorn is told that she is going to have a baby brother or sister she will take her role in the affair very seriously and become the ideal sibling.

Though if for some reason she feels at all cut out she may tend simply to ignore the new arrival, her reliability and sense of responsibility will usually develop very quickly under such circumstances. You can always appeal to her sense of pride, and suggest that because she is older she is the one who must set the example in behaviour; always stress, indeed, the fact that she is older, and how much you trust her — she will then do her utmost to develop a bond between herself and the younger child — a bond which will cement a relationship that should be lifelong.

It is possible that an element of rivalry will develop. If it does, make sure it is kept very healthy; allow the two children to have individual as well as joint interests. This usually happens in families, but with Capricorn it is perhaps rather more important than usual, because should it happen that the younger child overtakes the Capricorn she will most certainly feel inadequate and lose self-confidence. Here, incidentally, is another occasion when 'I'm no good at anything!' may be the cry.

There is an inherent caring quality in every Capricorn. Try to encourage it while you are still pregnant, by appealing to her to help you in any way she can. She should actually enjoy this, and when the baby appears it should be easier for you to expand Ms Capricorn's caring affection to include the new arrival.

When you have a Capricorn younger son or daughter who is a second or third child, a very great deal will depend on whether she falls into the ambitious, sure-footed category, or whether she is shy and retiring (you will have gathered she is likely to be one or the other). The former group contains children who will from a very early age be capable of spurring younger brothers and sisters into action, challenging them to keep pace with her. However, if there is any lack of self-confidence at all you could find that she will tend to slip into negative behaviour patterns such as nail-biting or thumb-sucking. She could also become extremely quiet when the others are having their say. Do watch out for these tendencies, for the sooner they are corrrected, the better. If you find you are having difficulty in getting them sorted out, I suggest that you seek professional advice, either from your doctor or from a specialist in child behaviour.

The family is important to Capricorns, so should she and her brother or sister attend the same school, you will find that the odd dispute at home will be set aside and Capricorn will stand up consistently for her sibling, all along the line. She will instinctively know that it is her duty to do this — all Capricorns also have a strong sense of duty as well as devotion to the family.

If she has to share a room, she may be rather tidier than the other child. If you find that she is tending to clear up for both of them, draw up a schedule which makes it clear that the other should do a fair share of the work! Bearing in mind the fact that Capricorns are one of the most musical signs of the Zodiac, there could also be problems when she wants to practice her instrument long and hard in her room, and brother or sister can't stand the noise! I suggest you call a family conference to sort the problem out — you might like to consider, too, whereabouts in the room the instrument is going to be stored (easy with a recorder, more difficult with a double bass!)

A great booster to Capricorn confidence will be to encourage her to help her brother or sister in some way — especially if she is the younger, and if there is perhaps a school subject that Capricorn finds easy and the brother or sister difficult. This will help develop her natural patience and prove to her that other people, too, must cope with difficult subjects and problems. Any occupation or activity that increases the young Capricorn's expression of love and affection for her fellow beings is particularly good for her; obviously recognizing the needs of other members of the family and helping them will do this, and the sharing of expensive toys and books, the making of gifts and particularly baby-sitting for you when she is old enough to cope, will all be excellent.

## Capricorns as Parents

The perpetuation of the family line is probably important to you, and was more than likely one of the main things you discussed with your partner when you decided to settle into a permanent relationship.

You and your partner, then, will have carefully planned the arrival of your children, and have thought carefully about spacing them so that you can care for them and bring them up just as you wish.

Family tradition is very important to you — just as important as the other accepted, conventional values of life. Ambitious in many spheres of your life, you will be ambitious for your children, too. Be careful: sometimes you may tend to drive them a little too hard, and they could then see you as a harsh taskmaster, even if, determined that they should make the most of their potential, you intend to encourage rather than bully them.

You need and work best under discipline and routine, and while members of some signs may think it somewhat old-fashioned to work out a routine and encourage children to work and play to it, the chances are that they will be all the better for it, learning to use their time wisely and discovering that life can be more exciting if you arrange it so that you can fit in as many activities as you wish.

It is sometimes important for Capricorn parents to look quite seriously at themselves, and ask themselves some pretty searching questions. The most important of these is 'Am I spending enough time with my children?' You may be so involved with your work (with the excellent motive of making more money to spend on them) that you are not giving them enough time — time to enjoy simply being with you and having fun together, time when you should be taking them out and enjoying simple pleasures like going to the park or the country. Of course it is splendid for children to have the advantage of an expensive private education (if it suits them), and obviously the more money you earn the more practical it is for you to encourage them to develop skills which need specialist training (dancing or music, for instance), but do be careful that in buying your children all these things, you are not in a sense buying them off. Watch that in your involvement with your own career and your enthusiasm for money making, you are not distancing yourself from your children, who may grow to see these occupations as something that stands between them and you. Think carefully — are you taking this line because you find it difficult to be spontaneously warm and affectionate?

I have mentioned, the fact that Capricorn is a conventional sign, and it is in this area that you may have to make allowances, especially when your children reach puberty and start developing opinions of their own and identifying their own objectives (which will largely be those of their own generation, rather than of yours). I cannot too strongly urge you to be aware of the fact that you (and your children) may suffer as a result of the generation gap. Consciously make allowances, and do all you can to develop an open mind which allows bridge-building between you, especially when they make sweeping statements about how they want to live and what they want their world to be like — for their opinions will often seem very foreign to you. Remember in all this that your dry, off-beat sense of humour can be an invaluable help, and indeed may be the thing that will see you through.

One way in which you can increase your involvement with your children's life is to take an active part in PTA events. You will be particularly good at balancing the books and devising ambitious money raising schemes. It seems unlikely that you will be at all apprehensive of speaking your mind and putting over the opinions of other parents in meetings with school managers, and if you are either at the top or well on the way to the top of your own profession you will find it all the easier to identify with the headmaster or headmistress' problems, so the chances are you will be an invaluable link with them.

To end with advice which doesn't apply to all Capricorns, but certainly does to some, you should consciously let your hair down from time to time, and have real, relaxed fun with your children, totally forgetting material problems and pressures of work.

## Case Study

David - Sun in Capricorn, Mercury in Sagittarius, Venus in Scorpio. Mercury Group 1, Venus Group 1.

From the Report: 'If David is set on taking up music as a full time profession he should be allowed to go ahead. He has ambition, persistence, originality and the inspiration to make a success of it. What is even more important is that he can blend the practical and the inspired to achieve what he wants to do. He has his aesthetic side, but also the ability to control and channel it constructively.'

Comment: David's mother approached me when her son was 21; she, being a very practical woman, was concerned that an uncertain career as a professional musician would prove unsuccessful. While music was strongly emphasized in his chart, so were marvellously practical and determined qualities which, it subsequently emerged, he had inherited from her (I worked also on her chart). He is now a very successful professional musician.

# The Sun-sign and Its Rulerships

*Countries and areas*: Afghanistan, Albania, the Antarctic, Bulgaria, India, Lithuania, Macedonia, Mexico, Orkney and Shetland, Saxony, Thrace, and the coastal strip of Yugoslavia.

*Cities*: Brussels, Constanta, Delhi, Ghent, Mecklenberg, Mexico City, Oxford, Port Said. The administrative centres of all capitals.

*Trees*: pine, yew, elm, aspen, poplar.

*Flowers and herbs*: amaranthus, belladonna, comfrey, hemlock, henbane, medlar, onion, pansy, quince, rye, wolf'sbane.

*Food*: all meat; malt; starchy food.

*Cell salts*: Calc. Phos., Calc. Fluor.

*Animals*: goats, all cloven-hoofed animals.

*Stone*: turquoise, amythyst.

*Metal*: lead (for jewellery, silver).

*Colour*: black, grey, dark brown, dark green.

# AQUARIUS

## (January 21 - February 18)

Note: Aquarius is a male sign, so for the most
part I refer throughout to 'he', but most of my
comments refer also to girls.

## General Characteristics

Your Aquarian child will be as bright and sunny as a clear, crisp winter morning,
with the Sun glinting on the frozen snow. He will be lively and intelligent and ready
to listen to everything you say — but you will find that from a very early age indeed
he will also be remarkably stubborn!

Aquarians are enormously friendly and very kind, but *extremely* independent,
and sometimes because the need for independence is so important to them they
tend to distance themselves even from those they love. While young Aquarius will
respond well to your instruction and encouragement, there will always be a part
of him which is essentially private and which no one is likely to be able to reach.
He will soon develop a tremendous sense of justice, and will want to see right done.
Supporting the underdog is an essential Aquarian activity, and you will find him
always interested to listen to discussion of the social questions of the day. He won't
just be content to listen, either; even when he is quite young, he will want to take
action when he hears of injustice — not because he will be emotionally moved,
and certainly not because he is a sentimentalist, but because he recognizes the need
for a system of social justice and fair play — and it must be supported by everyone
if it is to work well. This kind of behaviour is very characteristic indeed, and in
one way or another you will find it expressed by every Aquarian throughout his
life, though in a variety of ways.

The element of stubbornness I have mentioned is really one of the worst Aquarian
faults. This is an air sign (see p.15), high in logic and intellectual conviction; but
it is also one of the fixed signs (see again p.15). This is a contradiction in terms —
and you will discover that in an argument your small Aquarian may do his best
to convince you that he has changed his mind about something, just in the interests

of a more peaceful life, but in reality will remain convinced that he is right; Aquarius never merely *thinks* he's right — he *knows* it!

Aquarians seem always to show a certain perversity, and if in argument you seriously want to change their minds for them, one of the best ways may well be to appear to agree with them, but while doing so find a way of emphasizing all the things you don't like about the idea. They'll then find themselves agreeing with you, and because you're not *telling* them to reject their previous arguments, they'll be happy to do so!

Aquarians are notorious for their unpredictability. Say something to them, and whatever you think their response will be you can expect to hear the opposite. You should do what you can when your Aquarius is young to correct this tendency — later in life it can pose really serious problems and be extremely annoying to other people. It goes hand in hand with an inherent eccentricity. If that particular trait is controlled, it can be endearing; if it's not, it can also cause considerable annoyance.

Never underestimate Aquarian originality. Look out for it everywhere and encourage it all along the line, for the attribute usually has great potential which can be expressed in an enormous variety of ways — particularly creatively and scientifically.

Here is perhaps the friendliest, most trusting and unsuspicious of all the twelve Zodiac signs; Aquarians will take everyone at face value. Of course this can be very dangerous when they are young — and indeed later — and you should explain very carefully, and at an early age, the necessity to be wary of strangers, because these are high on the list of children vulnerable to approaches from strangers with bags of sweets — or even just a friendly word.

Aquarians are the humanitarians of the Zodiac, and it will not be difficult to encourage your child to be generous and charitable even with limited pocket-money. It is always good for children to take an active role and *work* for charity rather than simply giving to it, and the best way for Aquarians to do this is through creativity — perhaps playing a musical instrument, appearing in a play or pageant, or making something on behalf of charity, rather than simply handing over money.

Though generous, they are sensible enough to know that it's good to have a little extra money with which to buy one or two spectacular things — but remember that they like glamour and will sometimes spend rather a lot on show rather than practical things. Encourage them to appreciate quality and good value rather than surface glitter. You can always nurture their sense of pride by raising their pocket-money — especially when something has been achieved — a good result in examinations, for instance.

There is no doubt at all that Aquarians are *the* individuals of the Zodiac, and it is very likely indeed that yours will positively loath school uniform — or any other kind of uniform, for that matter; it reduces him to being just one of the crowd, and he will dislike that idea enormously. I expect he, like the inhabitants of some other signs, will scarcely be able to wait to throw off his things once he comes home from school, and get into clothes he likes. Far be it from me to make any suggestions about what any Aquarian, of either sex, should wear in private life — they would immediately climb into the opposite. But I think they will especially like the pale shade of turquoise which is their particular colour: I call it Aquarian blue, and most people of this sign look extremely attractive in it.

It is important to make sure that your Aquarian uses his physical energy evenly. Because they tend to be somewhat erratic in their behaviour it's very easy for them to be over-active one moment and lethargic the next. They may not think this matters too much — they like the changes of tempo, but their metabolism is best maintained on an even keel — see *Health and Diet*.

Your young Aquarian is unlikely to throw strong emotional tantrums, but he could suddenly become very cross for the most surprising and unexpected reason. When this happens, do all you can to calm him, and appeal to his sense of logic to show him the irrationality of his behaviour. If this kind of thing becomes a regular pattern it will be because his perverse and unpredictable streak is getting the better of him. Treat the situation seriously, and if necessary discipline him — he should not be allowed to get away with irrational anger — it will be a severe disadvantage later in life.

## The Three Ways of Thinking
Due to the influence of Mercury (see p.13) the Aquarian mind characteristically works in one of three ways.

★ In the first group are Aquarians who are extremely practical and thoughtful; loyalty and tradition are important to them. They are capable of careful thinking and are thorough, but be prepared for slow (but steady) progress when young Aquarius is at school.

★★ The second group comprises those who may quite strongly display the typical Aquarian perversity and eccentricity; there will also be a tendency towards intractibility. Their lively minds will support their originality. A tendency towards the undue dramatization of situations may emerge. Aquarian stubbornness is increased.

★★★ Woolly thinking may slightly impair the intellectual power of the third group of Aquarians, but they will be imaginative, and there is considerable potential if this attribute can be creatively developed. Watch out for forgetfulness and absent-mindedness.

## The Five Ways of Loving
Due to the influence of Venus (see p.13), Aquarians will tend to express their affection in one of five ways.

★ The first group is flirtatious and passionate. Aquarians with a wonderfully positive and optimistic attitude to love, they need independence within an emotional relationship, and intellectual *rapport* is also essential to them. A tendency to dual relationships can cause problems.

★★ Extremely loyal and faithful, the people in the second group can sometimes be a little cool in the expression of their feelings but once committed are very faithful partners. They will sometimes seek a partner older than themselves, or perhaps marry rank or position.

★★★ The third group contains perhaps the most glamorous Aquarians, often extremely good-looking and dynamically attractive to the opposite sex. But they have a tendency to distance themselves from their partners, and they are often reluctant to commit themselves body and soul to another person.

★★★★ Group four contains tender, loving and caring people, but they can suffer conflict when it comes to deciding which is more important — a relationship or their need for independence. A delightfully sentimental streak can sometimes be seen, and they are certainly extremely romantic.

★★★★★ The final group of Aquarians, like the first, is passionate and will enjoy a lively love life; they are enthusiastic in its expression. But here too considerable independence is very necessary to them, and they must remember that their tendency to be selfish can easily sour a relationship.

## Health and Diet

One of the most important means of keeping your young Aquarian healthy is making sure that he keeps warm — especially of course in cold weather.

Interestingly most members of this Sun-sign seem to enjoy the winter, and will be out and about taking long, brisk walks (when it is fine) or taking part in winter sports (for which many of them have talent). But the circulation is governed by Aquarius, and persistently cold hands and feet are a sure sign that something is wrong. It may be that even when your Aquarian is a tiny baby, he will throw off warm bedclothes if he has the chance — he will probably simply hate the weight of them and the restriction to his movements. Make a point, if you can, of providing very light bedclothes — a duvet would be best — or a sleepsuit, so that if he does throw the clothes off he will still be sufficiently covered.

With the circulation in mind, it is obviously important to encourage an Aquarian to take regular exercise — not for strength but for endurance, for these strengthen the heart and thus safeguard the circulation. Remembering that most Aquarians are artistic, it may be that both boys and girls will get greater pleasure all round from going to the ice rink or to dance classes, which will have the added advantage of strengthening their ankles, which happen to be ruled by the sign. It is for that reason the ankles are somewhat vulnerable, and it is always advisable to chose for Aquarian children shoes which adequately support them.

Because Aquarius is such a remarkably logical sign, its children can usually approach their problems rationally, and they do not usually worry too much about them. However they are often fairly high strung, and this can lead to a kind of twitchy tension and inability to relax. It's quite important that you bear this in mind, since tension once built-up will not be very easily thrown off. When faced with problems, they can uncharacteristically tend to be rather secretive, and you may have to encourage them to speak out about any difficulties, so that you can get at their source; having done so, they will release any attendant tension. This is really very important, for the more high strung Aquarian is sometimes prone to migraine.

Because this is such a friendly sign, your Aquarian will obviously be more likely to pick up colds and minor infections than a child who keeps himself to himself.

You won't want to argue about friendliness, of course, but a course of vitamin C will do no harm if there are colds around.

The Aquarian diet should be kept fairly light, with an accent on salads, even in the winter. Cooked vegetable salads or ratatouille are good for them and should be much enjoyed. Aquarius may be a bit 'picky' about food, and is not impossible that the occasional lunchtime drama may occur when he takes a sudden dislike to something on offer. Be advised: he's just being stubborn, and he, more than most children, will listen to the argument that he should eat up all his food when so many children have to go without. The only thing is, being logical he may demand that you parcel up his rice pudding and send it off to central Africa. And that, I'm afraid, is a demand you'll have to cope with as best you may!

I think you will find that Aquarius should sleep very well, provided too much excitment can be avoided just before bedtime and his volatile energy isn't on too much of a peak. It is really essential to keep a balanced routine and make sure that Aquarius is physically active for a certain period, but then spend some time on more intellectual pursuits. This is more difficult to achieve than it may seem — Aquarian enthusiasm may tend to encourage him to exercise for too long a period — or, if he gets involved in some sedentary hobby, he may tend to spend rather too long in one position, and give himself headaches through too much concentration.

Bearing in mind the fact that Aquarians are individualists, when it comes to between-meal snacks you could encourage him to experiment — one day, try him with prawn crackers, the next with a slightly unusual fruit — lychees or kiwi fruit. Apart from enjoying it, it will amuse him to produce this in the playground, for it will appeal to his natural sense of individuality.

## The First Five Years

Of all the Aquarian traits for which you can watch from the earliest days, independence is probably the one which will strike you first. Of course you should do all you can to encourage it and develop your child's interesting and imaginative originality.

Toys that stretch his imagination — and the simpler they are, the better — will be most appreciated, but as he gets a little older it will be an excellent idea to introduce him to puzzles and the sort of plaything about which he has to ask himself 'How does it work?' This will help in the development of what may prove to be a scientific mind. He will certainly enjoy his first books — again, let these be colourful and stimulating to his imagination, rather than purely factual.

You will probably notice an element of quirkiness in his behaviour; it will be interesting for you to watch for this too, for he is the least predictable of all young Zodiac children. This applies not only to his attitude and the way he responds to his toys but to his eating and sleeping habits. One day you may find him very ready to take his afternoon rest immediately after lunch, while the next he may be extremely lively at two o'clock, but ready for a sleep at four. Try not to let this interfere with your life-style, especially if you are planning an evening out and have employed a baby-sitter. The good thing is that because he is friendly, he adapts to people pretty easily, and I hardly think that he will be apprehensive or fearful of anyone who comes to look after him.

To develop his sense of responsibility, look again at *The Five Ways of Loving* (p.219-20) and try to work out which category you think he fits into; he will be a little young for this, and it may not be too easy, but if you think he is a really warm and sensitive Aquarian he will be quite capable of feeding the cat or perhaps caring for a plant or a corner of the garden. Leave it to him (though of course checking to make sure the cat is neither fat nor starving!). If he is a somewhat distant child, looking after or cleaning something inanimate is probably a better idea.

I think you must be prepared for the fact that Aquarius will not be very easy to discipline. If you have a *contretemps* there are one or two effective approaches, however: while it is no use coming over all emotional with an Aquarian, you can point out that what he has done has upset you — that you are a family, and that he as a kind, helpful child must be a responsible member of it and not upset the routine and weaken the ties between you. In general, always go for a logical rather than an emotional approach.

He should enjoy play group very much; he will make a lot of acquaintances, and probably tell you that every other child is his friend! The challenge of larger, more demanding toys and of being with children perhaps a little older and more advanced than he, will be excellent for him, certainly stimulating his mind and imagination, and standing him in good stead as an introduction to a more advanced school a little later on.

## School Years

The transition from nursery to day school should be an easy one for your Aquarian child. Should you encounter some stubbornness or find he doesn't want to go to school on the second day, you might have to fight a fairly hard battle to get him round to the conventional way of thinking!

You can always appeal to that independent streak: 'Now you're a big boy, there's no need for you to be at home with mummy all day — it's much better for you to be out by yourself, learning new things and having fun with your friends.' Aim to explain that within a few days he will realize that 'the big boys' school' is much more interesting and enjoyable than play group.

When it comes to making new friends, if he had no problems in this respect at nursery school he should go on to express his true Aquarian spirit by being kind and friendly towards the other children of his age, and very soon you will find you have the whole crowd of youngsters bursting in on you at about four o'clock in the afternoon!

As far as discipline is concerned, he will certainly try to pull a fast one on his teachers and will push them to see just how much he can get away with. It's not that he's a naughty child but simply that his spirit naturally rebels at any restriction, and at being told precisely what to do. Routine is something he probably won't like at all, and a school timetable which is totally predictable will bore him stiff with the repetitive routine. I don't think this should apply to the lessons themselves but simply to the way they crop up at the same time on the same day every week.

With this in mind Aquarius will respond particularly well to a school with a flexible timetable, and possibly a somewhat freer attitude to discipline and the work in general. This does not mean, however, that he should be allowed to slack, and if you find that he's not making as much progress as he should, you really must be very firm indeed with him, because in most Aquarians there is excellent potential asking to be developed.

Perhaps the only time at which you should encourage him into a steady routine is at examination time. He could become a little slap-happy, but his attitude of mind will depend on which group he belongs to in *The Three Ways of Thinking* (p.219). Be strict if you think he is one of the third group; compromise and be as logical as possible if he is in the second; if he is in the first group he will have a generally more serious attitude of mind, and the problem may not arise.

An Aquarian's progress in class may be very erratic. Again this depends to some extent on his way of thinking, but the usual pattern is uneven — excellent progress at some times, less at others. Don't worry too much if during his early years he seems to be getting on less well than you would like. This is often the case, and you will probably find that when he is a little older he will start to move forward in leaps and bounds.

There is only one time when he will need to curb his originality, and that is when he is answering examination papers — it is all too easy for Aquarians, in their free-thinking, original way, to try to impress the examiners with their own opinions and with interesting irrelevances rather than the facts required; this is something against which you and his teachers should continually warn him.

Bearing in mind the fact that the Aquarian circulation needs to be monitored, all sport and exercise is good for him. It is pretty well impossible to say just how much or how little he will enjoy school sports, but because he is open-minded there should be at least one which he will approve; athletics, fast games such as tennis and badminton, and, when he is older, squash, are all good possibilities. Simply because he is Aquarian you will be just as likely to find him an enthusiastic soccer or rugger player, or perhaps more especially scoring at cricket — and in his own highly creative and original way!

Because he is so fair-minded, with a well developed sense of right and wrong, he will make an ideal prefect or perhaps eventually head boy. He can take re-sponsibility and will cope with it in much the same way as children of his neighbour sign in the Zodiac, Capricorn. However, the difference is that he will probably be far more approachable. He is not a remote, lonely boss figure; should he become a prefect he will be unlikely to lose that special bond he has built up over the years with his classmates and will accept responsibility with a light heart and in precisely the spirit that the position demands. He will obviously have to come to terms with any stubbornness or unpredictability in his character when he accepts such a responsibility — at least as far as his behaviour and attitude at school are concerned.

If he has a choice of a school project unrelated to the syllabus and comes up with a suggestion you think zany, don't dismiss it too readily, especially if it has an inventive quality about it — here is Aquarius at his best, taking up something off-beat and making it his own.

# Out of School Activities

When considering activities that might interest your young Aquarian, consult the golden rule: Aquarians love the deep past and the distant future!

If you bear this in mind, it means of course that you can carry them off to the Science Museum or the Archaeological Museum — to an archaeological site or to an exhibition of space travel. Many children these days have a craze for studying dinosaurs and extinct animals, and if your young Aquarian catches the craze, he is likely to keep it much longer than his friends. He may also enjoy collecting stones and pebbles and will be over the moon if he manages to find a fossil.

In complete contrast, he will devour science fiction stories, novels and films, and will enjoy making models of spaceships and the very latest planes. Astronomy is also very popular with many Aquarians; why not get him interested by showing him the moon and planets through a good pair of binoculars? (much better than a cheap telescope). A youngster who looks towards the future, as he does, will have no difficulty in coming to terms with the computer. Most modern children find this relatively easy, but young Aquarius will probably be teaching his teachers the use of the keyboard almost before he has set a finger to it. With these two extremes in mind, there should really be no problems in entertaining and educating your young Aquarian — and indeed relying on him to entertain and educate himself outside school time.

Aquarius is basically a communicative type and may enjoy writing articles for the school magazine or perhaps setting up some kind of communications link with his friends — even if it is only a toy telephone system consisting of two empty cans with a string between them! His natural curiosity will lead him to enjoy a good children's encyclopaedia of the 'How it Works' type, and it will be an excellent investment.

Sports interests outside school are an excellent idea, for he must always be as active as possible. It is very often the case that members of this sign have a flair for drama and theatre, so the local amateur dramatic society may attract him — or indeed dance classes (he may be particularly interested in modern free dance). As I have already mentioned (see *Health and Diet*) winter sports are good for him, and he will probably enjoy them.

It may be that you have a potential inventor in the family, so do bear with him if ghastly smells emerge from his room when he is experimenting with his chemistry set.

The girls of the sign are instinctively attracted to shiny, shimmering objects, and will have fun making necklaces from clear plastic beads, or anything that glitters — they absolutely love sparkle. Very often they have considerable fashion flair, and will get a great deal of pleasure from creating dresses for their toys (when they are little) and, later, glamorous little numbers to wear to evening parties. If your daughter shows an interest in fashion or jewellery design, you should do everything possible to encourage her to pursue it and develop a good sewing or craft technique. A childhood interest of this kind can, especially with Aquarians, develop into a lucrative and extremely rewarding career. For either sex, an interest in anything out of the ordinary or unusual is marvellous, and should always be watched for and nurtured.

# Preparing for Life

Every Aquarian I have ever known has had something particularly individual about his or her life-style.

When your young son or daughter is beginning to grow up and come to terms with their personality, they will probably tend to take slightly longer than most youngsters to go through the emotional mill and come out at the other side a true adult. This is because they will need to work out for themselves precisely what kind of life-style they want. Do not worry if they do not settle into a permanent relationship at the same time as most of their contemporaries; they are fiercely independent and may not want to give up that independence even for someone for whom they feel deeply. This, incidentally, is true of both sexes.

Because Aquarians have very special needs, it is a good thing for them to take rather longer than usual to select a partner for life. Once committed, they are faithful, and usually one finds that one of the most rewarding elements of their relationship is a true rapport and friendship with their loved one.

It is very likely that your young Aquarian will be extremely attractive to the opposite sex, and like all young people will be eager to experiment sexually — but in no way should his need for independence and freedom be linked to sexual promiscuity; there should be no need to worry on that score. It is simply more than usually important that Aquarius should get everything just right before making a commitment. Having said that, we should remember that many Aquarians are extremely romantic and sometimes come over more than a little starry-eyed. You may have to keep a keen eye out for this tendency, especially when Aquarius is in love for the first time. As ever, try without dampening their enthusiasm to appeal to their natural logic and indeed to a very useful personality trait typical of the sign — the ability to distance themselves from their problems and view them almost as though they concerned someone else.

The first hint that puberty is beginning to grip young Aquarius is a glint of curiosity about everything and anything adult. He will begin to ask questions about scenes of love-making on television, for instance, and ask pertinent but subtle questions not only of you but of friends and relatives not too much older than himself. I don't think he will be over-influenced by what you, or anyone else, says; he is not gullible and will draw his own conclusions from your comments, finding out for himself just what it is all about, and documenting his own reactions in his mind almost as though they were someone else's. This will be very much the Aquarian's attitude to his or her sexual development; both the boys and girls may well take a very detached and clinical attitude to the physical changes of adolescence. A really good book which explains these simply but in careful detail would be the best possible way of educating them on the subject; unless you are an Aquarian yourself, you are probably unlikely to be able to answer all their questions in just the way they need them to be answered.

Of all the twelve Sun-signs, there is perhaps no other whose members are more likely to benefit from a coeducational school (one would almost say, a coeducational boarding school!). They accept the opposite sex entirely on their own terms; there should be no awkward age during which there is any mystery or embarrassment, and certainly no discrimination.

This is another sign which will probably benefit from and enjoy going on double dates — partly because Aquarians need a strong bond of friendship within an emotional relationship, and this is encouraged on a double date, where passion must to some extent be curbed. Aquarius should get a lot of simple fun and pleasure from his early romantic experiences, and if there is a number of them, that is all to the good, for it is probably true to say that the greater the bond of friendship and the more Aquarius has in common with his partner the stronger the relationship is likely to become, and dating a number of girl-friends is far better than becoming too involved with one, committing himself in some way, and then discovering too late that they really have very little in common.

It is during their adolescence that you should carefully reread *The Five Ways of Loving* (p.219-20); technically speaking, the influence of Venus on this sphere of Aquarians' lives is particularly relevant.

## Further Education

The prospect of moving on from school to college or university will send a starry glow of excitement and enthusiasm into your young Aquarian's eyes. He will certainly be ready to make the change to further education and will take the enormous stride forward in personal independence with the greatest possible assurance.

Now is the time when perhaps more than the people of any other Zodiac sign his own opinions and attitude to life will be set, and it is very likely that during student years he will be well ahead of his particular generation in ideas and matters which are important to him. However, it is a unique fact that Aquarians who very often are ahead of their generation, and have set their opinions, tend to cling on to them for the rest of their life, so that when they are much older they can have difficulty in readjusting to progress and the changing times.

You should find that he will have no difficulty in settling down to life at university. His circle of acquaintances will be extremely wide, as will his choice of extramural activities. He may become just a little too self-assured where study is concerned, perhaps tending to think that he knows more than he actually does; so when he has to take examinations, he may sometimes not prepare himself as well as he should. I suggest you look out for this tendency, and for reassurance read again *The Three Ways of Thinking* (p.219), and if he has been a steady plodder at school, try to encourage him to get back into that routine.

If he has young and enthusiastic tutors he will certainly treat them as equals; on the whole he is not the type automatically to respect his instructors — and this is in fact a good thing, because one Aquarian principle is that all men are equal, in personality if not in knowledge. It's not that he's disrespectful; he will simply challenge his tutors on every possible occasion.

If he is living at home while he studies at polytechnic or some other centre, you may find that after a term or two he will say he wants to move in with some friends. Perhaps you will feel that this is a little strange, but I do suggest that you don't treat his decision as a family tragedy but go along with his desire to fly the nest. When the situation arises he will have decided that he really is ready to cope with greater independence and freedom, and you should not attempt to cramp his style. Rest assured, he probably has rather more common sense than you realize. (This situation is a particularly tricky one for Cancerian parents.)

The very best way for him to progress in his studies will be to encourage him to experiment within the confines of the subjects he is studying. Generally speaking it is more advantageous for Aquarians to find things out for themselves than for them to have to absorb information from the experiences of others, however expert those others may be. This is because no matter which way his mind works, it is an enquiring mind, insatiable for knowledge and new experiences, especially when the individual is young and impressionable.

If you feel that he is not getting out enough, that he needs some additional fresh air, do suggest that he renew earlier sporting interests, or at least join some university club that will take him off perhaps to inexpensive winter sports holidays or on an expedition of some sort. Here is someone who will specially benefit from an adventurous journey to some remote area or another.

It's possible that at this time Aquarius may quite suddenly decide that he wants to give all his time to something which has perhaps preoccupied him for years but only as a spare time hobby or enthusiasm. So what has previously been just an engrossing interest may turn into a career. Don't try to oppose this, for he will really have given it serious consideration; any heavy-handed opposition will only provoke his stubborn side, and he will waste emotional energy on doing battle with you — energy which would be far better spent on developing the interest on which he has set his heart. Determination and that Aquarian flair which often approaches brilliance, will see him through.

## Unemployment: Stresses and Strains

Like the young people of his polar or opposite sign, Leo, Aquarius will feel a great loss of dignity and pride if he leaves full-time education to find that no one apparently wants to employ him.

He will have an inner urge to get on top of the situation as quickly as possible, so he will explore every avenue to find a job, displaying what experience and ability he has to the best advantage whenever he has the opportunity. He will enjoy preparing a well-presented and impressive c.v.; encourage him to make it look good and use his originality to make it as unusual as possible, so that it stands out among the many which will doubtless arrive in response to any advertisement.

Aquarius will probably want to spend some time with contemporaries who are also looking for work. It will not be time wasted, for when he has done the rounds of the job centre and the library he will probably want to turn his attention to any community work which needs doing in his area — and he will be very good at dragooning his friends into helping out.

If he is thinking of going on a youth employment scheme he will probably be attracted to work which is unusual and rather out of the ordinary — the more off-beat, the better it will be. Even if it does not develop into a career, the experience will certainly benefit him.

He may find it quite difficult to relax, for he will really want to give all his time to looking for work; he may experience periods of tension, perhaps accompanied by nervous headaches. Some kind of relaxation technique will help him unwind when he is under pressure; a sporting activity or an exercise regime will also help. He may respond well to yoga or perhaps one of the far Eastern techniques which marry physical with mental discipline.

His best way of coping with long days of inactivity will be for him to pack them with as much variety as possible; encourage him to be enterprising — though he may not think money tremendously important, he will certainly get a kick from being able to profit from a small private business venture of some sort, and it's likely that he will come up with a very original and unusual one which will be fun to devise and set up.

If Aquarians fall into the drug habit, it may be for the exceptionally silly reason that it is fashionable, that people he feels are particularly 'with it' use drugs. Once he is trapped, his natural stubbornness will make it difficult for you to persuade him to withdraw; you will have to find some way of making it *his* decision — and once he has decided, his natural determination and logic will help him. Remember that he has a natural ability to distance himself from problems and look at them coldly and objectively; if you can get him round to this approach, there is a very good chance that the battle can be won. You can also appeal to his natural sense of pride; just as he will feel a loss of dignity when unemployed, he will feel it acutely if drugs destroy his self-respect. The sight of drug users reduced to total mistery and degradation will appall him; similarly, the example of people he respects and who have kicked the habit will also count very strongly with him.

The escapist aspect of drug-taking is not, I think, particularly important to Aquarians; natural curiosity is much more likely to lead him to try drugs in the first place — he won't want to escape from the world. As to which drug is most likely to appeal to him, I think it will be the one which is most fashionable at the moment.

## Interests and Spare Time Activities

Aquarians usually have a very wide circle of friends and acquaintances and on the whole keep them for a lifetime, but you need not expect to be easily admitted to an Aquarian's private life, however much of a friend you believe yourself to be. They need their private lives and hug them to themselves more, even, than their closest friends.

It is very often the case, too, that from time to time Aquarius unwittingly offends his friends, maybe by some entirely thoughtless remark, but in any case for no very good reason; it is very difficult to know why this is so, but it does seem very often to happen. In contrast, should you ever need help, Aquarius is certainly the person to fly to — he will be ready and willing to support you and will give freely of his time and energy.

Even young male Aquarians who are just in the grip of awakening sexuality are able to accept women on equal terms and have really well-bonded ties of friendship with them. They like to be seen with an elegant partner — perhaps because they enjoy arousing the curiosity of others — but if their partner expects a romantic involvement, they may well be disappointed. It will be, 'thank you for a lovely evening, and goodnight'. Emotional involvement will be out — other things will be more important!

Groups of people sharing a common interest attract Aquarians, who get a great deal of pleasure from the cross-fertilization of ideas and the sharing of information and enthusiasm. They will do a great deal to further the development of such a group. They make ideal committee members provided they don't hold up the proceedings because of their stubbornness — in a minority, they can stand out against a particular decision until everyone else wants to scream. But their ability to look rationally at problems will be a great asset, and specific tasks can be assigned to them in full confidence that they will be responsibly carried through. They will chair a sub-committee reliably and well, for they will enjoy looking after one perhaps small but important facet of a project and seeing that it is perfectly accomplished.

Aquarians are acutely aware of social conditions, and it is particularly good for them to involve themselves in some kind of work which is of benefit to the local community. Do encourage your young Aquarian to take part in such projects; he will find it very satisfying, and the community will also benefit. Old people will be charmed by his lively, bright personality, for instance.

When it comes to hobbies, it is almost impossible to list preferences — they seem to be able to turn their enthusiasm to almost anything. But we certainly find many Aquarians who are very successful at designing their own clothes, the girls in particular specializing in dazzling evening clothes or stunning outfits with overtones of the glamorous TV 'soaps'. Others will be intrigued by astronomy and will want to own a telescope — and there are a great many Aquarians who become very competent astrologers, too; members of this sign are particularly fascinated by the subject. Aquarians often have a particular liking for the theatre, and frequently theatre or concert going become in themselves a hobby which is taken as seriously as their pockets allow. They can get a great deal of pleasure from joining an amateur theatre group, either as performers or perhaps as set or costume designers and painters, if they don't see themselves as performers. Many Aquarians are attracted to vintage motor cars and cycles, which they enjoy repairing, restoring and grooming.

Aquarians are attracted to the deep past and the distant future, and this can be a good line to remember if they are uncertain what hobby to pursue. On the one hand we find the young archaeologist, geologist or palaeontologist, while on the other we have the young inventor, or a science fiction and space exploration fanatic.

Many a delicious meal will be consumed at an Aquarian's table. Their inventiveness and flair accompany them into the kitchen, where they are brilliant improvisers, happy to spend as much as they can afford on wine or some expensive ingredient to enhance the meal. They are often attracted to unusual dishes, perhaps from the East, and cook them with as much skill as any Chinese or Japanese chef.

It is good for Aquarians to have a pet — though sometimes they will avoid committing themselves because of the responsibility involved — and the fact that from time to time pets can encroach upon the set pattern of their days and their need for independence. Before they choose one, they should be encouraged to think very carefully. Maybe they will choose an animal which is very little trouble to care for, but, ideally, it seems likely that a nice, lively dog would be particularly good, since taking him for walks will not only help that Aquarian circulation, but perhaps increase the circle of friends and acquaintances, since one usually then strikes up conversations with other dog owners.

## Ideal Careers

Generally speaking, Aquarians can cope with most working environments — provided they do not have very strong feelings about certain aspects of work: the Aquarian who is a militant non-smoker, for instance, would suffer enormously in a smoking environment. It is also true that if his job keeps him sitting in one position for a long time his joints will probably get stiff, or he will suffer from lower back pain; so moving around a little from time to time is advantageous — and I would also strongly recommend that in one way or another he acquire a back rest chair, since along with circulation problems he may well find that as he grows older his spine is vulnerable.

Ideally, an Aquarian should be in a job in which his logical, rational approach to problems, his ability to see fair play, and above all his originality, have plenty of free expression. He will be at his best when having been told what to do, he is allowed to get on with doing it in his own individual way. It is vital that he impress on employers the fact that he is trustworthy and reliable. If he is over-disciplined or over-supervised, he will certainly rebel and could head for trouble, because it is very easy for him to rub his superiors up the wrong way. Once they know what he is capable of they will no doubt be understanding, recognizing his value, but Aquarius may at least at first have to suffer a fool gladly in order to earn the respect he deserves.

Having reached that stage, there is no reason why he should not go from strength to strength, eventually accepting high responsibility and coping well with it. Should he reach a position of authority, he will never become a remote, distant figure — he will always be ready to listen to colleagues' ideas, even if his Aquarian stubbornness may be difficult to sway.

Looking at suitable careers, once more — as with Aquarian hobbies — the choice is extremely wide. With a scientific training, he will be good at experimentation, but may not score very highly when it comes to logging detailed research. He should allow his intuition and flair to guide him, both in science and in professions of a more artistic, creative nature. The Aquarian who is involved in the fine arts will show brilliance, and it should not be difficult for him to attract the attention of the critics and the public. The young, newly qualified designer ending an art school course will mount his final show with such panache that it is sure to interest prospective employers. The young actor leaving drama school will make the most of his graduation performance and will be noticed in the tiniest part on the screen. Aquarians have an interesting, dynamic, magnetic power of attraction which stands them in good stead where their careers are concerned, as well as in their personal life.

Aquarians who decide to enter the retail trades will probably particularly enjoy 'performing' — the junior girl assistant at an up-market boutique will enjoy adjusting her sale approach from customer to customer; she will love the element of fantasy in the clothes she is selling, which are so often allied to that in stage costumes or TV soap operas. The same will apply if she sells unusual or spectacularly trendy items for the home.

Any profession in which art is married to science will be ideal, so an Aquarian will be happy as a beautician or make-up artist, or perhaps a hairdresser. Very differently, for the Aquarian who has a highly developed social conscience, a career working in the social services or for a major charity is rewarding. He could be a major source of inspiration to colleagues and an enormous comfort to those he is serving. Because they are often idealistic in outlook Aquarians not only inspire others to give freely but also get great satisfaction from the work itself.

Deciding on a teaching profession, the Aquarian will probably cope better with older rather than younger children. His pupils will inevitably respond well to him, and he will be very much concerned with sharpening their outlook and expanding their minds. Because Aquarians are interested in so many different things, so many aspects of life, they are good at broadening young minds. I always feel that Muriel Spark's Jean Brodie is the quintessential Aquarian schoolteacher (in her faults as well as her virtues!)

# Travel

Even when Aquarians are very young, they will be fascinated by places with a long history — so you will find them enjoying exploring ruined palaces or castles, imagining them filled with courtiers or the clash of armed men.

Aquarians need plenty of variety; they will not want to return to the same place every year for a decade or more, looking forward to the same routine in the same hotel or holiday home, building the same sandcastles on the same beach. They will want to plan each holiday in a different place — and if possible an unusual and 'different' place, not one that is loudly advertised in every holiday brochure that they set eyes on. They will specially like meeting new people who lead a very different life to their own.

Any lack of enthusiasm they display about a coming holiday will probably be linked either to over-familiarity or to ignorance; if you are going to somewhere new, it is a very good idea to show them plenty of photographs of it and explain what there is to see there — bearing in mind the fact that they will be particularly interested in its history. You will find it very easy to stimulate their imaginations if you can get hold of a book which will tell them about any local archaeological sites or discoveries.

They love flying, and the flight to their holiday will be one of the best parts of it. They don't mind travel in general, though they might get bored during a long car journey, especially if they associate car travel with regular visits to boring relatives!

They will dive into a 'different' menu with great interest, ready to try everything from snails in garlic sauce to raw fish, even if the idea makes them shudder a little, their insatiable curiosity will encourage them to try everything once. Heavy food isn't specially good for them, however, so it is a good idea to try to keep the diet as light as possible. (See *Health and Diet*, p.220)

Try to encourage Aquarians to be adventurous, and they will love experimenting with wind surfing or aquaplaning; as they grow older their appetite for adventure may, indeed, outstrip your own ideas of what is desirable or safe. In view of Aquarian stubbornness, you will probably simply have to put up with that. But you can perhaps divert their attention — to local craftspeople, for instance, whose work will specially interest them if they can watch how it is done; they will be delighted to try to pick up the skill, and back at home may well become fascinated by a new hobby.

The stranger and more individual the souvenir an Aquarian can bring back from holiday, the better they will be pleased. They can sometimes unusually be attracted to mass-produced souvenirs, if they are sufficiently flashy. But with any luck they will turn to something far more original and far less expensive — some prettily coloured stones, shells or pebbles, for instance, or intriguing seeds to conceal in their sponge-bag.

## Aquarians as Brothers and Sisters

Young Aquarians will be very proud of a baby brother or sister.

Before the infant is born, he may well enjoy pretending to be doctor and asking you all kinds of questions — not only where the baby will come from, but how you are feeling and what you must do to take care of yourself. He will no doubt have overheard enough to give him the material for some pertinent and surprisingly adult remarks.

He will certainly mature a lot when the younger member of the family is small, but you must be careful, for he may tend to become rather bossy and perhaps think that the baby is capable of much more than is the case. A little later on, this could provide an interesting challenge for the younger one, but when for instance baby is still too young to crawl or walk, an Aquarian invitation to play football is perhaps not altogether a good thing. Quite a lot of careful explanation may be necessary if you are to avoid some hair-raising moments.

I do not think that generally speaking Aquarius will become jealous of a younger sibling; it doesn't seem in the nature of the sign to react in that way. If childhood jealousy does emerge, it may well be the case that it will take the form of diverting your attention from the young one and towards himself.

It is good for all children to have something specific to do to help out when there is a baby in the family, and I think you will find that for the most part Aquarius will be happy to do so. Should he, for reasons of his own, suddenly decide that he wants no part of it, you can be confident that he is making an indirect protest — perhaps against what he sees as favouritism — and you should take him aside and find out the reason for his behaviour. It may well be far more complicated than you think. He is quite likely just to say that he's bored with helping out, while the real reason for his lack of co-operation will only emerge if you appeal to his sense of justice and point out that you really do need to know what's bothering him, for you don't want to be unfair to him.

On the whole, because Aquarius is an independent child, you should find that he will be quite happy to go and play with his toys, living his life in his own way while you get on with the necessary business of looking after his brother or sister. As a reward for good behaviour, the very best thing you can do is treat him to a new toy or game which will stimulate his imagination and give him scope for creativity. Don't be afraid if you find, when you reach the toy shop, that such things are directed at an older age group than his; the challenge of a more grown up toy will be good for him.

An Aquarian with older brothers and sisters who feels at all in their shadow will seem to be stubbornly opposed to all your suggestions. He may suddenly take a dislike to foods that he's previously enjoyed and simply become in general rather difficult. It may be necessary for you to confer with the older child or children before going on to appeal to Aquarius' logic and reason, which may actually be strengthened as a result of a difficult period. If he is attending the same school as his brothers and sisters, his natural family loyalty (a trait he shares with the Capricornians) will almost certainly come into play should the other member of the family get into scrapes or suffer from the machinations of an unsympathetic teacher. You can rest assured that young Aquarius will see that justice is done and may even go as far as to make a fuss about it in the process! If you have to get explanations from him about what actually happened in a particular case (maybe a quarrel with a friend) remember that he is truthful and honest and capable of giving you a very fair description of the incident — one you can rely on if you have to sort it out with other people.

If Aquarius has for a while to share a room with a young brother or sister, there should in theory be few problems — but remember he is an individualist, and that this will show from a very early age. Allow him to have private space which he can call his own, and which shouldn't be invaded. And why not allow him to have his say if and when the room is to be redecorated? He could well come up with an interesting and unusual colour scheme.

## Aquarians as Parents

Before starting a family, Aquarians usually discuss the whole subject with great care and thoroughness, knowing that once the baby has arrived you will be far less independent than you were before.

Aquarian mothers are among those in the Zodiac who really need a few private hours each week in which to follow their own individual interests, and I would advise you, as soon as you have recovered from the birth, to work out a way of making this possible. You have a great deal to offer your children, even when they are very young, but if you allow your mind to stagnate, and simply get bored with them, this particular talent will atrophy, and they will be the losers.

Aquarians of either sex make wonderfully stimulating parents, very keen indeed to expand their children's minds as thoroughly as possible. You will want to ensure that your children have a busy round of activities out of school hours, and because you are fair and understanding of other people you will be eager to allow them to follow their own interests rather than (as some parents tend to do) foisting your own interests on them.

It will be a good thing for you to look back to *The Five Ways of Loving* (p.219-20) and decide in which group to place yourself; the few remarks there should have a strong bearing on the way in which you express your love towards your children.

Consider this very carefully; you may have to make some allowances — for instance, if you decide you come into the second or third category you will probably have a tendency to be rather cool towards your children, and perhaps may concentrate rather too much on working hard to provide them with all the advantages of life. If you feel (and your partner agrees!) that you are more warmly affectionate, there will be fewer adjustments to make on that score, because you will want to spend time with your children, having fun with them and at least temporarily forgetting any problems at work, or any money problems.

Something you must also bear in mind is the fact that you are on the whole unconventional and like plenty of freedom of expression. It may well be that your youngster needs a more rigid discipline than you would care for, or even care to extend; it offers him security. This would be the case, for instance, if your child is a young Taurus. You may feel he will thrive in a permissive school with a slack, easygoing discipline, but he will really be far more conventional than you and will make steadier progress in a rather different atmosphere. This could be a hard pill for you to swallow, but the situation is, I assure you, worth serious thought.

You may have read that Aquarians are very forward-looking and up to date in their ideas — ahead of their time, in fact. But as you may have gathered from my earlier comments it sometimes happens that ideas formed in youth are too rigidly adhered to throughout the whole of life. When your children are growing up and coming to their own conclusions about important issues, don't be surprised to discover that these are very different from your own — and that your convictions are not nearly as contemporary as you may like to think. Perhaps you have got out of touch, and are even slightly shocked by your children's opinions. So while in many respects there should be no generation gap problems between Aquarians and their children, it is sadly too often the case that this difficulty does arise and is even more serious than with some other signs where you would *expect* a yawning gap! In such a situation, use your Aquarian logic rather than stubbornly sticking to what may be outdated ideas.

You are probably ideally suited to take a really active and imaginative role in your children's PTA. It is likely that if you are asked to serve on the committee you will move the whole association forward a notch, because you certainly won't lack original ideas for the promotion of its development and for the support it can give to the school. If you can organize some events involving the raising of funds not only for the school but for charities, involving both parents and children, you will be doing a great deal of good not only for the local community but for mankind in general — and after all that's what being an Aquarian is all about.

## Case Study

**Philippa** - Sun Mercury and Venus in Aquarius. Mercury Group 2, Venus Group 3.

**From the Report:** 'Accepting the fact that a daughter has a very independent and freedom loving side to her personality is not the easiest thing for a mother, but these tendencies in Philippa do not suggest run-of-the-mill rebelliousness. They are of the highest possible order, and she has a very great deal to offer the world;

you need have no qualms about them. If she takes up a cause, profession or calling, you need not worry that it may be the wrong one — if she has decided upon it for herself, it will be right for her! It may be that she will be inclined towards unconventional way-out and unusual interests — this is excellent for her, and just as it should be. A negative trait in her personality which needs special care and discouragement on your part is too much outspoken stubbornness. This is balanced, however, by a very great deal of natural kindness and by humanitarian instincts which are very powerful in her personality.

'You may well find that as she grows up her attitude to boy-friends will be rather detached. She will enjoy their company but will want them as friends — and may quite openly take this attitude, perhaps being a little cool where emotional ties are concerned. This line of approach will be very much in character, but she is also the sort quite suddenly to fall madly in love and go through a sudden change of emotions and attitudes in these matters.'

Comment: Philippa's analysis was written for her mother not long after her father died. At the time, she was ten years old; she is now just over thirty. Her mother says that she has turned out to be a true Aquarian in the best sense of the term — kind and humanitarian and very independent. With guidance from her mother her Aquarian tendency to stubbornness has become single-mindedness. I also learned that her attitude towards men and relationships is exactly as described: coping rationally with a broken engagement when she was twenty, she did not commit herself to marriage until she was twenty-nine. She loves her husband very deeply, and expects her first baby at the time of writing; she has always been a rather private person — something very common among the friendly but detached people of this enigmatic Zodiac group.

## The Sun-sign and Its Rulerships

*Countries and areas*: Abyssinia, Cyprus, Iran, Israel, Polynesia, Sweden, Syria, Turkey, U.S.S.R.

*Cities*: Bremen, Hamburg, Moscow, Salzburg.

*Trees*: fruit trees.

*Flowers and herbs*: alder, amaranthus, artichoke, asparagus, beans, belladonna, brambles, cloves, columbine, comfrey, daisy, elder, foxglove, hemlock, henbane, marshmallow, medlar, mint, onion, orchid, pansy, poppy, primula, quince, rose, rye, sorrel, violent, wolf'sbane.

*Food*: apples; all cereals, especially wheat; all berries; grapes, pears; spices.

*Cell salts*: Nat. Mur., Mag. Phos.

*Animals*: large birds which fly long distances.

*Stone*: amethyst, aquamarine.

*Metal*: aluminium.

*Colour*: electric blue, pale turquoise.

# PISCES

## (February 19 - March 20)

Note: Pisces is a feminine sign, so for the most
part I refer throughout to 'she', but most of my
comments refer also to boys.

## General Characteristics

Young Pisces is emotional, kind, charitable, caring, and has a very colourful
imagination. She is also naturally intuitive, and you can usually count on her being
right about things when she simply 'feels' that they are so.

You should always encourage your Piscean to use her imagination in a creative
and positive way, for if it is not developed along those lines she will very easily become
deceptive, and you will hear all sorts of very convincing stories which, to your horror,
you will find are far from the truth.

You should also watch out for any tendency to evasiveness, and to counter this
trait it is important to question her in depth whenever it seems necessary. Try to
encourage a self-critical element in her, so that she will be able to assess herself logically
and less intuitively than she may otherwise tend to do. You will find that this will
help strengthen her character, which can sometimes be rather weak. She is gullible
and can be too easily led by other people, so you should also teach her to think
for herself and do everything you can to develop decisiveness. It is not that she
always sits on the fence, but she is very sensitive to the needs of other people and
will hate to hurt or upset them, so may well tend to procrastinate. Once she begins
to take a direct line of action for herself, the weaker side of her personality will be
under control.

Perhaps her worst fault is that strongly deceptive streak, and while she would
hate to be accused of dishonesty, she will tend to tell white lies and then go on
to add one or two black ones as a cover-up, as a result of which she can all too
easily find herself in a very difficult situation which will be hard to resolve. Similarly,
she can also be self-deceptive, and this too can cause considerable problems, especially
later in life.

Her emotional level is high, and she has a great deal of love and affection to give, so she will be an adorable child, always willing to help, and indeed to sacrifice her own interests and perhaps pleasures in order that she may do good to others — you, in particular.

Her physical energy level may not be particularly high, and to get her energy going I suggest that at a very early age you encourage her to learn to swim; remember, this is a water sign (see p.15), and like the other water-babies of the Zodiac, Cancer and Scorpio, she will probably get both physical and psychological benefit from attending mother-and-baby swimming lessons as early as you like.

She is extremely creative, but can be almost totally lacking in self-confidence — obviously not all young Pisceans are this way, but it is the case from time to time; so it will be enormously helpful if when she produces a painting, or perhaps writes a little verse, that you praise her and her work fulsomely — rather more than you might if she had any other Sun-sign. In this way you will again build her confidence. Any praise and encouragement will be valuable, otherwise some excellent potential may fail to develop simply because she has a bee in her bonnet which suggests that she is no good at anything and that everyone else's work is much better than hers (indeed, she may think that everyone else is not only cleverer but prettier). So why should she bother?

It will not be very easy for you to warn her about possibly dangerous strangers, for though she may well be a little shy she is definitely not naturally suspicious — and as on the one hand you are building her self-confidence, you don't want on the other to undo your good work by making her so. Your best approach will probably be to read her the story of Red Riding-Hood! She will adore fairy stories anyway, and you can point the moral of the tale, which is of course that the Big Bad Wolf is alive and well and may be living nearby.

Pisces is perhaps the most charitable of all the twelve signs, and like their neighbours in the Zodiac, the Aquarians, Pisceans have a strong humanitarian streak — so much so that you will have to make a special effort to train your child to be careful with her pocket-money, otherwise it will run through her fingers like water — and *not* because she is spending it all on herself. On the contrary, she will want to spend far too much on treats and presents for her friends (and will certainly choose some imaginative and pretty gifts), and will have a decided tendency to be impressed by sob-stories, lending money and not being sufficiently determined to make sure it is returned to her. As to charging interest — never!

It is when she is asked to support a charity with which she sympathizes that her emotions will really take over; she is wonderfully kind and generous, no doubt — but rather than simply giving all her money away, she should really be encouraged to make things to sell for charity, or perhaps produce a little play or some other performance with her friends, which will use her imaginative and creative capacity and strengthen her self-confidence, as well as probably raising more money than she could afford.

If she is at all absent-minded, you can expect her to have lost her gym kit or school scarf, or to have lent it to a friend who forgot hers. Don't neglect to put a name-tag on absolutely everything. I doubt if your Piscean will very much enjoy wearing her school uniform; she may well be very bored by it simply because it is rather dull, as well as probably being restrictive. And oh, those school shoes!

Out of school, I think she will love all clothes in pastel shades, especially delicate shades of green, and shimmery fabrics — satins and soft silks — and those with a metallic thread in them. Ideally, she would probably like to drift about in fancy dress or some gorgeous ball gown, or perhaps a ballet tutu; let her wear light-weight fabrics when it is warm enough, and at all times try for clothes which impede her movements as little as possible. The boys of the sign will love shiny, soft anoracs and gym shorts. Both will probably enjoy going around in bare feet, and this is by no means a bad thing when it is possible and safe; if you have wood or stone floors, an above-average supply of fairly thick socks will probably be a good thing!

You will discover soon enough, incidentally, that your young Piscean will like to sit on the floor and will certainly appreciate a sheepskin or greek flokati rug to curl up on.

## The Three Ways of Thinking

Due to the influence of Mercury (see p.13) the Piscean mind characteristically works in one of three ways.

★ Many Pisceans have inventive and original minds. If they can bring their abundant ideas to fruition, they will do extremely well in life, either in the sciences or the arts. Interestingly, this group can be quite stubborn and fixed in their opinions. Eccentricity may well be present.

★★ Pisceans of the second group notably lack the capacity to think constructively and practically. They should use their intuition and sixth sense when coming to their conclusions and making decisions. Forgetfulness can become quite a serious problem. Encourage them to make careful checklists.

★★★ In the third group are confident, straightforward thinkers with a potential for quick decision making, who will not hesitate to speak out. They should try to develop the ability to consider problems in real detail and avoid the tendency to jump from the frying pan into the fire.

## The Five Ways of Loving

Due to the influence of Venus (see p.13) Pisceans will tend to express their affection in one of five ways.

★ Perhaps shy and rather apprehensive when they first fall in love, Pisceans of the first group make faithful and loyal partners when they manage to break through their natural reticence and learn to relax into a partnership and express their feelings freely. Trusting their partners is the vital element.

★★ Stars will shine in the eyes of these young Pisceans, who will tend to glamourize their relationships. Dynamically attractive, they can sometimes be surprisingly cool and distant; they should be careful not to lead their lovers on, then go cold on them at the last moment.

★★★ Members of the third group will love very deeply and passionately but will sometimes drift up to cloud nine, since there is a strong tendency to become over-romantic — and it is all too easy for them to shy away from reality when assessing their prospective partners. Self-deception can be disastrous.

★★★★ The fourth group contains Pisceans with a passionate, less complicated attitude to romance; because of a tendency to fall in and out of love very quickly, the path of true love will not always run smoothly, but with the most positive Piscean approach to the subject they will have many rewarding relationships.

★★★★★ In the final group are those who will be extremely warm and affectionate, as well as emotional and sensuous. They will spend freely and will get a great deal of real pleasure from their relationships, but their possessive streak may provoke jealousy, damaging their relationships.

## Health and Diet

The Piscean constitution may not seem quite as robust as that of some other Zodiac types. It is not that Pisces is a weakling; it's simply that exterior influences and changing atmospheres — to say nothing of other people's attitudes — have an extremely potent effect on them. The result can be a surprising number of psychosomatic illnesses.

Though they may not admit it, Pisceans tend to conceal a strong tendency to worry. They are good at this, but you will soon realize when something is wrong because your youngster will either go off her food or develop a tummy or headache. If she becomes fidgety and restless, that is a danger signal. To avoid this situation, you must encourage her to be open and talk through her problems, and make her face up to reality and see situations as they really are, not as she thinks or wishes they might be. Worry can lead to apprehension and tension. Get her to unwind by encouraging her to become involved in her favourite interests, which will probably naturally be tension-free and relaxing. Remember that her incredible imagination can work against as well as for her in all spheres of her life.

The Piscean body area is the feet, and your child will either have very beautiful feet which will look delightful in or out of all kinds of shoes and sandals, or they will be the source of all sorts of problems. Be prepared to have to cope with shoe shop dramas. I cannot too strongly advise you to seek a really well-trained and professional assistant to help you out. Always buy an established make of children's shoes right from the start, expensive though this may be. Youngsters of this sign really can suffer as a result of ill-fitting shoes, very easily developing corns and hammer-toes. When young Pisces (son or daughter) becomes aware of fashion they will be attracted to the most extreme shoe styles; all you can do is warn them. Foot exercise sandals will be helpful, both in the home and in summer as outdoor wear.

Young Pisces should sleep really quite well; I would suggest that you encourage her, as soon as she is old enough to write coherently, to keep a dream diary. She is the type who should find dream recall easy, and it will be a wonderful exercise for her to make a record of her dreams. If she elaborates on them, turning them into stories or poems, that will be excellent, for she will be stretching her Piscean imagination and using it creatively.

When she goes down with childish illnesses she should be a reasonably docile patient. Keep her well supplied with story-books and books of amusing, somewhat unusual verse (I recommend that of Charles Causley). Pisces has always been the natural poet and poetry lover of the Zodiac. Simple hobbies and puzzles that can be done in bed will also help take her mind off her aches and pains. Watch out for feverishness, since she could tend to be more vulnerable to this than many Zodiac types.

You may find that she will prefer food which has a smooth, creamy texture. That does not necessarily mean that she will only love custard or cream cakes — but cream soup will be more enjoyable to her than *minestrone*. Pisces is of course the sign of the fish, and most of its denizens thrive very well on a fish diet. Yoghurt and dairy products are good for her, but it is sometimes the case that Pisceans tend to put on weight more easily than many other signs, so you may have to count her calories if you think she is developing a sweet tooth. A carton of (perhaps low-calorie) yoghurt would make an excellent snack; grapes, fresh plums, peaches and nectarines will be much enjoyed.

Your young Piscean will certainly need a lot of physical exercise and may have to be encouraged to take it. Because they are gentle and sensitive, they may not take naturally to the rough and tumble of school sports but will probably benefit enormously, both physically and psychologically, from all kinds of dancing and ice or roller skating. If at all possible I advise you to encourage either boy or girl, at as early age as practicable, to attend a babies' dance or skating class; this will bring out their natural grace, and give it a good physical basis, as well as helping them develop self-confidence.

## The First Five Years

When your young Piscean son or daughter becomes mobile, be prepared to step on a toy every time you move — they will be all over the floor, for he or she is bound to be pretty careless and leave things lying about all over the place.

Piscean children are perhaps more easily satisfied, where toys are concerned, than those of any other sign; give them a saucepan lid and it will immediately become a space ship or a cymbal, a circus ring or a swimming pool for their tiniest dolls. So if you can't afford expensive toys, don't worry; the Piscean imagination will help you out. Any toys you do give them should be very carefully chosen to stretch their imagination, for though every child benefits from imaginative toys, Pisceans will specially enjoy and make good use of them.

Generally speaking they are unaggressive (even perhaps becoming pacifists when they are older) so toy forts, guns and soldiers will probably be less popular with them than with other children. They will specially love playing with water and sand!

They will respond particularly well to nursery rhymes, when they are young, and to stories about animals — Peter Rabbit, Paddington Bear, Winnie-the-Pooh — and they love really imaginative, good illustrations. Fairy stories (Cinderella springs to mind as the most Piscean character in fiction!) will be popular.

Do everything you can to encourage young Pisces to be helpful in the home, though it will be absolutely no use to ask her to help you tidy anything; untidiness is the natural state of all Pisces, and they will react with amazement to the idea that anything

The Zodiac Family

has a place in which it should be! But helping you in other household tasks will develop her practicality (not her most natural attribute). She will probably love washing-day — so you can certainly encourage her to wash a few handkerchiefs. She will be naturally kind and caring, and looking after any pet will come naturally to her — but being Piscean, goldfish (in a properly spacious tank, please, and *not* just a bowl!) will be a particularly good idea if circumstances preclude your having dog or cat.

When the time comes for her to go to play group, she may be rather shy but will soon enjoy the facilities which aren't available at home. And, anyway, mixing with other children and a change of pattern to her day will help her to develop that adaptibility which is one of the most marked attributes of Pisces. Once she has settled in you will find that she will be rather easily influenced by the children around her — hopefully in a positive way.

It is important to remember that it will not be easy to discipline a young Piscean, because over-strictness will very easily damage her susceptible self-confidence. But right from the start you should be careful to instruct her in right and wrong and try to encourage her to be strictly truthful, pointing out that owning up right away not only hurts you less but will make life a great deal easier for herself.

## School Years

Almost as soon as she has settled into her first term at school you will know in which subjects Pisces is going to do well. Most children do well in some subjects and badly in others, but with Pisces the dividing line will be quite clearly marked; this is because practical subjects will on the whole tend to bore her and she will simply not be bothered to pay attention, while those which exercise the imagination will enthrall and captivate her, and she will be prepared to work very hard at them.

Of course you will have to try to impress on her the fact that it is difficult to live life without a certain amount of knowledge of practical school subjects; with luck she may have a teacher capable of engaging her enthusiasm by pointing out that mathematics, algebra, geometry also have their romantic and imaginative sides — though this is sadly rare. Similarly, history (which she will probably enjoy very much as a subject) can make her aware of current events, for there are often interesting parallels to be drawn.

I think you will find that Pisces either idealizes or is in fear and trepidation of her teachers; hopefully there will be a good mix — if she seems to be slipping in some subjects it may well be because the teacher has forfeited her good will by being sarcastic or impatient. This will make her feel inadequate, and her work will suffer as a result. Try to encourage the offender to be more sympathetic; with patience the wound can be healed.

If you have a choice of school, choose one where there is a special emphasis on creative expression — but one where there is a reasonably disciplined structure, in order that she may feel free to express her talents while at the same time feeling reasonably secure. She must know where she stands if she is to accept direction and make progress.

When examination time comes, I suggest you work out a careful timetable for revision. It is important that you know just how much Pisces has to do, because it will not be possible to count on her not to be forgetful or to procrastinate, and it will be up to you to keep her nose reasonably close to the grindstone. Happily, attention is usually focussed on assessment of a whole term's or year's work, rather than just on examination results. Bear this in mind when helping her through school projects. She will certainly not lack original ideas of her own, and if she has to make a scrapbook or a collection of information sheets she will get an enormous amount of material together — but her presentation is likely to be rather poor and untidy. She simply won't be able to understand why people have to be helped to see the wood for the trees and will place far too much emphasis on quantity rather than quality. So help her with her weeding and making her work look neat and attractive; if she happens to enjoy drawing and painting she may tend to over-decorate her project and make it look too pretty rather than businesslike. You can't too often point out that neatness and a certain slickness will impress the assessors and will also actually help to cover any gaps which may inadvertantly have been left when she got the material together.

If she enjoys the usual run of school sports, that's fine, but be prepared for her to scorn them — Pisceans don't like being knocked about and are not particularly competitive. If anything, swimming will appeal to her most strongly, and should be encouraged from a very early age. If she wins prizes at sports, it will probably be for swimming — not because she wants to win medals, but just because this is something she happens to do better than other people!

If the school has a choir, orchestra or drama group, they will be popular with her, and membership will be rewarding; they will satisfy her creative and artistic bent — and you may find that she particularly enjoys and is good at playing stringed instruments.

Although it is important for children to choose their own friends, parents like to keep an eye on the sort of children with whom they are mixing, and this is actually rather important for parents of a young Piscean, for they are very impressionable, and can be easily led astray by children with perhaps stronger minds or personalities, and seem sometimes to have a positive instinct for choosing their friends unwisely. If your young Pisces' closest friend is exuberant, lively and extrovert (a Leo or Sagittarian, perhaps), the friendship could be extremely good for her, for she will catch the enthusiasm and energy and be spurred into action.

Pisceans tend sometimes to be more than usually susceptible to bullying. Up to a point she must learn to take the rough and the smooth in life, so pampering her is a bad idea (anyway, she may well be fantasizing a little); this is a sensitive area, and you should certainly not ignore the problem if it comes up. Try to find out, tactfully, the truth of the situation and deal with it through tackling the alleged bully's parents.

## Out of School Activities

There will be times when you may think that your young Piscean is sitting doing nothing. She may well have that appearance, but I assure you that plenty will be going on in her head, for she will be daydreaming.

Daydreaming is sometimes sneered at by others, but it is important for Pisceans, for high among the dreamers of dreams she needs that kind of stimulation. However she should not be encouraged to live entirely in a fantasy life, and she must be encouraged to act her fantasies out in highly imaginative play (it will be a help to encourage her to collect a fancy dress box for the purpose) or to paint or draw them. She should enjoy all kinds of creative or artistic hobbies, and, remembering that she adores helping and caring for people, you will probably find that from time to time she will appear as a 'doctor' or 'vet'.

It will be interesting for you to watch her progress if she attends dance class or music lessons or takes part in any activity that requires special tuition outside school hours. As she makes progress, her personal self-confidence will develop alongside her technique. If she passes an examination, it will be a very good idea to give her a special treat as a reward, for this will underline the achievement and her pleasure in pleasing you will be an added spur to further effort.

She may enjoy learning to ride — often an expensive hobby, I know, but one that could prove well worthwhile (she will enjoy simply being in the presence of horses, quite apart from mounting them).

It may be that religion will be important to her, whatever your own attitude to it; activities involving church groups of various kinds may be more satisfying than you realize. Generally speaking, Pisceans are not specially adventurous, and you should keep this in mind when helping her to choose out of school activities. If she really adores swimming, it might be worth discovering whether there are facilities anywhere nearby which would allow her to become part of a sequence swimming team, or she might like to train in scuba diving with an eye to eventually taking part in underwater exploration or archaeology.

Most Pisceans have intense and long lasting love affairs with their hobbies and interests, and once she has decided on them I think you will find that she will continue to be intrigued and fascinated by them for many years to come. The only thing which might discourage her and cause a major set back will be a failure in some kind of test or examination, or someone more confident and showy inflicting a put-down, sapping her confidence.

Miss and Master Pisces will benefit from spending as much time as possible on or by river or sea; boats are something all water-signs enjoy. If there is no water nearby, I suggest an occasional outing to the seaside, lake or river; Pisces will love the day out and will remember it for ages.

## Preparing for Life

A Piscean child at coeducational school will be more easily and smoothly prepared for life than in perhaps any other way, for much of the 'mystery' of the opposite sex will simply never present itself.

The Piscean imagination can tend to work overtime at puberty, and all sorts of fanciful notions about love and sex may jostle for place in his or her head. So it is important for parents and teachers to take a really pragmatic attitude to her sex education, leaving absolutely nothing to that imagination!

The romantic attitude is strong in both sexes, and there is something of a tendency

to be in love with love. In the first instance Pisceans will probably set their sights
on their favourite pop star or performer, and this stage may last rather longer with
them than with many other Zodiac types. When it comes to dating a real live boy
or girl, a gentle modesty will make its presence felt. This is delightful and captivating,
but of course can get a little out of control and make the partner rather impatient
if Pisces is physically inhibited by it. The modesty can take another form, because
sometimes Pisceans can convince themselves that there is nothing whatsoever in
them that could possibly attract anybody else. They are, of course, almost always
wrong, but they believe it all right and can take refuge in wishful thinking ('If only
I were handsome . . . if only I were beautiful . . .'). Try to encourage your young Piscean
to take a realistic view of themselves, and underline the fact that the company of
the opposite sex can be light-hearted fun — and that moreover they must realize
that their partner may also be feeling shy and apprehensive; once this is realized,
anxiety should take a back seat.

At this point it will be good for you to look back to *The Five Ways of Loving*
(p.239-40) and try to assess the category your youngster fits into. This may give you
some kind of guidance about her attitude. Encourage the positive qualities I mention,
but be on the look out for the negative ones, for the chances are that because Pisces
is not among the strongest signs of the Zodiac these will emerge quite potently in
one way or another (the influence of Venus being very strong for them).

Having overcome possible initial shyness, and irrespective of the influence of
Venus, Pisceans are keen to experiment sexually because this is such an intense
form of emotional expression. They will fall in love very deeply and probably
quite often. There will be times when your young Piscean will be deeply hurt.
All you can do is comfort and encourage them, and listen to what they have
to say, remembering that they will only really learn as a result of their own
experiences. At such times as these you can point out that she may be seeing their
loved ones through rose-coloured spectacles, and do as much as you can to encourage
her not to rush too hastily into a positive declaration of love, and certainly
not into a permanent relationship, but to allow herself time for her and her
partners' feelings to mature and settle. Pisces is one of the signs which encourages
its inhabitants to dramatize, and the relationship may well be just one of those
things.

There is more than a hint of sentimentality in the Piscean attitude to love, and
it is likely that both sexes will send an above-average number of Valentine cards
and collect all kinds of souvenirs and love letters or verses — which, incidentally,
they will be good at writing. Perhaps the first indication you will get that young
Pisces is becoming interested in love and sex will be when she starts first reading
love poetry and then writing it. Whether she actually posts her letter or poems
is another matter!

The natural Piscean modesty should keep them out of trouble when sex comes
up — unless they become really besotted with someone, when their desire to please
could overcome their rather tentative approach. Under such circumstances they
can find themselves very easily led into danger, perhaps particularly by older and
more experienced people; again, thorough sex education is the answer — the best
contraceptive is knowledge!

# Further Education

Moving from the discipline of school to the freer, more adult atmosphere of further education, young Pisces will be stunned by the enormous variety of activity and opportunity which confronts her.

Eager to study her subject, she must be warned that because there will be so many outside interests she could easily be distracted from the purpose of her course and her work might suffer as a result.

At first, especially if she is at university, she may be somewhat confused and could take a little while to settle down, but if she allows herself time to consider just what she really wants to achieve there, she should benefit enormously from the atmosphere and from the various extramural activities (and the wide variety of people also involved in them).

In some respects her progress will be very similar to that of her school years. Provided she is able to work with lecturers and tutors who are gently encouraging and supportive, she will gain even more self-confidence both in her work and her personality. There is no reason why she should not end her course with a good degree or diploma.

Hopefully, her choice of college will be made in order that she may develop one of her much-loved interests — she may find herself an art or dance student — but whatever she decides to do, provided she has a real feeling for and love of her subject she should be enormously successful. If on the other hand she has been forced to take a course of study in subjects which have no real appeal, she may well become disillusioned and confused and her university years may not be quite as rewarding as they might have been.

She should try if possible to avoid changing course in mid-career; while some people can adapt to such a situation, the additional pressures which it will bring about may make a Piscean particularly tense and worried.

Sometimes youngsters have a spare year between school and university, and if that is the case it can be a mixed blessing for a Piscean. On the one hand the time to drift will allow her to come to terms with the important issues of her life; on the other, if she is allowed to wander in an undisciplined way she may tend to think she can always take the easy option in the future — and that may include a decision not to bother to go to college after all.

Pisceans are probably at their best when they achieve a decided pattern to their lives. This does not necessarily mean an intense discipline which will ensure that they are always doing precisely the same thing at precisely the same time every day; but they should aim to set targets for themselves — if they have a particular task to do, they should determine to complete it by a particular time. This regime is something that the Piscean student will find particularly valuble, for it will ensure that she delivers essays on time, completes courses of study by the date on which they should be completed, and hopefully, when examination time comes round, will have done an adequate amount of revision over a decent period, rather than trying to cram it into the previous twenty-four hours. If good habits of this kind can be acquired during student years, she will find it much easier to cope with the stresses and strains of a busy and demanding career later on. For instance, Pisceans generally tend to delude themselves that they work best under pressure. I think that in fact a lot of unnecessary tension and worry can build up when someone is breathing down the back of their necks. It is always worth their while to consider whether organizing a solid routine of work under a carefully devised discipline will not be the best way, in fact, of securing their job and advancing in it.

Pisceans are among the members of the Zodiac who will benefit particularly from viewing the ordinary driving test as a first step and going on to take advanced driving lessons. It is not that they are naturally reckless drivers, but when behind the wheel they can tend to allow their minds to drift a little, perhaps listening too closely to the conversation of their passengers, or getting too involved with a radio discussion — and this can lead to carelessness, and then to accidents.

## Unemployment: Stresses and Strains

It will be very easy indeed for a young Piscean who cannot find work to get discouraged and distressed, and you may well have to give her a very great deal of support and encouragement if she is to continue to make a real effort to find a job. Her self-confidence will need constant boosting, and you may well have to nag her more than a little if she is not to give up trying.

It is terribly important that she really fills her day. Of course there will — or should — be a continual round of going through the newspapers at the library, going to the job centre, writing letters, and so on, but when she has done that, do encourage her to go on to work on her favourite hobbies, so that she has no time in which to sit around feeling sorry for herself.

If she is creative you will have no problem, and the best way of helping her out financially will probably be to buy her the materials she needs in order to pursue her interest or maybe pay for some kind of study course or evening institute class (though many of these are free to the unemployed). Remembering the possibility that she may not have her life terribly well organized, I suggest you make a fairly careful check on the appearance of her letters of application and c.v. If her image veers towards the untidily romantic, encourage her to think twice about her personal appearance when she goes for an interview; she may need to dress a little more formally than her taste suggests. A Piscean boy in this situation may also not care to get out of his most comfortable jeans and well-worn tee-shirt. He should be persuaded.

It is important that an unemployed Piscean keep in touch with what's happening to her friends — she may well tend to become reclusive when she is not in work, almost ostracizing her friends, especially if they are employed. But it is important that she *does* keep in touch, for through them she may hear of situations vacant, which might solve her problem. Besides which, friends can be a considerable source of encouragement, perhaps helping to avoid her becoming entirely disheartened.

We must always remember that Pisceans can react negatively even to medically prescribed or administered drugs, and that they have a tendency to take the easy way out of difficult situations. It can be a lethal combination, for they can for instance tend to rely, under stress, on alcohol, or turn to cigarettes to alleviate tension. At the best of times Piscean smokers tend to smoke too much and often find it difficult to give up the habit. Should your young Piscean become very depressed because she can't find a job, you should be on the safe side and look out for any evidence that she may be slipping into drug taking — tobacco at the easy end, hard drugs in extremity.

Because she tends to be secretive by nature she will be particularly good at disguising or hiding the evidence, and if you confront her too aggressively may well be adamant that she is innocent. Remember her natural proclivity for romanticizing, not to say deception; she may not be speaking the truth. It is not too easy to make practical suggestions for helping her; she could respond well however to the help and support of an older friend or confidante whom she has known and respected for some time. That person might well be able to get through to her and help her more easily than close relatives. The realization of the extent of the problem — that drugs could rule her life and be very distressing for her family — could be of most help in encouraging her to kick the habit. Once she has done so, she will be a wonderful help to those working in the field, and she will be most persuasive in helping others to avoid the trap.

## Interests and Spare Time Activities

Romantic notions and strong emotions may tend to inhibit simple ties of friendship with the opposite sex. Joint interests may bring Ms Pisces together with a male contemporary, but if some young man merely wants to be *friendly* with your Piscean daughter, he will have to make this quite clear from the beginning — which requires a lot of tact, and even then is not always easy.

Pisceans tend to be fairly selective in their choice of friends, and it often takes some time to prove a friendship, for they need to build up real confidence, real ties of trust. Once a friend is made the ties of friendship mean a great deal to them, but they have a tendency to lose touch, especially if they are separated, for they are often not very good at writing letters or even making telephone calls. However, when meeting again after an absence, the threads of the friendship will be picked up very easily, and life will go on as though the separation had never occurred.

Pisceans will try their hand at a great variety of hobbies, and sometimes have a tendency to throw in the towel too easily when they encounter difficulties. It can be the case that because of this a lot of excellent potential remains undeveloped; all the encouragement family and friends can give them to stick to a course of action until they see it through, will be extremely worthwhile. Indeed, when the Piscean really becomes proficient in some spare time activity there is a high possibility that this can provide a worthwhile source of income — but Pisces is not the best saleswoman in the world, especially when it comes to selling her own work; far better stay behind the scenes producing the work and get a more extrovert, assertive friend to sell it.

One of the most rewarding hobbies for Pisceans is photography; they have a natural eye for composition, and whether they are working with a still, ciné or video camera, they should achieve marvellously creative results. It is never too early to give a young Piscean her first camera. There is also a natural flair for design; Pisceans almost always seem to have a keen eye for beauty and should be encouraged to express it in one way or another. Anything from arranging dried flowers to creating fabulous fabric designs will appeal.

We must not forget the Piscean's need for physical activity of one sort or another. Hobbies which burn up energy are a subtle form of relaxation. But in addition to the activities I have already mentioned (dance, skating and swimming, for instance) when they are older they may care to consider taking a course of yoga or some meditative spiritual discipline; these often exercise the body and sooth the mind. There are some dance techniques which have the same effect.

I have always thought that the Piscean woman can look marvellous either in a designer model or a lovely piece of fabric that she has simply draped around herself, held in place with safety pins! Their attitude to fashion varies considerably from person to person, but while some Zodiac types seem to court disaster in this area no matter how much money they spend, Pisceans seem to be able to look stunning in anything. Texture is important to them, and they will favour soft, shimmery fabrics or the intriguing dark intensity of black velvet. Shoes will probably always be a problem, and many tend to go barefoot; if you have taken my advice (see *Health and Diet*) no doubt your own individual Piscean will have less trouble in this area than the others.

When a young Piscean joins a club or society she will probably feel she is contributing more if she has some behind-the-scenes work to do. This is fine, up to a point, but should she be asked to serve on a committee she should try to accept the invitation, for she probably has more to contribute than she realizes. She must not, however, allow herself to become a lackey while others swan around doing little to promote the common cause. She will probably be at her best if the committee work she undertakes is firmly linked to a charity; she will then be able to express her splendid sympathy and natural enthusiasm for helping the underdog. If she is reluctantly forced into high office, she should learn to speak up and say what she thinks and not hesitate to let other members of the committee take up their share of the burden. A good secretary will be necessary, since Ms Pisces is not the best of organizers.

Pisces is an inventive cook, excellent at adapting recipes to suit her own book, and usually with excellent results — even if the reason she does this is generally that she has forgotten to buy all the listed ingredients. Any substituted herb or spice will have an interesting and acceptable effect. When entertaining she should be careful not to get into too much of a muddle, and leave enough time to enjoy her own parties as much as the friends invited to them!

Pisces is perhaps a cat rather than a dog person; one Piscean friend of mine had an adorable house-trained rabbit (which tended to believe he was a cat). Fish or terrapins are also popular, though.

## Ideal Careers

Although on the whole Pisceans can adapt to most working conditions, they are probably happiest working in a peaceful and relaxed atmosphere — I would like to say 'quiet', but in the modern world that is perhaps asking too much.

Because they are not generally speaking particularly materialistic, they are unlikely to slog away at a boring, repetitive job simply because they need the money. It is terribly important that they find some kind of work which is thoroughly congenial to them and allows them to feel satisfied at the end of the working day.

Like their Zodiac partners, the Virgoans, they have an inner need to serve, so all the caring professions will have a strong appeal for them. Here are wonderful nurses, sometimes specializing in geriatrics or psychiatric nursing. Others make excellent social or charity workers.

Over the centuries there has been a very strong link between Pisces and religion, and the vocation of priest or nun is essentially Piscean in nature. Should a young member of this sign express a desire for this kind of life, be he Christian, Buddhist or whatever, it will be as well to take the matter seriously, and encourage him to spend some time gaining practical experience of what the life is really like — it could well be that he has a real vocation.

Rather differently, the prison service can also have its attractions. And since Pisces is a water sign, all professions related to water are often extremely rewarding — ship building, the Navy or Merchant Navy, working as stewards on cruise ships — not to mention the fishing industry.

Because Pisces is one of the more creative signs, the fine arts are well represented in the list of careers which promise well for members of the sign — along with cinema, television and photography. Many a young amateur photographer will turn professional, and many a young Piscean who has slogged her way through ballet class since the age of six will, with complete dedication — and a similar sense of vocation to that of the nun or priest — step into the life of a professional dancer. The same is true of those dedicated to sport. The art student will perhaps be more successful if she specializes in illustration or graphics than if she turns to, say, sculpture — though obviously this differs from individual to individual. I have met, over the years, several young creative Pisceans who have an ambition to design shoes!

Those of a scientific bent will find medical research rewarding, especially if it is of the kind that is working towards cures for cancer and fatal illnesses; the knowledge that the results of their work could be of crucial help to thousands of people will inspire them to making much even of the most boring and repetitive areas of the work, when experiment after experiment must be repeated before a conclusion can be assured.

We should recognize the fact that many Pisceans are genuinely psychic. Any young man or woman who feels that this may be the case should be extremely careful how they go about using their powers and resist any attempt to lead them along dubious paths — apart from the damage they may do to others, they could seriously damage their own psyches if they become involved with some of the cults or occult practices which are, unfortunately, around. They should recognize that it is possible to be sensibly trained in order that their special gifts can be positively expressed and should seek out the proper bodies to supervise their studies. Some may be natural healers, others clairvoyants; they should get in touch with those who can teach them to learn and discipline the proper techniques. It is also advisable for them to develop counselling techniques and skills. The same advice applies if they are interested in astrology or palmistry.

# Travel

Well, yes, of course — a fishing trip! But though Pisces is a water sign, it is not necessarily true that every Piscean child will adore being on the end of the pier all day with a piece of string and a bent pin.

However, it is probably the case that your son or daughter will enjoy a holiday which involves water or water sports in one way or another. The seaside is an obvious solution — or the lakeside, or a holiday on a canal or inland waterway. A cruise on a river boat down the Rhine, the Nile, or the Mississippi should be a great success.

It is fortunate for young contemporary Pisceans that the old, regimented kind of holiday camp is well out of the way, for they do not warm to the sort of holiday where the whole day is carefully mapped out in half-hour segments by the Camp Commandant! They like wandering aimlessly about, collecting impressions, making sketches, and just generally relaxing in the way everyone would like to do if they were as talented at it as Pisces! They have plenty of imagination, and this will be wonderfully stimulated by a new landscape, especially if it has a romantic air — a castle in the middle distance, or a mysterious valley with a crag on which an eagle might just be perching. They will like to photograph, draw or paint some of the scenery, and a pocket watercolour box and small pad of paper may make a very good holiday present. By the way, do make sure that they have comfortable shoes for every conceivable activity from beachcombing to cragclimbing!

This talent for amusing themselves and getting thoroughly involved in the landscape can of course be dangerous, for they will be so intent on exploration and inventing splendidly romantic stories to fit it that they may well lose all notion of time and place, and it is a rare Piscean child who hasn't got lost from time to time, or simply been two hours late home, plunging everyone into hysterics (especially if their command of SerboCroat is not perhaps impeccable). It is quite a good idea to keep more than half an eye on them until they are at least in their teens, and even then to make sure that when they wander off they at least have a piece of paper on them with the name and telephone number of the hotel in which you are staying.

Choosing a country to visit should not be too much of a problem, for Pisceans are not in general worried by extremes of climate. When other children are reduced to tears by streams of rain, Pisces will often look on this as a rather interesting change from continual bright sun — intriguing to see how it changes the landscape. There should not be too many difficulties with diet, either, though occasionally there could be a tummy upset caused not so much by some new local delicacy as by general excitement; take a good first aid kit with the usual remedies.

## Pisceans as Brothers and Sisters

Young Pisceans' eyes, always on the brink of tears of joy or sorrow, will certainly brim over when she hears she is going to have a baby brother or sister.

In order that she shall accept the situation with as few problems as possible, you should appeal to her naturally kind and loving nature and willingness to help. If you are not very careful, she may easily invent all kinds of fantasic stories about where babies come from; no matter how young she is, explain the whole business as simply and honestly as possible. She will be fascinated to listen to the baby's heart beating before birth and will enjoy helping to 'look after daddy' if the confinement is not at home.

I do not think that you should have too many jealous scenes or tantrums, but you may find that young Pisces will from time to time become a little introverted and quiet — probably because she is thinking deeply and seriously, in her childish way, about her own relationship with her infant brother or sister: whether his arrival is a good or bad thing, just how much she will care for him. Should she decide she is not very keen on the whole idea she may become rather moody and sulky — or perhaps develop some unkind, rather sneaky behaviour pattern. The more she can be encouraged to help out in the home, the more it will help her feelings to mature. Do all you can to show that you trust her and appreciate her efforts. She will then fall easily into the role of 'big sister'.

One difficulty may arise because Pisceans are very romantic, and having heard of the imminent arrival she will immediately see visions of every beautiful and good baby there ever was, lying impeccably clean and quiet in a cot and smiling angelically. The reality, inevitably including a good deal of noise and smell, may not strike her as ideal. It is this kind of thing that may lead to some disgruntlement and indeed some jealousy ('How could anyone prefer *that* to me?'). If she suddenly reverts to bed-wetting, it will be a signal that something is really seriously wrong, and you will need to have a good talk with her and work the situation out between you, or perhaps get professional advice.

If she becomes really fond of her brother or sister it is likely that she will make many sacrifices — perhaps to the point that she will want to give up all her toys. If this happens, be careful; she may be beginning to feel that she's inferior, and a tendency to live in the younger child's shadow could easily develop. This can be quite a problem, and it is important to remember that Piscean children are not very self-confident at the best of times.

When Pisces is the younger child, it is very likely that she will look up to her older sibling with great love and respect — but here we have the mimics of the Zodiac, so any bad habits the older child falls into will very quickly be imitated. You must of course correct this, at the same time pointing out to young Pisces that she must not become a mirror image of an elder brother or sister, but be herself.

When all your children are at the same school, the others should be invited to watch out for any unfair treatment or bullying of the Piscean; it may be that he or she won't want to admit that it is happening. Meanwhile, Pisces can do her bit by being kind and protective in a more subtle and sensitive way, even if the siblings are older. It will be good for you to encourage her, for instance, to make sure that her brother or sister remembers to take to school whatever is needed for the day — it will help her to be less forgetful herself, and encourage her to be more practical and better organized. You will know when the time is right to trust her to take her younger brother or sister to school. Remember that the added sense of responsibility will increase her self-confidence and encourage her to deal in her own way with the minor problems that may arise.

It is not the easiest thing in the world to share a room with a Piscean; even when the child is very young, there could be problems, partly because they tend to be untidy, and partly because they may have very individual interests and hobbies which are totally different from those of their brother or sister, and this could cause complications. However, if room sharing is necessary, do your best to encourage compromise, if necessary working out some kind of timetable to enable each child to have the room to herself for a specific period: Pisces can practise the recorder for 40 minutes, then brother or sister can set out the model railway until bedtime. Fortunately, you can usually appeal successfully to Piscean adaptability.

## Pisceans as Parents

So you're a Piscean parent? Remember, you're a soft touch and your children can twist you round their little finger!

That's probably the way you want it, actually, because you love them so dearly — and in return all you ask is that they love you. But do remember that it's just possible that they may take advantage of your kindness — we find many the son or daughter of a Piscean parent living happily at home until their mid-thirties, with Pisces still cleaning the bathroom after them, making their beds and mending their clothes and practically cleaning their teeth for them.

The Piscean motto is 'Whatever will be, will be', and this probably colours your attitude to family planning, with the result that you may be equally surprised whether a child turns up or not! If it does, you will have to exercise all your Piscean adaptability, because you almost certainly won't have expected it! Happily, however, you will certainly be a marvellous source of inspiration for your children, and in the best possible way for them — encouraging them to march to the sound of their own drum rather than yours, not attempting to foist your own opinions on them. You can rest assured that they will be eternally grateful for your having taken that attitude and can be confident that your parental role has been well and truly played. Remember, however, that because of this very attitude, your children may not know precisely how they stand with you, and perhaps will have to turn to your partner for reassurance; don't be hurt by this. Be careful that if your family goes through a difficult period you make quite sure the children understand exactly what is going wrong; don't try to throw a Piscean veil over the whole problem and hope it will go away before they notice. If you do this, you will cause a lot of confusion on all sides, and when they find out the truth — as they inevitably will — they will think you have consciously deceived them, which may hurt quite as much as the problem itself.

If a Piscean mother's job is not specially important to her, she will not hesitate to give it up in order to look after her children. She should however think about herself — and her partner — a little, since if she spends absolutely all her time with a months-old child, her mind will amost inevitably atrophy and she will be extremely dull company. Both fathers and mothers of this sign will positively enjoy spending time with their children and taking them to all kinds of interesting events and locations in order to have fun with them and to stimulate their imagination. Even if the family funds are low, great efforts will be made to give the children a happy, contented and even memorable childhood.

It may be that when the children are older you could be rather surprised by your teen-age son or daughter's opinions and attitudes, but you are happily unlikely to become stuffy about it or rebuke them for their views. The element of detective in your nature will encourage you to do a little private research and discover their reasons for thinking differently from you; these could be more interesting and entertaining than you may think and should lead to a closer understanding. Who knows, you may end up changing your opinions.

When your children are at school there will probably be a PTA group which may approach you for help. It will be best for you to be creatively involved in some way — perhaps making costumes for the school play or helping to organize unusual money making events. Like all Pisceans who become involved in a club or society, you should remember there is a tendency for others to put upon you, and even if you really enjoy what you are doing, you should try not to allow yourself to be exploited. Remember too that such groups as the PTA can be quite demanding on your pocket; you are generous to a fault, and it may be necessary for you consciously to curb your generosity if you are not to over-spend.

If by chance your son or daughter is following in your footsteps and happens to share your enthusiasm, or is studying something you desperately wanted to study as a child but for some reason could not, you will be specially happy. I don't think you will force issues, but if the eventual outcome of such an interest might take your child into a risky or uncertain profession, aim to be practical as well as encouraging, since all young people must face up to reality and not kid themselves that the world owes them a living.

## Case Study

**Ralph** - Sun in Pisces, Mercury in Aquarius, Venus in Aries; Mercury Group 1, Venus Group 4.

**From the Report**: 'As Ralph grows up an enormously powerful sense of duty will develop. He has a very great deal of ability to carry responsibility and will not only enjoy doing so, but will do so with determination and tenacity. These are of course qualities of the first order, and for someone who will in the future have to carry responsibility he could scarcely be better endowed. In fulfilling his obligations he may however fall into a certain remoteness, and it could be that because he is likely to take his responsibilities so seriously he may tend to cut himself off from or neglect other important spheres of his life.

'Ralph is extremely intuitive. He may not actually realize this for some time, and when he does he may not like to trust his intuition. Honestly, I do not think you will be able to persuade him to do so even if you try; he will probably take no notice of anything you say about this facet of his personality. He may gradually come to realize that when he "feels" something about a situation, or "thinks" that someone will react in such-and-such a way, he will in 99% of cases be right. He will not, then, be able to ignore the gift completely.

'He will desperately want to respond to a powerful humanitarian streak, and his real *metier* in life could well be working to eliminate suffering in the broadest sense of the word: I mean perhaps working for the United Nations or in some advisory capacity to another body. Any leaning in that direction should be encouraged, for I really do think he has the ability to move mountains, and should those mountains be peaks of pain and suffering, what more could one ask?'

Comment: Ralph's analysis was written for his parents in 1974, when he was five. Now, into his twenties, it is apparent that his Piscean Sun-sign is a less powerful factor of his personality than his Capricorn Rising-sign; his father tells me he has a very strong sense of duty, and because he will eventually inherit a large estate this quality will certainly come into its own when the time comes. We must not forget however that Pisces is a creative sign, and while when I wrote the report I felt that perhaps he would turn out to be extremely musical, he in fact trained as a television graphics designer. He has intuition, but it does seem to be something he tends to keep under cover. He is very kind and humanitarian (the Moon was in Aquarius with Mercury when he was born), but these qualities are not expressed in their universal sense, being positively shown to the people of his father's estate.

## The Sun-sign and Its Rulerships

*Countries and areas*: Portugal, many small Mediterranean islands, the Sahara, Samoa, Scandinavia.

*Cities*: Alexandria, Bournemouth, Compostella, Seville, Worms.

*Trees*: those growing near water, especially the willow.

*Flowers and herbs*: those listed for Cancer and Sagittarius, which flower in Piscean colours: acanthus, balm, bilberry, borage, cinnamon, colvolvulus, dandelion, dock, lilies, mosses, pinks, sage, saxifrage, thistles, water-lily, white rose, white poppy.

*Food*: fruits and vegetables with high water content: cucumber, melon, pumpkin; mushroom, cabbage, turnip, lettuce.

*Cell salts*: Ferr. Phos., Kali. Sulph.

*Animals*: all fish; mammals that like water.

*Stone*: moonstone.

*Metal*: platinum, tin and titanium.

*Colour*: soft sea-green.

# OF FURTHER INTEREST

Other books by Derek and Julia Parker which enable those who are interested to explore astrology further:

*The New Compleat Astrologer* (London, 1984), is an excellent introduction to the technique of calculating, drawing and interpreting a full birth chart; an ephemeris of planetary positions is included, complete from 1910 to 2001.

*The Astrologer's Handbook* (London, 1985) explores the effects of the rising-sign and planetary positions in many areas of life, and contains simplified tables and aids to finding lunar and planetary positions and the rising-sign.

*Life Signs* (1986) is confined to Sun-sign astrology, but gives helpful advice on how these general astrological trends affect many areas of life.

Those who wish to study in particular the way in which astrology can be of help in the education and upbringing of children will find Lynne Burmyn's *Sun-signs for Children* (London, 1985) extremely helpful.

Those who wish to contact a professional astrologer are advised to write to The Secretary of the Astrological Association at 2, Waltham Close, Abbey Park, West Bridgford, Nottingham NG2 6LE.